NEW YORK
TRAVEL GUIDE

SHOPS, RESTAURANTS, ATTRACTIONS & NIGHTLIFE

The Most Positively
Reviewed and Recommended
by Locals and Travelers

EGP
Editorial

NEW YORK
TRAVEL GUIDE

SHOPS, *RESTAURANTS*, *ATTRACTIONS* & *NIGHTLIFE*

NEW YORK CITY TRAVEL GUIDE 2022
Shops, Restaurants, Entertainment & Nightlife

© Robert A. Davidson
© E.G.P. Editorial

Printed in USA.

ISBN-13: 9798748721950

INDEX

NEW YORK CITY TRAVEL GUIDE

Shops, Restaurants, Entertainment & Nightlife

*This directory is dedicated to New York City Business Owners and Managers
who provide the experience that the locals and tourists enjoy.
Thanks you very much for all that you do and thank for being the "People Choice".*

*Thanks to everyone that posts their reviews online and
the amazing reviews sites that make our life easier.*

*The places listed in this book are the most positively reviewed
and recommended by locals and travelers from around the world.*

*Thank you for your time and enjoy the directory that is
designed with locals and tourist in mind!*

TOP 500 SHOPS

Most Recommended by Locals & Trevelers
Ranking (from #1 to #500)

#1
A&J Lingerie and More
Discount Store, Adult
Average price: Inexpensive
District: Flatiron
Address: 41 W 28th St
New York, NY 10001
Phone: 1+ (212) 779-1141

#2
Fuego 718
Home Decor, Art Supplies
Average price: Moderate
District: Williamsburg - North Side
Address: 249 Grand St
Brooklyn, NY 11211
Phone: 1+ (718) 302-2913

#3
Proper Cloth
Men's Clothing
Average price: Expensive
District: SoHo
Address: 481 Broadway
New York, NY 10013
Phone: 1+ (260) 207-4478

#4
Beau by Aksel Paris
Men's Clothing, Bespoke Clothing
Average price: Moderate
District: SoHo, TriBeCa
Address: 311 W Broadway
New York, NY 10013
Phone: 1+ (888) 992-5735

#5
Blue In Green
Men's Clothing
Average price: Expensive
District: SoHo, TriBeCa
Address: 8 Greene St
New York, NY 10013
Phone: 1+ (212) 680-0555

#6
Brooklyn Superhero Supply Co
Toy Store, Community Service
Average price: Moderate
District: Park Slope
Address: 372 5th Ave
Brooklyn, NY 11215
Phone: 1+ (718) 499-9884

#7
David S Diamonds
Jewelry
Average price: Moderate
District: Midtown West
Address: 550 5th Ave
New York, NY 10036
Phone: 1+ (212) 921-8029

#8
Bra Tenders
Women's Clothing, Department Store
Average price: Expensive
District: Hell's Kitchen, Midtown West,
Theater District
Address: 630 9th Ave
New York, NY 10036
Phone: 1+ (212) 957-7000

#9
Meg
Women's Clothing
Average price: Moderate
District: East Village
Address: 312 E 9th St
New York, NY 10003
Phone: 1+ (212) 260-6329

#10
New York Running Company
Sports Wear, Shoe Store
Average price: Moderate
District: Upper East Side
Address: 1051 3rd Ave.
New York, NY 10065
Phone: 1+ (212) 223-8109

#11
Bonnie Slotnick Cookbooks
Bookstore
Average price: Moderate
District: West Village
Address: 163 W 10th St
New York, NY 10014
Phone: 1+ (212) 989-8962

#12
WORD
Bookstore
Average price: Moderate
District: Greenpoint
Address: 126 Franklin St
Brooklyn, NY 11222
Phone: 1+ (718) 383-0096

#13
Kinokuniya Bookstore
Bookstore, Cards, Stationery
Average price: Moderate
District: Midtown West, Theater District
Address: 1073 Ave of the Americas
New York, NY 10018
Phone: 1+ (212) 869-1700

#14
oo35mm
Toy Store, Skin Care, Jewelry
Average price: Moderate
District: Chinatown
Address: 81 Mott St
Canal Street, NY 10013
Phone: 1+ (718) 496-8163

#15
BookCourt
Bookstore
Average price: Moderate
District: Cobble Hill
Address: 163 Court St
Brooklyn, NY 11201
Phone: 1+ (718) 875-3677

#16
Fishs Eddy
Kitchen & Bath
Average price: Moderate
District: Flatiron
Address: 889 Broadway
New York, NY 10003
Phone: 1+ (212) 420-9020

#17
Little King Jewelry
Jewelry
Average price: Moderate
District: SoHo
Address:
New York, NY 10013
Phone: 1+ (212) 260-6140

#18
AY Jewelry
Jewelry, Watches
Average price: Inexpensive
District: Midtown West
Address: 20 West 47th St
New York, NY 10036
Phone: 1+ (212) 575-6322

#19
Bike Slug
Bikes
Average price: Inexpensive
District: Bedford Stuyvesant
Address: 1050 Bedford Ave
Brooklyn, NY 11205
Phone: 1+ (718) 247-7347

#20
Scent Elate
Home Decor
Average price: Moderate
District: Hell's Kitchen, Midtown West,
Theater District
Address: 313 W 48th St
New York, NY 10036
Phone: 1+ (212) 258-3043

#21
Victors Villa Furniture
Furniture Store
Average price: Moderate
District: Astoria
Address: 3209 Broadway
Queens, NY 11106
Phone: 1+ (718) 545-0244

#22
Miomia
Skin Care, Cosmetics, Beauty Supply
Average price: Expensive
District: Williamsburg - South Side
Address: 318 Bedford Ave
Brooklyn, NY 11211
Phone: 1+ (718) 490-5599

#23
Kitchen Arts & Letters
Bookstore
Average price: Moderate
District: Upper East Side
Address: 1435 Lexington Ave
New York, NY 10128
Phone: 1+ (212) 876-5550

#24
Army & Navy Bags
Luggage, Men's Clothing, Hobby Shop
Average price: Inexpensive
District: Lower East Side
Address: 177 E Houston St
New York, NY 10002
Phone: 1+ (212) 228-5267

#25
Babeland
Adult
Average price: Moderate
District: Lower East Side
Address: 94 Rivington St
New York, NY 10002
Phone: 1+ (212) 375-1701

#26
Fab 208
Women's Clothing
Average price: Moderate
District: East Village
Address: 72 E 7th St
New York, NY 10003
Phone: 1+ (212) 673-7581

#27
Pippin Vintage Jewelry
Jewelry, Antiques
Average price: Moderate
District: Chelsea
Address: 112 W 17th St
New York, NY 10011
Phone: 1+ (212) 505-5159

#28
Self Edge
Men's Clothing
Average price: Expensive
District: Lower East Side
Address: 157 Orchard St
New York, NY 10002
Phone: 1+ (212) 388-0079

#29
Sacred Tattoo
Tattoo, Cosmetics, Beauty Supply
Average price: Moderate
District: SoHo
Address: 424 Broadway
New York, NY 10013
Phone: 1+ (212) 226-4286

#30
Goorin Bros.
Accessories, Hats
Average price: Moderate
District: Park Slope
Address: 195 5th Avenue
Brooklyn, NY 11217
Phone: 1+ (718) 783-4287

#31
The Evolution Store
Home Decor, Hobby Shop
Average price: Expensive
District: SoHo
Address: 120 Spring St
New York, NY 10012
Phone: 1+ (212) 343-1114

#32
Random Accessories
Jewelry, Cards, Stationery,
Baby Gear & Furniture
Average price: Moderate
District: East Village
Address: 77 E 4th St
New York, NY 10003
Phone: 1+ (212) 358-0650

#33
Red Lantern Bicycles
Bikes, Coffee & Tea, Bar
Average price: Inexpensive
District: Fort Greene
Address: 345 Myrtle Ave
Brooklyn, NY 11205
Phone: 1+ (347) 889-5338

#34
Midtown Comics
Comic Books, Toy Store
Average price: Moderate
District: Midtown West, Theater District
Address: 200 W 40th St
New York, NY 10018
Phone: 1+ (212) 302-8192

#35
Saks Fifth Avenue Shoes
Department Store
Average price: Exclusive
District: Midtown East
Address: 611 5th Ave
New York, NY 10022
Phone: 1+ (212) 753-4000

#36
West End Jewelers
Jewelry
Average price: Moderate
District: Bath Beach, Bensonhurst
Address: 2078 86th St
Brooklyn, NY 11214
Phone: 1+ (718) 372-0530

#37
Brooklyn Vaper
Tobacco Shop
Average price: Inexpensive
District: Williamsburg - North Side
Address: 240 Kent Ave
Brooklyn, NY 11249
Phone: 1+ (347) 871-7718

#38
Bergdorf Goodman
Women's Clothing, Men's Clothing,
Children's Clothing
Average price: Exclusive
District: Midtown West
Address: 754 5th Ave
New York, NY 10019
Phone: 1+ (800) 558-1855

#39
Babeland
Adult
Average price: Expensive
District: SoHo
Address: 43 Mercer St
New York, NY 10013
Phone: 1+ (212) 966-2120

#40
Reciprocal NYC
Sporting Goods, Arcade
Average price: Moderate
District: East Village
Address: 402 E 11th St
New York, NY 10009
Phone: 1+ (212) 388-9191

#41
Pearl River Mart
Department Store, Home Decor
Average price: Moderate
District: SoHo
Address: 477 Broadway
New York, NY 10013
Phone: 1+ (800) 878-2446

#42
MoMA Design Store Soho
Home Decor, Watches
Average price: Expensive
District: SoHo
Address: 81 Spring St
New York, NY 10012
Phone: 1+ (646) 613-1367

#43
Orchard Corset Center
Lingerie
Average price: Moderate
District: Lower East Side
Address: 157 Orchard St
New York, NY 10002
Phone: 1+ (212) 674-0786

#44
Designs By Ahn
Florist, Party & Event Planning
Average price: Moderate
District: Chelsea, Midtown West
Address: 208 West 30th St
New York, NY 10001
Phone: 1+ (212) 929-0660

#45
Pink Olive
Children's Clothing, Cards, Stationery
Average price: Moderate
District: East Village, Alphabet City
Address: 439 E 9th St
New York, NY 10009
Phone: 1+ (212) 780-0036

#46
Argyle Yarn Shop
Knitting Supplies
Average price: Moderate
District: South Slope, Windsor Terrace
Address: 288 Prospect Park W
Brooklyn, NY 11215
Phone: 1+ (347) 227-7799

#47
Uniqlo
Women's Clothing, Men's Clothing,
Children's Clothing
Average price: Moderate
District: SoHo
Address: 546 Broadway
New York, NY 10012
Phone: 1+ (877) 486-4756

#48
Bencraft Hatters
Accessories, Men's Clothing
Average price: Moderate
District: Williamsburg - South Side,
South Williamsburg
Address: 236 Broadway
Brooklyn, NY 11211
Phone: 1+ (718) 384-5517

#49
Book-Off
Bookstore, Comic Books, Music & DVDs
Average price: Inexpensive
District: Midtown West
Address: 49 W 45th St
New York, NY 10036
Phone: 1+ (212) 685-1410

#50
Article&
Women's Clothing, Accessories
Average price: Expensive
District: Cobble Hill, Gowanus
Address: 198 Smith St
Brooklyn, NY 11231
Phone: 1+ (718) 852-3620

#51
Village Tannery
Leather Goods
Average price: Expensive
District: Greenwich Village
Address: 173 Bleecker St
New York, NY 10012
Phone: 1+ (212) 673-5444

#52
Rockefeller Center
Landmarks/Historical,
Shopping Center
Average price: Moderate
District: Midtown West
Address: 30 Rockefeller Plz
New York, NY 10012
Phone: 1+ (212) 632-3975

#53
Erie Basin
Jewelry, Antiques
Average price: Moderate
District: Red Hook
Address: 388 Van Brunt St
Brooklyn, NY 11231
Phone: 1+ (718) 554-6147

#54
Uniqlo
Women's Clothing, Men's Clothing,
Children's Clothing
Average price: Moderate
District: Midtown West
Address: 31 W 34th St
New York, NY 10001
Phone: 1+ (877) 486-4756

#55
Warby Parker
Eyewear, Optician, Optometrist
Average price: Moderate
District: SoHo
Address: 121 Greene St
New York, NY 10012
Phone: 1+ (646) 568-3720

#56
AuH2O
Used, Vintage, Thrift Store
Average price: Inexpensive
District: East Village
Address: 84 E 7th St
New York, NY 10003
Phone: 1+ (212) 466-0844

#57
Stray Vintage
Used, Vintage
Average price: Moderate
District: Woodside
Address: 4809 Skillman Ave
Sunnyside, NY 11104
Phone: 1+ (718) 779-7795

#58
Saffron Brooklyn
Flowers & Gifts
Average price: Moderate
District: Fort Greene
Address: 31 Hanson Pl
Brooklyn, NY 11217
Phone: 1+ (718) 852-6053

#59
My Plastic Heart
Toy Store
Average price: Moderate
District: Lower East Side
Address: 210 Forsyth St
New York, NY 10002
Phone: 1+ (646) 290-6866

#60
Cadillac's Castle
Used, Vintage, Women's Clothing,
Accessories
Average price: Moderate
District: East Village
Address: 333 E 9th St
New York, NY 10003
Phone: 1+ (212) 475-0406

#61
Rosebud Vintage
Used, Vintage, Antiques
Average price: Moderate
District: Crown Heights
Address: 726 Franklin Ave
Brooklyn, NY 11238
Phone: 1+ (347) 413-7799

#62
Avalon Chemists
Drugstore
Average price: Moderate
District: East Village, Lower East Side
Address: 7 2nd Ave
New York, NY 10003
Phone: 1+ (212) 260-3131

#63
Casa Magazines
Newspapers, Magazines, Print Media
Average price: Moderate
District: West Village
Address: 22 8th Ave
New York, NY 10014
Phone: 1+ (212) 645-1197

#64
Maison Martin Margiela
Men's Clothing, Women's Clothing,
Leather Goods
Average price: Exclusive
District: West Village
Address: 803 Greenwich St
New York, NY 10014
Phone: 1+ (212) 989-7612

#65
Bash & Bow
Gift Shop, Jewelry, Women's Clothing
Average price: Moderate
District: Gramercy
Address: 210 E 21st St
New York, NY 10010
Phone: 1+ (646) 494-9412

#66
Kamakura Shirts
Men's Clothing, Women's Clothing,
Formal Wear
Average price: Moderate
District: Midtown East
Address: 400 Madison Ave
New York, NY 10017
Phone: 1+ (212) 308-5266

#67
Main Drag Music
Musical Instruments
Average price: Moderate
District: Williamsburg - South Side
Address: 330 Wythe Ave
Brooklyn, NY 11211
Phone: 1+ (718) 388-6365

#68
Longboard Loft
Outdoor Gear
Average price: Moderate
District: Lower East Side
Address: 132 Allen St
Manhattan, NY 10002
Phone: 1+ (212) 673-7947

#69
Fragrance Shop New York
Cosmetics, Beauty Supply
Average price: Moderate
District: East Village
Address: 65 E 4th St
New York, NY 10003
Phone: 1+ (212) 254-8950

#70
Jeremy Argyle
Men's Clothing
Average price: Expensive
District: SoHo
Address: 160 Spring St
New York, NY 10012
Phone: 1+ (646) 781-9050

#71
C'Est Magnifique
Jewelry
Average price: Moderate
District: East Village
Address: 328 E 9th St
New York, NY 10003
Phone: 1+ (212) 475-1613

#72
Brooklyn Vintage Bicycles
Bikes
Average price: Moderate
District: Gerritson Beach
Address: 51 Fane Ct
Brooklyn, NY 11229
Phone: 1+ (347) 733-2079

#73
The Market NYC
Women's Clothing, Men's Clothing, Jewelry
Average price: Moderate
District: Greenwich Village
Address: 159 Bleecker St
New York, NY 10012
Phone: 1+ (212) 580-8995

#74
Printed Matter
Bookstore, Art Gallery
Average price: Moderate
District: Chelsea
Address: 195 10th Ave
New York, NY 10011
Phone: 1+ (212) 925-0325

#75
Patagonia
Outdoor Gear
Average price: Expensive
District: SoHo
Address: 101 Wooster St
New York, NY 10012
Phone: 1+ (212) 343-1776

#76
John Fluevog
Shoe Store
Average price: Expensive
District: Nolita
Address: 250 Mulberry St
New York, NY 10012
Phone: 1+ (212) 431-4484

#77
Brooklyn Denim
Accessories, Men's Clothing,
Women's Clothing
Average price: Expensive
District: Williamsburg - North Side
Address: 85 N 3rd St
Brooklyn, NY 11249
Phone: 1+ (718) 782-2600

#78
Acustom Apparel
Men's Clothing
Average price: Expensive
District: South Village, TriBeCa
Address: 330 W Broadway
New York, NY 10013
Phone: 1+ (212) 219-8620

#79
Milan Optique
Eyewear, Optician
Average price: Moderate
District: Park Slope
Address: 83 5th Ave
Brooklyn, NY 11217
Phone: 1+ (718) 636-4526

#80
Maraya
Tobacco Shop, Lounge
Average price: Moderate
District: Lower East Side
Address: 87 Orchard St
New York, NY 10002
Phone: 1+ (212) 334-3499

#81
Culturefix
Art Gallery, Bar
Average price: Moderate
District: Lower East Side
Address: 9 Clinton St
New York, NY 10002
Phone: 1+ (646) 863-7171

#82
Louis Purple
Men's Clothing, Bespoke Clothing
Average price: Expensive
District: NoHo
Address: 323 Lafayette
New York, NY 10012
Phone: 1+ (212) 219-8559

#83
Kiehl's Since 1851
Cosmetics, Beauty Supply, Skin Care
Average price: Expensive
District: East Village
Address: 109 Third Ave
New York, NY 10003
Phone: 1+ (212) 677-3171

#84
FAO Schwarz
Toy Store
Average price: Expensive
District: Midtown East
Address: 767 5th Ave
New York, NY 10153
Phone: 1+ (212) 644-9400

#85
Warshaw Hardware
Hardware Store
Average price: Inexpensive
District: Gramercy
Address: 248 3rd Ave
New York, NY 10010
Phone: 1+ (212) 475-5820

#86
Sustainable NYC
Accessories, Home Decor
Average price: Moderate
District: East Village, Alphabet City
Address: 139 Ave A
New York, NY 10009
Phone: 1+ (212) 254-5400

#87
Sycamore
Bar, Florist, Music Venues
Average price: Moderate
District: Flatbush
Address: 1118 Cortelyou Rd
Brooklyn, NY 11218
Phone: 1+ (347) 240-5850

#88
H and B Digital
Electronics, Photography Store, Services
Average price: Moderate
District: Midtown West
Address: 29 W 46th St
New York, NY 10036
Phone: 1+ (212) 354-1341

#89
Baked In Brooklyn
Arts &Crafts, Party & Event Planning
Average price: Moderate
District: Williamsburg - North Side
Address: 242 Wythe Ave
Brooklyn, NY 11211
Phone: 1+ (718) 384-2300

#90
Linda's Bra Salon
Lingerie, Swimwear
Average price: Expensive
District: Midtown East, Murray Hill
Address: 552 3rd Ave
Manhattan, NY 10016
Phone: 1+ (646) 736-1949

#91
Union Square Holiday Market
Shopping Center
Average price: Moderate
District: Union Square, Flatiron, East Village
Address: Union Sq & W 14th St
New York, NY 10003
Phone: 1+ (212) 529-9262

#92
Jack's
Discount Store
Average price: Inexpensive
District: Midtown West
Address: 110 W 32nd St
New York, NY 10001
Phone: 1+ (212) 268-9962

#93
Whisk
Kitchen & Bath
Average price: Moderate
District: Williamsburg - North Side
Address: 231 Bedford Ave
Brooklyn, NY 11211
Phone: 1+ (718) 218-7230

#94
Rain Africa
Skin Care, Cosmetics, Beauty Supply
Average price: Moderate
District: Midtown West
Address: 59 W 49th Street
New York, NY 10112
Phone: 1+ (212) 239-3070

#95
Circa Tabac
Lounge, Cocktail Bar, Tobacco Shop
Average price: Moderate
District: South Village
Address: 32 Watts St
New York, NY 10013
Phone: 1+ (212) 941-1781

#96
Cigarillos
Tobacco Shop
Average price: Moderate
District: South Village
Address: 191 Spring St
New York, NY 10012
Phone: 1+ (212) 334-2250

#97
By Robert James
Men's Clothing
Average price: Expensive
District: Lower East Side
Address: 74 Orchard St
New York, NY 10002
Phone: 1+ (212) 253-2121

#98
Bettie Page
Women's Clothing, Plus Size Fashion
Average price: Moderate
District: East Village, NoHo
Address: 303 Bowery St
New York, NY 10003
Phone: 1+ (646) 478-7006

#99
Toy Tokyo
Toy Store
Average price: Moderate
District: East Village
Address: 91 2nd Ave
New York, NY 10003
Phone: 1+ (212) 673-5424

#100
The Smoking Shop
Tobacco Shop
Average price: Moderate
District: West Village
Address: 45 Christopher St
New York, NY 10014
Phone: 1+ (212) 929-1151

#101
Beyond Vape
Tobacco Shop
Average price: Moderate
District: East Village
Address: 19-23 St Marks Pl
New York, NY 10003
Phone: 1+ (646) 707-3648

#102
The Jewelry Patch
Jewelry
Average price: Moderate
District: Midtown West
Address: 501 Fashion Ave
New York, NY 10018
Phone: 1+ (212) 840-8279

#103
Paper Source
Hobby Shop, Cards, Stationery
Average price: Moderate
District: Cobble Hill, Boerum Hill
Address: 102 Smith St
Brooklyn, NY 11201
Phone: 1+ (718) 858-4524

#104
Kawaii Optical
Eyewear, Optician
Average price: Moderate
District: West Village
Address: 44 Carmine St
New York, NY 10014
Phone: 1+ (212) 620-0366

#105
Desert Island
Comic Books, Bookstore
Average price: Moderate
District: Williamsburg - North Side
Address: 540 Metropolitan Ave
Brooklyn, NY 11211
Phone: 1+ (718) 388-5087

#106
Cinders
Art Gallery
Average price: Moderate
District: Williamsburg - North Side
Address: 28 Marcy Ave
Brooklyn, NY 11211
Phone: 1+ (718) 388-2311

#107
Obscura Antiques
Antiques
Average price: Expensive
District: East Village, Alphabet City
Address: 207 Ave A
New York, NY 10009
Phone: 1+ (212) 505-9251

#108
Henri Bendel
Jewelry, Accessories
Average price: Expensive
District: Midtown West
Address: 712 5th Ave
New York, NY 10019
Phone: 1+ (800) 423-6335

#109
Kate Spade
Leather Goods, Accessories
Average price: Expensive
District: SoHo
Address: 454 Broome St
New York, NY 10013
Phone: 1+ (212) 274-1991

#110
Babeland
Adult
Average price: Moderate
District: Park Slope
Address: 462 Bergen St
Brooklyn, NY 11217
Phone: 1+ (718) 638-3820

#111
Crumpler Store
Luggage, Accessories
Average price: Expensive
District: Nolita
Address: 45 Spring St
New York, NY 10012
Phone: 1+ (212) 334-9391

#112
Japan Society
Museum, Art Gallery, Language School
Average price: Moderate
District: Midtown East
Address: 333 E 47th St
New York, NY 10017
Phone: 1+ (212) 832-1155

#113
Black Gold Records
Coffee & Tea, Vinyl Records
Average price: Moderate
District: Carroll Gardens
Address: 461 Court St
Brooklyn, NY 11231
Phone: 1+ (347) 227-8227

#114
Grand Optician
Eyewear, Optician, Optometrist
Average price: Moderate
District: Brooklyn Heights
Address: 151 Montague St
Brooklyn, NY 11201
Phone: 1+ (718) 625-6545

#115
The Compleat Strategist
Hobby Shop
Average price: Expensive
District: Midtown East
Address: 11 E 33rd St
New York, NY 10016
Phone: 1+ (212) 685-3880

#116
The Brooklyn Kitchen
Kitchen & Bath, Cooking School
Average price: Moderate
District: Williamsburg - North Side
Address: 100 Frost St
Brooklyn, NY 11211
Phone: 1+ (718) 389-2982

#117
Dave's New York
Shoe Store, Men's Clothing
Average price: Moderate
District: Flatiron
Address: 581 Ave of the Americas
New York, NY 10011
Phone: 1+ (212) 989-6444

#118
Americas Florist
Florist
Average price: Moderate
District: Midtown West
Address: 1020 Ave of the Americas
New York, NY 10018
Phone: 1+ (212) 921-8150

#119
Noble Planta
Nursery, Gardening
Average price: Moderate
District: Chelsea
Address: 106-A W 28th St
New York, NY 10001
Phone: 1+ (212) 206-1164

#120
STORY
Accessories, Men's Clothing,
Women's Clothing
Average price: Moderate
District: Chelsea
Address: 144 10th Ave
New York, NY 10011
Phone: 1+ (212) 242-4853

#121
Szeki
Women's Clothing, Jewelry
Average price: Moderate
District: Lower East Side
Address: 157 Rivington St
New York, NY 10002
Phone: 1+ (646) 243-1789

#122
Christian Louboutin
Shoe Store
Average price: Exclusive
District: Upper East Side
Address: 965 Madison Ave
New York, NY 10022
Phone: 1+ (212) 396-1884

#123
Greenlight Bookstore
Bookstore
Average price: Moderate
District: Fort Greene
Address: 686 Fulton St
Brooklyn, NY 11217
Phone: 1+ (718) 246-0200

#124
La Petite Coquette
Lingerie
Average price: Expensive
District: Greenwich Village
Address: 51 University Pl
New York, NY 10003
Phone: 1+ (212) 473-2478

#125
Human Head Records
Vinyl Records
Average price: Inexpensive
District: East Williamsburg
Address: 168 Johnson Ave
Brooklyn, NY 11206
Phone: 1+ (347) 987-3362

#126
Juice Pedaler
Café, Bikes, Juice Bar
Average price: Inexpensive
District: Windsor Terrace
Address: 154 Prospect Park SW
Brooklyn, NY 11218
Phone: 1+ (718) 871-7500

#127
353 Watch Station
Watch Repair, Watches
Average price: Inexpensive
District: Midtown East
Address: 875 3rd Ave.
New York, NY 10022
Phone: 1+ (212) 421-2749

#128
Apple Store
Computers
Average price: Expensive
District: SoHo
Address: 103 Prince St
New York, NY 10012
Phone: 1+ (212) 226-3126

#129
JackRabbit Sports
Sports Wear
Average price: Expensive
District: Upper East Side
Address: 1255 Lexington Ave
New York, NY 10028
Phone: 1+ (212) 727-2980

#130
In God We Trust
Women's Clothing, Jewelry, Men's Clothing
Average price: Expensive
District: SoHo, Nolita
Address: 265 Lafayette St
New York, NY 10012
Phone: 1+ (212) 966-9010

#131
Papél New York
Cards, Stationery
Average price: Moderate
District: Cobble Hill
Address: 225 Court St
Brooklyn, NY 11201
Phone: 1+ (718) 422-0255

#132
Alter
Men's Clothing, Women's Clothing,
Accessories
Average price: Moderate
District: Greenpoint
Address: 109 Franklin St
Brooklyn, NY 11222
Phone: 1+ (718) 784-8818

#133
Upper 90 Soccer + Sport
Sports Wear
Average price: Moderate
District: Downtown Brooklyn, Boerum Hill
Address: 359 Atlantic Ave
Brooklyn, NY 11217
Phone: 1+ (646) 863-7076

#134
Delphinium Home
Home Decor, Cards, Stationery
Average price: Moderate
District: Hell's Kitchen, Midtown West,
Theater District
Address: 353 W 47th St
New York, NY 10036
Phone: 1+ (212) 333-7732

#135
RePop
Art Gallery, Antiques
Average price: Moderate
District: Williamsburg - North Side
Address: 143 Roebling St
New York, NY 11211
Phone: 1+ (718) 260-8032

#136
Fitzgerald Jewelry
Jewelry, Art School
Average price: Expensive
District: Williamsburg - North Side
Address: 174 North 11th Street
Brooklyn, NY 11211
Phone: 1+ (718) 387-6200

#137
Goorin Bros.
Accessories, Hats
Average price: Expensive
District: West Village
Address: 337 Bleecker Street
New York, NY 10014
Phone: 1+ (212) 256-1895

#138
Uniqlo
Women's Clothing, Men's Clothing
Average price: Moderate
District: Midtown West
Address: 666 5th Ave
New York, NY 10103
Phone: 1+ (877) 486-4756

#139
Nintendo World Store
Videos, Video Game Rental, Toy Store
Average price: Moderate
District: Midtown West
Address: 10 Rockefeller Plz
New York, NY 10020
Phone: 1+ (646) 459-0800

#140
Epaulet Shop
Men's Clothing
Average price: Expensive
District: Lower East Side
Address: 144 Orchard St
New York, NY 10002
Phone: 1+ (212) 228-3626

#141
Etsy Labs
Art Gallery
Average price: Moderate
District: DUMBO
Address: 55 Washington St
Brooklyn, NY 11201
Phone: 1+ (718) 855-7955

#142
Mysterious Island
Comic Books, Bookstore,
Newspapers, Magazines
Average price: Inexpensive
District: Chelsea
Address: 207 W 14th St
New York, NY 10011
Phone: 1+ (212) 691-0380

#143
Cog & Pearl
Home Decor, Jewelry
Average price: Expensive
District: Park Slope
Address: 190 5th Ave
Brooklyn, NY 11217
Phone: 1+ (718) 623-8200

#144
Seaport Flowers
Florist
Average price: Expensive
District: Brooklyn Heights
Address: 309 Henry St
Brooklyn, NY 11201
Phone: 1+ (718) 858-6443

#145
Yesterday's News
Antiques
Average price: Inexpensive
District: Carroll Gardens
Address: 428 Court St
Brooklyn, NY 11231
Phone: 1+ (718) 875-0546

#146
Verameat Jewelry
Jewelry, Accessories
Average price: Moderate
District: East Village
Address: 315 E 9th St
Manhattan, NY 10003
Phone: 1+ (212) 388-9045

#147
Cook's Arts & Crafts
Arts & Crafts
Average price: Moderate
District: Glendale
Address: 80-09 Myrtle Ave
Glendale, NY 11385
Phone: 1+ (718) 366-6085

#148
Lockwood
Women's Clothing, Toy Store, Home Decor
Average price: Moderate
District: Astoria
Address: 32-15 33rd St
Astoria, NY 11106
Phone: 1+ (718) 626-6030

#149
Red Wing Shoes
Shoe Store
Average price: Expensive
District: Sunnyside
Address: 4701 Queens Blvd
Sunnyside, NY 11104
Phone: 1+ (718) 392-2242

#150
INTIMACY - bra fit stylists
Women's Clothing, Lingerie
Average price: Expensive
District: Upper East Side
Address: 1252 Madison Avenue
New York, NY 10128
Phone: 1+ (212) 860-8366

#151
Last Rites Tattoo & Art Gallery
Tattoo, Art Gallery
Average price: Exclusive
District: Hell's Kitchen, Midtown West
Address: 325 W 38th St
New York, NY 10018
Phone: 1+ (212) 529-0666

#152
Domus Unaffected Living
Home Decor, Jewelry, Cards, Stationery
Average price: Moderate
District: Hell's Kitchen, Midtown West
Address: 413 W 44th St
New York, NY 10036
Phone: 1+ (212) 581-8099

#153
Make A Frame
Framing
Average price: Expensive
District: Cobble Hill
Address: 180 Atlantic Avenue
Brooklyn, NY 11201
Phone: 1+ (718) 875-6150

#154
Optical Solutions
Eyewear, Optician
Average price: Inexpensive
District: Fort Greene
Address: 711 Fulton St
Brooklyn, NY 11217
Phone: 1+ (718) 222-8122

#155
Sabon
Cosmetics, Beauty Supply
Average price: Expensive
District: Greenwich Village
Address: 434 6th Ave
New York, NY 10011
Phone: 1+ (212) 473-4346

#156
Brooklyn General
Fabric Store, Hobby Shop
Average price: Moderate
District: Carroll Gardens, Columbia Street
Waterfront District
Address: 128 Union St
Brooklyn, NY 11231
Phone: 1+ (718) 237-7753

#157
Chess Forum
Hobby Shop
Average price: Inexpensive
District: Greenwich Village
Address: 219 Thompson St
New York, NY 10012
Phone: 1+ (212) 475-2369

#158
Ballard Pharmacy
Drugstore
Average price: Moderate
District: South Slope, Windsor Terrace
Address: 226 Prospect Park W
Brooklyn, NY 11215
Phone: 1+ (718) 768-1325

#159
Erstwhile Jewelry
Antiques, Jewelry
Average price: Expensive
District: Midtown East
Address: 589 5th Ave
New York, NY 10017
Phone: 1+ (212) 390-1144

#160
LUSH
Cosmetics, Beauty Supply
Average price: Moderate
District: Midtown West, Koreatown
Address: 1293 Broadway
New York, NY 10001
Phone: 1+ (212) 564-9120

#161
Anthropologie
Women's Clothing, Home Decor
Average price: Expensive
District: Midtown West
Address: 50 Rockefeller Plz
New York, NY 10020
Phone: 1+ (212) 246-0386

#162
The Container Store
Home & Garden
Average price: Moderate
District: Flatiron
Address: 629 6th Ave
New York, NY 10010
Phone: 1+ (212) 366-4200

#163
Harmon Face Values
Cosmetics, Beauty Supply
Average price: Inexpensive
District: Chelsea
Address: 675 6th Ave
New York, NY 10010
Phone: 1+ (212) 243-3501

#164
APC
Men's Clothing, Women's Clothing
Average price: Expensive
District: SoHo
Address: 131 Mercer St
New York, NY 10012
Phone: 1+ (212) 966-9685

#165
Rena Reborn
Thrift Store
Average price: Inexpensive
District: East Village, Alphabet City
Address: 117 E 7th St
New York, NY 10009
Phone: 1+ (212) 253-2595

#166
Every Thing Goes Book Café
and Neighborhood Stage
Music & DVDs, Bookstore, Coffee & Tea
Average price: Inexpensive
District: Tompkinsville
Address: 208 Bay St
Staten Island, NY 10301
Phone: 1+ (718) 447-8256

#167
Other Music
Music & DVDs
Average price: Moderate
District: NoHo
Address: 15 E 4th St
New York, NY 10003
Phone: 1+ (212) 477-8150

#168
Ben Moses Jewelry Designer
Jewelry
Average price: Moderate
District: Midtown West
Address: 15 W 47th Street Unit 3
New York, NY 10036
Phone: 1+ (212) 221-1017

#169
Michael F & Company
Jewelry
Average price: Moderate
District: Midtown West
Address: 7 W 47th St
New York, NY 10036
Phone: 1+ (212) 278-8585

#170
Stick, Stone & Bone
Hobby Shop
Average price: Moderate
District: West Village
Address: 111 Christopher St
New York, NY 10014
Phone: 1+ (212) 807-7024

#171
MiN New York
Cosmetics, Beauty Supply,
Barbers, Home Decor
Average price: Expensive
District: SoHo
Address: 117 Crosby St
New York, NY 10012
Phone: 1+ (212) 206-6366

#172
MoMA PS1
Museum, Art Gallery
Average price: Inexpensive
District: Hunters Point, Long Island City
Address: 22-25 Jackson Ave
Long Island City, NY 11101
Phone: 1+ (718) 784-2084

#173
Brunello Cucinelli
Men's Clothing, Women's Clothing
Average price: Exclusive
District: West Village
Address: 379 Bleecker St
New York, NY 10014
Phone: 1+ (212) 627-9202

#174
Film Biz Recycling
Thrift Store, Art Supplies
Average price: Moderate
District: Gowanus
Address: 540 President St
Brooklyn, NY 11215
Phone: 1+ (347) 384-2336

#175
Union Garage NYC
Bespoke Clothing, Motorcycle Dealer
Average price: Moderate
District: Columbia Street Waterfront District
Address: 103 Union St
Brooklyn, NY 11231
Phone: 1+ (718) 594-7093

#176
Saks Fifth Avenue
Department Store, Men's Clothing
Average price: Exclusive
District: Midtown West, Midtown East
Address: 611 5th Ave
New York, NY 10022
Phone: 1+ (212) 753-4000

#177
By Brooklyn
Cards, Stationery, Jewelry
Average price: Moderate
District: Cobble Hill, Gowanus
Address: 261 Smith St
Brooklyn, NY 11231
Phone: 1+ (718) 643-0606

#178
Hooti Couture
Thrift Store, Accessories,
Used, Vintage
Average price: Moderate
District: Prospect Heights
Address: 321 Flatbush Ave
Brooklyn, NY 11217
Phone: 1+ (718) 857-1977

#179
Guvnor's Vintage Apparel
Used, Vintage, Thrift Store
Average price: Moderate
District: Park Slope
Address: 178 5th Ave
Brooklyn, NY 11227
Phone: 1+ (718) 230-4887

#180
Crate & Barrel
Furniture Store
Average price: Moderate
District: Greenwich Village
Address: 611 Broadway
New York, NY 10012
Phone: 1+ (212) 308-0011

#181
LightHouse Films
Videographers, Photography Store, Services
Average price: Moderate
District: Chelsea, Midtown West
Address: 115 W 29th St
New York, NY 10001
Phone: 1+ (646) 649-3600

#182
Apple Store
Electronics
Average price: Expensive
District: Midtown East
Address: 767 5th Ave
New York, NY 10022
Phone: 1+ (212) 336-1440

#183
The Bike Truck
Bikes
Average price: Moderate
District: Greenpoint
Address: 27 West St
Brooklyn, NY 11222
Phone: 1+ (718) 734-8833

#184
The Reed Space
Accessories, Men's Clothing
Average price: Expensive
District: Lower East Side
Address: 151 Orchard St
New York, NY 10002
Phone: 1+ (212) 253-0588

#185
Mast Books
Bookstore
Average price: Moderate
District: East Village, Alphabet City
Address: 66 Ave A
New York, NY 10009
Phone: 1+ (646) 370-1114

#186
Town & Village Hardware
Hardware Store
Average price: Moderate
District: Stuyvesant Town, Gramercy
Address: 337 1st Ave
New York, NY 10003
Phone: 1+ (212) 673-3192

#187
Odin
Men's Clothing
Average price: Expensive
District: SoHo
Address: 199 Lafayette St
New York, NY 10012
Phone: 1+ (212) 966-0026

#188
Bonobos Guideshop
Men's Clothing, Formal Wear
Average price: Expensive
District: Flatiron
Address: 45 W 25th St
New York, NY 10010
Phone: 1+ (646) 738-3314

#189
Gray & Davis
Jewelry
Average price: Moderate
District: Midtown West
Address: 15 W 47th St
New York, NY 10036
Phone: 1+ (212) 719-4698

#190
Forever 21
Women's Clothing, Men's Clothing
Average price: Inexpensive
District: Midtown West, Theater District
Address: 1540 Broadway
New York, NY 10036
Phone: 1+ (212) 302-0594

#191
Lion In The Sun
Cards, Stationery
Average price: Moderate
District: Park Slope
Address: 232 7th Ave
Brooklyn, NY 11215
Phone: 1+ (718) 369-4006

#192
Warby Parker HQ
Eyewear, Optician, Optometrist
Average price: Moderate
District: South Village
Address: 161 Avenue of the Americas
New York, NY 10012
Phone: 1+ (646) 517-5223

#193
The Wall Street Humidor
Tobacco Shop
Average price: Moderate
District: Civic Center, TriBeCa
Address: 18 Warren St
New York, NY 10007
Phone: 1+ (212) 962-4427

#194
Onassis Clothing
Men's Clothing
Average price: Moderate
District: SoHo
Address: 71 Greene St
New York, NY 10012
Phone: 1+ (212) 966-8869

#195
Flight Club
Shoe Store, Sports Wear
Average price: Expensive
District: Greenwich Village, East Village
Address: 812 Broadway
New York, NY 10003
Phone: 1+ (888) 937-8020

#196
Makerbot Store
Electronics
Average price: Expensive
District: NoHo
Address: 298 Mulberry St
New York, NY 10012
Phone: 1+ (347) 457-5758

#197
Brooklyn Charm
Jewelry, Accessories
Average price: Moderate
District: Williamsburg - North Side
Address: 145 Bedford Ave
Brooklyn, NY 11211
Phone: 1+ (347) 689-2492

#198
Tierra
Jewelry
Average price: Moderate
District: SoHo
Address: 65 Spring St
New York, NY 10012
Phone: 1+ (646) 476-5343

#199
Stella Dallas
Used, Vintage
Average price: Moderate
District: Greenwich Village
Address: 218 Thompson St
New York, NY 10012
Phone: 1+ (212) 674-0447

#200
Video Games New York
Videos, Video Game Rental
Average price: Expensive
District: East Village
Address: 202 E 6th St
New York, NY 10003
Phone: 1+ (212) 539-1039

#201
Marc Jacobs
Men's Clothing, Women's Clothing
Average price: Expensive
District: SoHo
Address: 163 Mercer St
New York, NY 10012
Phone: 1+ (212) 343-1490

#202
Jillery
Jewelry, Used, Vintage
Average price: Moderate
District: East Village, Alphabet City
Address: 107 Ave B
New York, NY 10009
Phone: 1+ (212) 674-9383

#203
BAGGU Summer Store
Accessories
Average price: Inexpensive
District: Williamsburg - North Side
Address: 242 Wythe Ave
Brooklyn, NY 11249
Phone: 1+ (800) 605-0759

#204
The Brooklyn Circus
Men's Clothing, Women's Clothing
Average price: Expensive
District: Boerum Hill
Address: 150 Nevins St
Brooklyn, NY 11217
Phone: 1+ (718) 858-0919

#205
Rue St Denis Clothier
Used, Vintage,
Men's Clothing, Women's Clothing
Average price: Moderate
District: East Village, Alphabet City
Address: 170 Avenue B
New York, NY 10009
Phone: 1+ (212) 260-3388

#206
Daytona Trimmings Company
Fabric Store
Average price: Inexpensive
District: Midtown West
Address: 251 W 39th St
New York, NY 10018
Phone: 1+ (212) 354-1713

#207
White House Black Market
Women's Clothing
Average price: Moderate
District: Flatiron
Address: 136 5th Ave
New York, NY 10011
Phone: 1+ (212) 741-8685

#208
Skinnyskinny
Skin Care, Nursery, Gardening, Gift Shop
Average price: Expensive
District: Williamsburg - South Side
Address: 268 Grand St
Brooklyn, NY 11211
Phone: 1+ (718) 388-2201

#209
Sur La Table
Kitchen & Bath
Average price: Expensive
District: SoHo
Address: 75 Spring St
New York, NY 10012
Phone: 1+ (212) 966-3375

#210
Saint Laurent
Men's Clothing, Women's Clothing,
Accessories
Average price: Exclusive
District: Midtown East
Address: 3 E 57th St
New York, NY 10022
Phone: 1+ (212) 980-2970

#211
No Relation Vintage
Used, Vintage, Thrift Store
Average price: Inexpensive
District: East Village
Address: 204 1st Ave
New York, NY 10009
Phone: 1+ (212) 228-5201

#212
Kiki de Montparnasse
Adult, Lingerie
Average price: Exclusive
District: SoHo
Address: 79 Greene St
New York, NY 10012
Phone: 1+ (212) 965-8070

#213
Guenevere Rodriguez
Jewelry
Average price: Moderate
District: Williamsburg - South Side
Address: 309 Bedford Ave
Brooklyn, NY 11211
Phone: 1+ (718) 387-4878

#214
Skate Brooklyn
Outdoor Gear, Sports Wear
Average price: Moderate
District: Park Slope, Gowanus
Address: 78 St. Marks Pl
Brooklyn, NY 11217
Phone: 1+ (718) 857-5283

#215
Forbidden Fruit NYC
Desserts, Flowers & Gifts
Average price: Inexpensive
District: Greenwich Village
Address: 106 Macdougal St
New York, NY 10012
Phone: 1+ (212) 671-1222

#216
Facial Index
Eyewear, Optician
Average price: Expensive
District: SoHo
Address: 104 Grand St
New York, NY 10013
Phone: 1+ (646) 613-1055

#217
Piccolini
Baby Gear & Furniture, Toy Store
Average price: Moderate
District: Nolita
Address: 230 B Mulberry St
Manhattan, NY 10012
Phone: 1+ (212) 775-1118

#218
Devonshire Optical
Eyewear, Optician
Average price: Expensive
District: Greenwich Village
Address: 51 University Pl
New York, NY 10003
Phone: 1+ (212) 982-3762

#219
The Ink Pad
Art Supplies
Average price: Moderate
District: West Village
Address: 37 7th Ave at W 13th St
New York, NY 10011
Phone: 1+ (212) 463-9876

#220
Milly & Earl
Accessories, Jewelry
Average price: Moderate
District: Williamsburg - North Side
Address: 351 Graham Ave
Brooklyn, NY 11211
Phone: 1+ (718) 389-0901

#221
Adeline Adeline
Bikes
Average price: Expensive
District: TriBeCa
Address: 147 Reade St
New York, NY 10013
Phone: 1+ (212) 227-1150

#222
Smiley's Yarn Store
Knitting Supplies
Average price: Inexpensive
District: Woodhaven
Address: 92-06 Jamaica Ave
Woodhaven, NY 11421
Phone: 1+ (718) 849-9873

#223
Michiyo Art Studio
Art Gallery, Art School
Average price: Moderate
District: Chinatown, Civic Center
Address: 59 Franklin St
Manhattan, NY 10013
Phone: 1+ (646) 801-3282

#224
Patricia Field
Accessories, Women's Clothing, Costumes
Average price: Expensive
District: NoHo
Address: 306 Bowery
New York, NY 10012
Phone: 1+ (212) 966-4066

#225
Community Optical
Optometrist, Eyewear, Optician
Average price: Moderate
District: Carroll Gardens
Address: 453 Ct St
Brooklyn, NY 11231
Phone: 1+ (718) 625-7300

#226
Poppy
Women's Clothing, Accessories
Average price: Expensive
District: Nolita
Address: 281 Mott St
New York, NY 10012
Phone: 1+ (212) 219-8934

#227
Good Records NYC
Music & DVDs
Average price: Moderate
District: East Village
Address: 218 E 5th St
New York, NY 10003
Phone: 1+ (212) 529-2081

#228
The Mysterious Bookshop
Bookstore
Average price: Moderate
District: TriBeCa
Address: 58 Warren St
New York, NY 10007
Phone: 1+ (212) 587-1011

#229
Lori McLean
Jewelry, Accessories
Average price: Moderate
District: West Village
Address: 49 Grove St
New York, NY 10014
Phone: 1+ (212) 242-3204

#230
Kelima K
Bridal
Average price: Expensive
District: SoHo, Greenwich Village, NoHo
Address: 611 Broadway
New York, NY 10012
Phone: 1+ (212) 334-6546

#231
Dig
Nursery, Gardening
Average price: Moderate
District: Boerum Hill
Address: 479 Atlantic Ave
Brooklyn, NY 11217
Phone: 1+ (718) 554-0207

#232
MALIN + GOETZ
Skin Care, Cosmetics, Beauty Supply
Average price: Expensive
District: Chelsea
Address: 177 7th Ave
New York, NY 10011
Phone: 1+ (212) 727-3777

#233
Selima Optique
Eyewear, Optician
Average price: Expensive
District: SoHo
Address: 59 Wooster St
New York, NY 10012
Phone: 1+ (212) 343-9490

#234
MOSCOT
Optometrist, Eyewear, Optician
Average price: Expensive
District: Lower East Side
Address: 108 Orchard St
New York, NY 10002
Phone: 1+ (212) 477-3796

#235
Comptoir Des Cotonniers
Women's Clothing, Children's Clothing
Average price: Expensive
District: SoHo
Address: 155 Spring St
New York, NY 10012
Phone: 1+ (212) 274-0830

#236
Angel Orensanz Foundation
Art Gallery
Average price: Expensive
District: Lower East Side
Address: 172 Norfolk St
New York, NY 10002
Phone: 1+ (212) 529-7194

#237
Guitar New York
Musical Instruments
Average price: Moderate
District: Midtown West
Address: 1350 Ave of the Americas
New York, NY 10019
Phone: 1+ (646) 380-2467

#238
Beauty 35
Cosmetics, Beauty Supply
Average price: Inexpensive
District: Hell's Kitchen, Midtown West
Address: 505 8th Ave
New York, NY 10018
Phone: 1+ (212) 563-1010

#239
The Sample Room NY
Bridal
Average price: Expensive
District: Flatiron
Address: 40 W 17th St
New York, NY 10011
Phone: 1+ (212) 929-8868

#240
Kidding Around
Toy Store
Average price: Moderate
District: Flatiron
Address: 60 W 15th St
New York, NY 10011
Phone: 1+ (212) 645-6337

#241
192 Books
Bookstore
Average price: Moderate
District: Chelsea
Address: 192 10th Ave
New York, NY 10011
Phone: 1+ (212) 255-4022

#242
The Little Lebowski Shop
Books, Mags, Music & Video, Hobby Shop
Average price: Moderate
District: Greenwich Village
Address: 215 Thompson St
New York, NY 10012
Phone: 1+ (212) 388-1466

#243
Burton Snowboards Flagship Store
Outdoor Gear
Average price: Expensive
District: SoHo
Address: 106 Spring St
New York, NY 10012
Phone: 1+ (212) 966-8070

#244
Alphabets
Toy Store
Average price: Moderate
District: East Village, Alphabet City
Address: 115 Ave A
New York, NY 10009
Phone: 1+ (212) 475-7250

#245
Global Gold & Silver
Jewelry, Gold Buyers
Average price: Exclusive
District: Midtown West
Address: 7 W 45th St
New York, NY 10036
Phone: 1+ (212) 302-4653

#246
From The Source
Furniture Store, Home Decor, Antiques
Average price: Expensive
District: Greenpoint
Address: 69 West St
Brooklyn, NY 11222
Phone: 1+ (718) 532-1671

#247
Argosy Book Store
Antiques, Art Gallery, Bookstore
Average price: Expensive
District: Midtown East
Address: 116 E 59th St
New York, NY 10022
Phone: 1+ (212) 753-4455

#248
John Paradiso Diamond Jewelry
Jewelry
Average price: Expensive
District: Little Italy, Chinatown
Address: 76 Bowery
New York, NY 10013
Phone: 1+ (212) 343-1917

#249
Joy's Flowers and Gifts
Florist
Average price: Moderate
District: Lower East Side
Address: 40 Hester St
New York, NY 10002
Phone: 1+ (212) 777-7701

#250
Fanaberie
Women's Clothing
Average price: Moderate
District: Greenpoint
Address: 102A Nassau Ave
Brooklyn, NY 11222
Phone: 1+ (347) 987-3929

#251
Shut Skates
Outdoor Gear
Average price: Moderate
District: Lower East Side
Address: 158 Orchard Street
Manhattan, NY 10002
Phone: 1+ (212) 420-7488

#252
Downtown Yarns
Knitting Supplies
Average price: Moderate
District: East Village, Alphabet City
Address: 45 Ave A
New York, NY 10009
Phone: 1+ (212) 995-5991

#253
New York Running Company
Sports Wear, Shoe Store
Average price: Moderate
District: Hell's Kitchen, Midtown West
Address: 10 Columbus Circle
New York, NY 10019
Phone: 1+ (212) 823-9626

#254
Le Labo
Cosmetics, Beauty Supply
Average price: Expensive
District: Nolita
Address: 233 Elizabeth St
New York, NY 10012
Phone: 1+ (212) 219-2230

#255
**Gemological Appraisal
Laboratory of America**
Jewelry
Average price: Moderate
District: Midtown West
Address: 10 W 47th St
New York, NY 10036
Phone: 1+ (212) 382-2888

#256
Hartley Chemists
Drugstore
Average price: Moderate
District: Morningside Heights
Address: 1219 Amsterdam Ave
New York, NY 10027
Phone: 1+ (212) 749-8481

#257
New York City Pharmacy
Drugstore
Average price: Moderate
District: East Village
Address: 206 1st Ave
New York, NY 10009
Phone: 1+ (212) 253-8686

#258
Clover's Fine Art Gallery
Coffee & Tea, Art Gallery, Venues
& Event Spaces
Average price: Moderate
District: Boerum Hill
Address: 338 Atlantic Ave
Brooklyn, NY 11201
Phone: 1+ (718) 625-2121

#259
Artikal N.Y.C.
Accessories, Bridal
Average price: Moderate
District: East Village, Alphabet City
Address: 510 E 12th St
New York, NY 10009
Phone: 1+ (212) 260-0278

#260
The Lego Store
Toy Store
Average price: Moderate
District: Midtown West
Address: 620 5th Ave
New York, NY 10020
Phone: 1+ (212) 245-5973

#261
KITEYA SOHO
Accessories, Cards, Stationery,
Home Decor
Average price: Moderate
District: SoHo
Address: 464 Broome St
New York, NY 10013
Phone: 1+ (212) 219-7505

#262
MAC Cosmetics
Cosmetics, Beauty Supply, Makeup Artists
Average price: Expensive
District: Flatiron
Address: 1 East 22 Street
New York, NY 10010
Phone: 1+ (212) 677-6611

#263
Owl & Thistle General Store
Gift Shop
Average price: Moderate
District: Crown Heights
Address: 833 Franklin Ave
New York, NY 11225
Phone: 1+ (347) 722-5836

#264
Town Shop
Lingerie
Average price: Expensive
District: Upper West Side
Address: 2270 Broadway
New York, NY 10024
Phone: 1+ (212) 787-2762

#265
Barneys New York
Department Store
Average price: Exclusive
District: Upper East Side
Address: 660 Madison Ave
New York, NY 10065
Phone: 1+ (212) 826-8900

#266
Barnes & Noble
Newspapers, Magazines, Bookstore
Average price: Moderate
District: Upper East Side
Address: 150 E 86th St
New York, NY 10028
Phone: 1+ (212) 369-2180

#267
A K Fabric
Fabric Store
Average price: Moderate
District: Midtown West
Address: 257 W 39th St
New York, NY 10018
Phone: 1+ (212) 944-5693

#268
A Cook's Companion
Kitchen & Bath
Average price: Expensive
District: Brooklyn Heights
Address: 197 Atlantic Ave
Brooklyn, NY 11201
Phone: 1+ (718) 852-6901

#269
Greenwich Letterpress
Cards, Stationery
Average price: Expensive
District: West Village
Address: 39 Christopher St
New York, NY 10014
Phone: 1+ (212) 989-7464

#270
Kim's Jewelry
Jewelry
Average price: Moderate
District: Midtown West
Address: 26 W 47th St
New York, NY 10036
Phone: 1+ (212) 575-2317

#271
S H Zell & Sons
Jewelry
Average price: Moderate
District: Midtown West
Address: 23 W 47th St
New York, NY 10036
Phone: 1+ (212) 921-9693

#272
Eastern Mountain Sports
Outdoor Gear, Sports Wear
Average price: Moderate
District: SoHo
Address: 530 Broadway
New York, NY 10012
Phone: 1+ (212) 966-8730

#273
Leathernecks Tattoo
Art Gallery, Tattoo, Piercing
Average price: Moderate
District: South Slope
Address: 667A 5th Ave
Brooklyn, NY 11215
Phone: 1+ (718) 499-9465

#274
Enfleurage
Cosmetics, Beauty Supply
Average price: Moderate
District: West Village
Address: 237 W 13 St
New York, NY 10011
Phone: 1+ (212) 691-1610

#275
Saturdays Surf NYC
Coffee & Tea, Sporting Goods
Average price: Moderate
District: SoHo
Address: 31 Crosby St
New York, NY 10013
Phone: 1+ (212) 966-7875

#276
Steinlauf & Stoller
Fabric Store
Average price: Moderate
District: Midtown West
Address: 239 W 39th St
New York, NY 10018
Phone: 1+ (212) 869-0321

#277
Bloomingdale's SoHo
Department Store
Average price: Expensive
District: SoHo
Address: 504 Broadway
New York, NY 10012
Phone: 1+ (212) 729-5900

#278
Soho Art Materials
Art Supplies
Average price: Moderate
District: SoHo, TriBeCa
Address: 7 Wooster St.
New York, NY 10013
Phone: 1+ (212) 431-3938

#279
Marni USA Store
Shoe Store, Women's Clothing
Average price: Exclusive
District: SoHo
Address: 161 Mercer St
New York, NY 10012
Phone: 1+ (212) 343-3912

#280
Save Khaki
Men's Clothing
Average price: Expensive
District: NoHo
Address: 317 Lafayette St
New York, NY 10012
Phone: 1+ (212) 925-0130

#281
Adidas Originals
Shoe Store
Average price: Moderate
District: SoHo
Address: 136 Wooster St
New York, NY 10012
Phone: 1+ (212) 673-0398

#282
Housing Works Thrift Shop
Used, Vintage, Thrift Store
Average price: Inexpensive
District: Upper West Side
Address: 306 Columbus Ave
New York, NY 10023
Phone: 1+ (212) 579-7566

#283
Pinkyotto
Women's Clothing, Jewelry
Average price: Expensive
District: East Village
Address: 307 E 9th St
New York, NY 10003
Phone: 1+ (212) 533-4028

#284
Lot Less Closeouts
Department Store
Average price: Inexpensive
District: Civic Center, TriBeCa
Address: 97 Chambers St
New York, NY 10007
Phone: 1+ (212) 233-0607

#285
Leisure Pro
Sporting Goods, Diving
Average price: Moderate
District: Flatiron
Address: 42 W 18th St
New York, NY 10011
Phone: 1+ (888) 805-3600

#286
Gramercy Typewriter Co
IT Services & Computer Repair,
Office Equipment
Average price: Moderate
District: Flatiron
Address: 174 5th Ave
Manhattan, NY 10010
Phone: 1+ (212) 674-7700

#287
Black Lapel Custom Clothiers
Men's Clothing, Formal Wear
Average price: Moderate
District: Chelsea
Address: 121 W 27th St
New York, NY 10001
Phone: 1+ (212) 389-2043

#288
Frank's Bike Shop
Bike Rentals, Bikes
Average price: Inexpensive
District: Lower East Side
Address: 553 Grand St
New York, NY 10002
Phone: 1+ (212) 533-6332

#289
Floating Piano Factory
Musical Instruments
Average price: Moderate
District: Williamsburg - North Side
Address: 272 Willoughby Ave
Brooklyn, NY 11205
Phone: 1+ (718) 283-4283

#290
SlapBack
Women's Clothing
Average price: Moderate
District: Williamsburg - North Side
Address: 490 Metropolitan Ave
Brooklyn, NY 11211
Phone: 1+ (347) 227-7133

#291
Jack's World
Discount Store
Average price: Inexpensive
District: Midtown West
Address: 45 W 45th St
New York, NY 10036
Phone: 1+ (212) 354-6888

#292
Diptyque
Cosmetics, Beauty Supply
Average price: Expensive
District: Upper East Side
Address: 971 Madison Ave
New York, NY 10021
Phone: 1+ (212) 879-3330

#293
Langdon Florist
Florist
Average price: Moderate
District: Civic Center, TriBeCa
Address: 62 Reade St
New York, NY 10007
Phone: 1+ (212) 962-4370

#294
Mr. Throwback
Thrift Store
Average price: Moderate
District: East Village, Alphabet City
Address: 428 E 9th St
New York, NY 10009
Phone: 1+ (646) 410-0310

#295
Cloak & Dagger
Women's Clothing, Jewelry, Accessories
Average price: Expensive
District: East Village, Alphabet City
Address: 441 E 9th St
New York, NY 10009
Phone: 1+ (212) 673-0500

#296
Housing Works Thrift Shop
Used, Vintage, Thrift Store
Average price: Inexpensive
District: West Village
Address: 245 W 10th St
New York, NY 10014
Phone: 1+ (212) 352-1618

#297
Costco
Wholesale Store
Average price: Moderate
District: East Harlem
Address: 517 E 117th St
New York, NY 10035
Phone: 1+ (212) 896-5900

#298
Mongo
Home Decor, Jewelry, Antiques
Average price: Moderate
District: Cobble Hill, Carroll Gardens
Address: 246 Smith St
Brooklyn, NY 11217
Phone: 1+ (917) 671-7696

#299
Socrates Sculpture Park
Art Gallery
Average price: Inexpensive
District: Hunters Point, Long Island City
Address: 32-01 Vernon Blvd
Long Island City, NY 11106
Phone: 1+ (718) 956-1819

#300
Bond No. 9
Cosmetics, Beauty Supply
Average price: Expensive
District: NoHo
Address: 9 Bond St
New York, NY 10012
Phone: 1+ (212) 228-1732

#301
Rudy's Music Soho
Musical Instruments
Average price: Expensive
District: SoHo
Address: 461 Broome St
Chinatown, NY 10013
Phone: 1+ (212) 625-2557

#302
JB Prince Company
Kitchen & Bath
Average price: Expensive
District: Midtown East
Address: 36 E 31st St
New York, NY 10016
Phone: 1+ (212) 683-3553

#303
Cosmophonic Sound
Electronics
Average price: Moderate
District: Yorkville, Upper East Side
Address: 1622 1st Ave
New York, NY 10028
Phone: 1+ (212) 734-0459

#304
Mini Mini Market
Women's Clothing, Accessories, Jewelry
Average price: Moderate
District: Williamsburg - North Side
Address: 218 Bedford Ave
Brooklyn, NY 11211
Phone: 1+ (718) 302-9337

#305
Foxy & Winston
Cards, Stationery, Children's Clothing
Average price: Moderate
District: Red Hook
Address: 392 Van Brunt St
Brooklyn, NY 11231
Phone: 1+ (718) 928-4855

#306
Christian Louboutin
Shoe Store
Average price: Exclusive
District: West Village
Address: 59 Horatio St
New York, NY 10184
Phone: 1+ (212) 255-1910

#307
Muji
Department Store
Average price: Moderate
District: Flatiron
Address: 16 W 19th St
New York, NY 10011
Phone: 1+ (212) 414-9024

#308
J Lindeberg Store
Men's Clothing
Average price: Expensive
District: SoHo
Address: 126 Spring St
New York, NY 10012
Phone: 1+ (212) 625-9403

#309
Billy Reid
Men's Clothing, Women's Clothing
Average price: Expensive
District: NoHo
Address: 54 Bond St
New York, NY 10012
Phone: 1+ (212) 598-9355

#310
Rainbow Ace Hardware
Hardware Store
Average price: Moderate
District: Yorkville, Upper East Side
Address: 1449 1st Ave
New York, NY 10021
Phone: 1+ (212) 288-4868

#311
The Upper Rust Antiques
Antiques
Average price: Moderate
District: East Village, Alphabet City
Address: 445 E 9th St
New York, NY 10009
Phone: 1+ (212) 533-3953

#312
Paul Stuart
Men's Clothing
Average price: Exclusive
District: Midtown East
Address: 10 E 45th St
New York, NY 10001
Phone: 1+ (212) 682-0320

#313
Freebird Books & Goods
Bookstore
Average price: Inexpensive
District: Columbia Street Waterfront District
Address: 123 Columbia St
Brooklyn, NY 11231
Phone: 1+ (718) 643-8484

#314
Leigh Jay Nacht
Jewelry
Average price: Moderate
District: Midtown West
Address: 10 W 47th St
New York, NY 10036
Phone: 1+ (212) 719-2888

#315
**Community Book Store
of Park Slope**
Books, Mags, Music & Video
Average price: Moderate
District: Park Slope
Address: 143 7th Ave
Brooklyn, NY 11215
Phone: 1+ (718) 783-3075

#316
Kate Spade
Women's Clothing
Average price: Exclusive
District: Upper East Side
Address: 789 Madison Ave
New York, NY 10065
Phone: 1+ (212) 988-0259

#317
Free People
Fashion
Average price: Expensive
District: Cobble Hill, Boerum Hill
Address: 113 Smith St
Brooklyn, NY 11201
Phone: 1+ (718) 250-0050

#318
ANNIE The Musical
Performing Arts, Musical Instruments
Average price: Expensive
District: Hell's Kitchen, Midtown West,
Theater District
Address: between 46th & 47th St
New York, NY 10036
Phone: 1+ (877) 250-2929

#319
Westside Skate and Stick
Outdoor Gear, Sports Wear
Average price: Expensive
District: Flatiron
Address: 174 5th Ave
New York, NY 10010
Phone: 1+ (212) 228-8400

#320
Alexander West
Men's Clothing, Formal Wear
Average price: Expensive
District: Flatiron
Address: 333 Park Ave S
New York, NY 10010
Phone: 1+ (866) 647-1740

#321
Molasses Books
Café, Bookstore, Bar
Average price: Inexpensive
District: Bushwick
Address: 770 Hart St
Brooklyn, NY 11237
Phone: 1+ (631) 882-5188

#322
Tekserve
Computers, Electronics
Average price: Moderate
District: Chelsea
Address: 119 W 23rd St
New York, NY 10011
Phone: 1+ (212) 929-3645

#323
Earrings Plaza
Jewelry
Average price: Inexpensive
District: Midtown West, Koreatown
Address: 1263 Broadway
New York, NY 10001
Phone: 1+ (212) 481-3666

#324
Swallow
Gift Shop
Average price: Expensive
District: Carroll Gardens, Gowanus
Address: 361 Smith St
Brooklyn, NY 11231
Phone: 1+ (718) 222-8201

#325
Vinnie's Styles
Women's Clothing, Men's Clothing
Average price: Expensive
District: Park Slope, Prospect Heights,
Boerum Hill
Address: 160 Flatbush Ave
Brooklyn, NY 11217
Phone: 1+ (718) 636-9787

#326
Lululemon Athletica
Sports Wear, Women's Clothing, Yoga
Average price: Expensive
District: SoHo
Address: 481 Broadway
New York, NY 10013
Phone: 1+ (212) 334-8276

#327
Jack Spade
Men's Clothing
Average price: Expensive
District: SoHo
Address: 56 Greene St
New York, NY 10012
Phone: 1+ (212) 625-1820

#328
Camper
Shoe Store
Average price: Expensive
District: SoHo
Address: 125 Prince St
New York, NY 10012
Phone: 1+ (212) 375-9786

#329
ABC Carpet And Home
Furniture Store
Average price: Exclusive
District: Flatiron
Address: 888 Broadway
New York, NY 10003
Phone: 1+ (212) 473-3000

#330
Fox & Fawn
Used, Vintage
Average price: Moderate
District: Greenpoint
Address: 570 Manhattan Ave
Brooklyn, NY 11222
Phone: 1+ (718) 349-9510

#331
Shown To Scale
Men's Clothing, Women's Clothing
Average price: Moderate
District: Greenpoint
Address: 67 W St
Brooklyn, NY 11222
Phone: 1+ (347) 987-4729

#332
Cure Thrift Shop
Antiques, Thrift Store
Average price: Moderate
District: East Village
Address: 111 E 12th St
New York, NY 10003
Phone: 1+ (212) 505-7467

#333
Journelle
Lingerie
Average price: Expensive
District: SoHo
Address: 125 Mercer St
Manhattan, NY 10012
Phone: 1+ (212) 255-7803

#334
Fresh
Cosmetics, Beauty Supply, Skin Care
Average price: Expensive
District: Union Square, Flatiron
Address: 872 Broadway
New York, NY 10003
Phone: 1+ (212) 477-1100

#335
Lululemon Athletica
Sports Wear, Women's Clothing
Average price: Expensive
District: Union Square, Flatiron
Address: 15 Union Sq W
New York, NY 10003
Phone: 1+ (212) 675-5286

#336
Dolly G's
Used, Vintage, Women's Clothing
Average price: Moderate
District: East Williamsburg
Address: 320 Graham Ave
Brooklyn, NY 11211
Phone: 1+ (718) 599-1044

#337
Tom Ford
Fashion
Average price: Exclusive
District: Upper East Side
Address: 845 Madison Ave
New York, NY 10021
Phone: 1+ (212) 359-0300

#338
ProAudioStar
Musical Instruments
Average price: Expensive
District: Greenpoint
Address: 217 Russell St
Brooklyn, NY 11222
Phone: 1+ (718) 522-1071

#339
Lot-Less Closeouts
Discount Store
Average price: Inexpensive
District: Midtown West, Theater District
Address: 206 West 40th Street
New York, NY 10018
Phone: 1+ (212) 704-9856

#340
Book Culture
Bookstore
Average price: Moderate
District: Morningside Heights
Address: 536 W 112th St
New York, NY 10025
Phone: 1+ (212) 865-1588

#341
PS Fabrics
Fabric Store
Average price: Inexpensive
District: Chinatown
Address: 359 Broadway
New York, NY 10013
Phone: 1+ (212) 226-1534

#342
Room & Board
Furniture Store, Mattresses
Average price: Expensive
District: SoHo
Address: 105 Wooster St
New York, NY 10012
Phone: 1+ (212) 334-4343

#343
Sur La Table
Appliances
Average price: Moderate
District: Hell's Kitchen, Midtown West
Address: 306 West 57th
New York, NY 10019
Phone: 1+ (212) 574-8334

#344
Harvest Cyclery- Vintage & Used Bicycle Shop
Bike Repair/Maintenance, Bikes
Average price: Inexpensive
District: Bushwick
Address: 606 Bushwick Ave
Brooklyn, NY 11206
Phone: 1+ (929) 234-3555

#345
Housing Works Thrift Shop
Used, Vintage, Thrift Store
Average price: Moderate
District: Chelsea
Address: 143 W 17th St
New York, NY 10011
Phone: 1+ (718) 838-5050

#346
567 Framing East Village
Framing, Printing Services, Photographer
Average price: Moderate
District: East Village, Alphabet City
Address: 228 Ave B
New York, NY 10009
Phone: 1+ (212) 533-6669

#347
Midtown Comics Grand Central
Comic Books
Average price: Moderate
District: Midtown East
Address: 459 Lexington Ave
New York, NY 10017
Phone: 1+ (212) 302-8192

#348
ENZ's
Women's Clothing
Average price: Moderate
District: East Village
Address: 125 2nd Ave
New York, NY 10003
Phone: 1+ (917) 841-5989

#349
M&J Trimming
Fabric Store, Hobby Shop
Average price: Expensive
District: Midtown West
Address: 1008 6th Ave
New York, NY 10018
Phone: 1+ (212) 391-6200

#350
Leather Spa
Shoe Repair, Luggage
Average price: Expensive
District: Midtown West
Address: 55 W 55th St
New York, NY 10019
Phone: 1+ (212) 262-4823

#351
Reiss
Men's Clothing, Women's Clothing
Average price: Expensive
District: West Village
Address: 313 Bleecker St
New York, NY 10014
Phone: 1+ (212) 488-2411

#352
Eye D Vision Optical
Optometrist, Eyewear, Optician
Average price: Moderate
District: Bath Beach, Bensonhurst
Address: 2057 86th St
Brooklyn, NY 11214
Phone: 1+ (718) 355-9656

#353
Pema NY
Women's Clothing, Accessories
Average price: Moderate
District: Williamsburg - North Side
Address: 225 Bedford Ave
Brooklyn, NY 11211
Phone: 1+ (718) 388-8814

#354
AC Gears
Electronics, Toy Store, Watches
Average price: Moderate
District: Greenwich Village
Address: 69 E 8th St
New York, NY 10003
Phone: 1+ (212) 375-1700

#355
Trunk Show Designer Consignment
Personal Shopping, Used, Vintage
Average price: Exclusive
District: Harlem
Address: 275-277 W 113th St
New York, NY 10026
Phone: 1+ (212) 662-0009

#356
Reiss
Women's Clothing, Men's Clothing
Average price: Expensive
District: SoHo
Address: 387 W Broadway
New York, NY 10012
Phone: 1+ (212) 925-5707

#357
D V V S
Jewelry
Average price: Moderate
District: Chelsea
Address: 263A W 19th St
New York, NY 10011
Phone: 1+ (212) 366-4888

#358
Burberry
Leather Goods, Shoe Store, Men's Clothing,
Women's Clothing, Children's Clothing
Average price: Exclusive
District: Midtown East
Address: 9 E 57th St
New York, NY 10022
Phone: 1+ (212) 407-7100

#359
Village Party Store
Costumes, Party Supplies
Average price: Inexpensive
District: Greenwich Village
Address: 13 E 8th St
New York, NY 10003
Phone: 1+ (212) 675-9697

#360
Artist & Craftsman Supply
Art Supplies
Average price: Moderate
District: East Williamsburg
Address: 761 Metropolitan Ave
Brooklyn, NY 11211
Phone: 1+ (718) 782-7765

#361
Mario Badescu Skin Care
Skin Care, Cosmetics,
Beauty Supply, Day Spas
Average price: Moderate
District: Midtown East
Address: 320 E 52nd St
New York, NY 10022
Phone: 1+ (212) 223-3728

#362
Sao Mai
Vietnamese, Asian Fusion, Shopping
Average price: Moderate
District: East Village
Address: 203 1st Ave
New York, NY 10003
Phone: 1+ (212) 358-8880

#363
Purlsoho
Fabric Store
Average price: Expensive
District: SoHo
Address: 459 Broome St
New York, NY 10013
Phone: 1+ (212) 420-8796

#364
Trash & Vaudeville
Men's Clothing, Women's Clothing,
Accessories
Average price: Expensive
District: East Village
Address: 4 St Marks Pl
New York, NY 10003
Phone: 1+ (212) 982-3590

#365
SRG Fashion
Bespoke Clothing, Men's Clothing
Average price: Inexpensive
District: Steinway
Address: 1971 41st St
Astoria, NY 11105
Phone: 1+ (718) 626-9600

#366
Village Style
Used, Vintage
Average price: Moderate
District: East Village, Alphabet City
Address: 111 E 7th St
New York, NY 10009
Phone: 1+ (212) 260-6390

#367
American Eagle Outfitters
Women's Clothing, Men's Clothing,
Accessories
Average price: Moderate
District: Midtown West, Theater District
Address: 1551-1555 Broadway
Manhattan, NY 10036
Phone: 1+ (212) 205-7260

#368
Madewell
Women's Clothing, Accessories, Shoe Store
Average price: Moderate
District: SoHo
Address: 486 Broadway
New York, NY 10013
Phone: 1+ (212) 226-6954

#369
Free People Clothing Boutique
Fashion
Average price: Expensive
District: Union Square, Flatiron
Address: 79 5th Ave
New York, NY 10003
Phone: 1+ (212) 647-1293

#370
Zarin Fabrics
Fabric Store, Shades & Blinds,
Furniture Store
Average price: Expensive
District: Lower East Side
Address: 72 Allen St
New York, NY 10002
Phone: 1+ (212) 925-6112

#371
Rudy's Hobby & Art
Hobby Shop, Art Supplies
Average price: Inexpensive
District: Astoria
Address: 3516 30th Ave
Astoria, NY 11103
Phone: 1+ (718) 545-8280

#372
Steven Alan
Men's Clothing, Women's Clothing
Average price: Expensive
District: TriBeCa
Address: 103 Franklin St
New York, NY 10013
Phone: 1+ (212) 343-0692

#373
Classic Tile & Marble
Kitchen & Bath
Average price: Moderate
District: Bath Beach, Bensonhurst
Address: 1635 86th St
Brooklyn, NY 11214
Phone: 1+ (718) 331-2615

#374
3.1 Phillip Lim
Women's Clothing, Men's Clothing
Average price: Expensive
District: SoHo
Address: 115 Mercer St
New York, NY 10012
Phone: 1+ (212) 334-1160

#375
Bed Bath & Beyond
Kitchen & Bath
Average price: Moderate
District: TriBeCa
Address: 270 Greenwich St
New York, NY 10007
Phone: 1+ (212) 233-8450

#376
PhotoManhattan
Specialty School, Adult Education,
Photography Store, Services
Average price: Moderate
District: Flatiron
Address: 51 W 14th St
New York, NY 10011
Phone: 1+ (212) 929-3302

#377
Ricky's & Revolver Salon
Cosmetics, Beauty Supply, Hair Salon
Average price: Moderate
District: SoHo
Address: 590 Broadway
New York, NY 10012
Phone: 1+ (212) 226-5552

#378
Exit 9 Gift Emporium
Cards, Stationery, Accessories, Toy Store
Average price: Moderate
District: Cobble Hill, Boerum Hill
Address: 127 Smith St
Brooklyn, NY 11201
Phone: 1+ (718) 422-7720

#379
Odin - East Village
Men's Clothing
Average price: Expensive
District: East Village
Address: 328 E 11th St
New York, NY 10003
Phone: 1+ (212) 475-0666

#380
Prada Broadway
Shoe Store, Leather Goods
Average price: Exclusive
District: SoHo
Address: 575 Broadway
New York, NY 10012
Phone: 1+ (212) 334-8888

#381
Buy Buy Baby
Baby Gear & Furniture
Average price: Moderate
District: Chelsea
Address: 270 7th Ave
New York, NY 10001
Phone: 1+ (917) 344-1555

#382
Bank of America Winter Village at Bryant Park
Skating Rinks, Shopping
Average price: Moderate
District: Midtown West, Theater District
Address: W 42nd St and 6th Ave
New York, NY 10018
Phone: 1+ (212) 768-4242

#383
Muji
Home Decor, Furniture Store
Average price: Moderate
District: SoHo
Address: 455 Broadway
New York, NY 10013
Phone: 1+ (212) 334-2002

#384
Puro Chile
Home Decor, Ethnic Food
Average price: Moderate
District: Chinatown
Address: 221 Ctr St
New York, NY 10013
Phone: 1+ (212) 925-7876

#385
AG Adriano Goldschmied
Men's Clothing, Women's Clothing
Average price: Expensive
District: SoHo
Address: 111 Greene Street
New York, NY 10012
Phone: 1+ (212) 680-0581

#386
Gizmo Notion
Fabric Store
Average price: Moderate
District: East Village
Address: 160 1st Ave
New York, NY 10009
Phone: 1+ (212) 477-2773

#387
A Uno Tribeca
Women's Clothing
Average price: Expensive
District: TriBeCa
Address: 123 W Broadway
New York, NY 10013
Phone: 1+ (212) 227-6233

#388
DeNatale Jewelers
Jewelry, Watches
Average price: Expensive
District: Financial District
Address: 111 Broadway
New York, NY 10006
Phone: 1+ (212) 349-8900

#389
Rolling Orange Bikes
Bikes, Bike Rentals, Bike Repair
Average price: Moderate
District: Cobble Hill
Address: 269 Baltic St
Brooklyn, NY 11201
Phone: 1+ (718) 935-0695

#390
Soula Shoes
Shoe Store
Average price: Expensive
District: Cobble Hill, Boerum Hill
Address: 185 Smith St
Brooklyn, NY 11201
Phone: 1+ (718) 834-8423

#391
Yaf Sparkle
Jewelry, Leather Goods, Accessories
Average price: Moderate
District: Lower East Side
Address: 158 Orchard St
New York, NY 10002
Phone: 1+ (212) 254-0460

#392
Sesame Letterpress
Cards, Stationery
Average price: Moderate
District: DUMBO
Address: 55 Washington Street
Brooklyn, NY 11201
Phone: 1+ (646) 263-7916

#393
Pageant Print Shop
Antiques, Bookstore
Average price: Moderate
District: East Village
Address: 69 4th St E
New York, NY 10003
Phone: 1+ (212) 674-5296

#394
D L Cerney
Fashion
Average price: Expensive
District: East Village
Address: 13 E 7th St
New York, NY 10003
Phone: 1+ (212) 673-7033

#395
Verizon Wireless One World
Mobile Phones, Electronics Repair,
IT Services & Computer Repair
Average price: Inexpensive
District: East Village
Address: 133 2nd Ave
New York, NY 10016
Phone: 1+ (212) 673-3801

#396
Cynthia Rowley
Women's Clothing
Average price: Expensive
District: West Village
Address: 376 Bleecker St
New York, NY 10014
Phone: 1+ (212) 242-3803

#397
**Selene Alterations
& Custom Designs**
Bridal, Sewing & Alterations
Average price: Moderate
District: East Village, Alphabet City
Address: 271 E 10th St
New York, NY 10009
Phone: 1+ (212) 777-1908

#398
Mooshoes
Shoe Store
Average price: Expensive
District: Lower East Side
Address: 78 Orchard St
New York, NY 10002
Phone: 1+ (212) 254-6512

#399
Urban Motion
Bikes, Toy Store
Average price: Inexpensive
District: East Village, Alphabet City
Address: 508 E 12th St
Manhattan, NY 10009
Phone: 1+ (718) 772-2105

#400
Altman Luggage
Luggage
Average price: Moderate
District: Lower East Side
Address: 135 Orchard St
New York, NY 10002
Phone: 1+ (800) 372-3377

#401
Urban Jungle
Used, Vintage, Thrift Store
Average price: Inexpensive
District: East Williamsburg, Bushwick
Address: 118 Knickerbocker St
Brooklyn, NY 11237
Phone: 1+ (718) 381-8510

#402
Lot Less Closeouts
Department Store
Average price: Inexpensive
District: Chinatown, Civic Center
Address: 299 Broadway
New York, NY 10184
Phone: 1+ (212) 233-2146

#403
Prive Designer Sales
Women's Clothing, Men's Clothing
Average price: Moderate
District: Chelsea, Meatpacking District
Address: 75 9th Ave
New York, NY 10011
Phone: 1+ (212) 543-4300

#404
Lot Less Closeouts
Discount Store
Average price: Inexpensive
District: Financial District
Address: 95 Fulton St
New York, NY 10038
Phone: 1+ (212) 566-8504

#405
Academy Records & CDs
Music & DVDs
Average price: Moderate
District: Flatiron
Address: 12 W 18th St
New York, NY 10011
Phone: 1+ (212) 242-3000

#406
Spandex House
Fabric Store
Average price: Moderate
District: Midtown West
Address: 263 W 38th St Fl 3
New York, NY 10018
Phone: 1+ (212) 354-6711

#407
Bowne & Co Stationers
Cards, Stationery, Antiques
Average price: Moderate
District: South Street Seaport
Address: 211 Water St
New York, NY 10038
Phone: 1+ (212) 748-8651

#408
Mary Adams the Dress
Bridal, Women's Clothing
Average price: Expensive
District: Midtown East, Murray Hill
Address: 31 E 32nd St
New York, NY 10016
Phone: 1+ (212) 473-0237

#409
Little Shop of Crafts
Arts & Crafts
Average price: Moderate
District: Upper West Side
Address: 711 Amsterdam Ave
New York, NY 10025
Phone: 1+ (212) 531-2723

#410
East Village Books
Bookstore, Music & DVDs
Average price: Inexpensive
District: East Village, Alphabet City
Address: 99 St Marks Pl
New York, NY 10009
Phone: 1+ (212) 477-8647

#411
Spoonbill & Sugartown Booksellers
Bookstore
Average price: Moderate
District: Williamsburg - North Side
Address: 218 Bedford Ave
Brooklyn, NY 11211
Phone: 1+ (718) 387-7322

#412
Jay Seth Photography
Photographer, Photography Store, Services
Average price: Moderate
District: Midtown West
Address: 142 W 36th St
New York, NY 10018
Phone: 1+ (646) 437-1680

#413
University Housewares
Home Decor
Average price: Expensive
District: Morningside Heights
Address: 2901 Broadway
New York, NY 10025
Phone: 1+ (212) 882-2798

#414
Moulded Shoe Company
Shoe Store
Average price: Expensive
District: Midtown East
Address: 10 E 39th St Lbby
New York, NY 10016
Phone: 1+ (212) 683-9389

#415
Jacks 99 Cent Store
Discount Store
Average price: Inexpensive
District: Midtown East
Address: 16 E 40th St
New York, NY 10016
Phone: 1+ (212) 696-5767

#416
Line & Label
Women's Clothing, Leather Goods
Average price: Moderate
District: Greenpoint
Address: 568 Manhattan Ave
Brooklyn, NY 11222
Phone: 1+ (347) 384-2678

#417
Saja Boutique
Bridal
Average price: Moderate
District: Nolita
Address: 250 Elizabeth St
New York, NY 10012
Phone: 1+ (212) 226-7570

#418
Arth
Accessories
Average price: Expensive
District: SoHo
Address: 75 W Houston St
New York, NY 10012
Phone: 1+ (212) 539-1431

#419
Suresh Beauty Co.
Makeup Artists, Cosmetics, Beauty Supply
Average price: Expensive
District: Midtown West, Theater District
Address: 130 W 42nd St
New York, WA 10036
Phone: 1+ (646) 796-4876

#420
Opera Gallery
Art Gallery
Average price: Exclusive
District: SoHo
Address: 115 Spring St
New York, NY 10012
Phone: 1+ (212) 966-6675

#421
Henry Westpfal & Co
Kitchen & Bath
Average price: Moderate
District: Chelsea
Address: 115 W 25th St
New York, NY 10001
Phone: 1+ (212) 563-5990

#422
Chanel
Women's Clothing
Average price: Exclusive
District: Upper East Side
Address: 735 Madison Ave
New York, NY 10021
Phone: 1+ (212) 535-5505

#423
Lotus Bridal
Bridal
Average price: Moderate
District: Sheepshead Bay, Midwood
Address: 1822 Ave U
Brooklyn, NY 11229
Phone: 1+ (718) 332-4385

#424
Pacific Optometry, PC
Optometrist, Eyewear, Optician
Average price: Moderate
District: Little Italy
Address: 87-89 Elizabeth St
New York, NY 10013
Phone: 1+ (212) 219-8260

#425
Talent Cycles
Bike Repair/Maintenance, Bike Rentals
Average price: Moderate
District: Harlem
Address: 502 W 139th St
Manhattan, NY 10031
Phone: 1+ (212) 368-5609

#426
East Side Vision
Eyewear, Optician, Optometrist
Average price: Moderate
District: East Village
Address: 159 1st Ave
New York, NY 10003
Phone: 1+ (212) 228-0950

#427
The National Arts Club
Art Gallery
Average price: Exclusive
District: Gramercy, Flatiron
Address: 15 Gramercy Park S
New York, NY 10003
Phone: 1+ (212) 475-3424

#428
Barbara Feinman Millinery
Hats
Average price: Expensive
District: East Village
Address: 66 E 7th St
New York, NY 10003
Phone: 1+ (212) 358-7092

#429
Greschlers Hardware
Hardware Store, Building Supplies
Average price: Inexpensive
District: South Slope
Address: 660 5th Ave
Brooklyn, NY 11215
Phone: 1+ (718) 499-3100

#430
John Derian
Home Decor
Average price: Exclusive
District: East Village
Address: 6 E 2nd St
New York, NY 10003
Phone: 1+ (212) 677-3917

#431
Crockett & Jones
Shoe Store
Average price: Expensive
District: Midtown West
Address: 7 W 56th St
New York, NY 10019
Phone: 1+ (212) 582-3800

#432
Brooklyn Art Library
Libraries, Art Gallery
Average price: Inexpensive
District: Williamsburg - North Side
Address: 103A N 3rd St
Brooklyn, NY 11249
Phone: 1+ (718) 388-7941

#433
Philip Williams Posters
Art Gallery
Average price: Moderate
District: TriBeCa
Address: 122 Chambers St
New York, NY 10007
Phone: 1+ (212) 513-0313

#434
Dave's Wear House
Sports Wear, Bikes
Average price: Inexpensive
District: Little Italy, Chinatown
Address: 123 Baxter St
Manhattan, NY 10013
Phone: 1+ (212) 334-1958

#435
Value Furniture Warehouse
Furniture Store
Average price: Moderate
District: Downtown Brooklyn, Boerum Hill
Address: 254 Livingston St
Brooklyn, NY 11201
Phone: 1+ (718) 243-2600

#436
Alexis Bittar Studio
Jewelry
Average price: Exclusive
District: SoHo
Address: 465 Broome St
New York, NY 10013
Phone: 1+ (212) 625-8340

#437
Alton Lane
Men's Clothing, Bespoke Clothing
Average price: Moderate
District: Flatiron
Address: 11 W 25th St
New York, NY 10010
Phone: 1+ (646) 896-1212

#438
Hermes Wall Street
Fashion
Average price: Exclusive
District: Financial District
Address: 15 Broad St
New York, NY 10005
Phone: 1+ (212) 785-3030

#439
Space Cowboy Boots
Leather Goods, Shoe Store, Accessories
Average price: Expensive
District: Nolita
Address: 234 Mulberry St
Manhattan, NY 10012
Phone: 1+ (646) 559-4779

#440
MoVapes
Tobacco Shop
Average price: Moderate
District: Crown Heights
Address: 1413 Bedford Ave
Brooklyn, NY 11216
Phone: 1+ (718) 427-2170

#441
Alexis Bittar
Jewelry
Average price: Expensive
District: West Village
Address: 353 Bleecker St
New York, NY 10014
Phone: 1+ (212) 727-1093

#442
Acorn Toy Shop
Toy Store
Average price: Moderate
District: Downtown Brooklyn, Boerum Hill
Address: 323 Atlantic Ave
Brooklyn, NY 11201
Phone: 1+ (718) 522-3760

#443
Orthotic Solutions
Shoe Store, Podiatrist
Average price: Expensive
District: Upper West Side
Address: 1841 Broadway
New York, NY 10023
Phone: 1+ (212) 265-3463

#444
Lush
Cosmetics, Beauty Supply
Average price: Expensive
District: Greenwich Village, Union Square,
Flatiron
Address: 7 E 14th St
New York, NY 10003
Phone: 1+ (212) 255-5133

#445
Meg
Women's Clothing
Average price: Expensive
District: Williamsburg - North Side
Address: 54 N 6th St
Brooklyn, NY 11211
Phone: 1+ (347) 294-0777

#446
East Coast Trimming
Fabric Store
Average price: Moderate
District: Midtown West
Address: 142 W 38th St
New York, NY 10018
Phone: 1+ (212) 221-0050

#447
James Leonard Optician
Eyewear, Optician, Optometrist
Average price: Moderate
District: Gowanus
Address: 309 Smith St
Brooklyn, NY 11231
Phone: 1+ (718) 222-8300

#448
The Travel Store
Luggage
Average price: Moderate
District: South Williamsburg
Address: 908 Driggs Ave
Brooklyn, NY 11211
Phone: 1+ (718) 367-8434

#449
Palma Chemist
Drugstore
Average price: Inexpensive
District: Park Slope
Address: 159 7th Ave
Brooklyn, NY 11215
Phone: 1+ (718) 638-9617

#450
Agora Gallery
Art Gallery
Average price: Expensive
District: Chelsea
Address: 530 W 25th St
New York, NY 10001
Phone: 1+ (212) 226-4406

#451
David Zwirner Gallery
Art Gallery
Average price: Exclusive
District: Chelsea
Address: 525 W 19th St
New York, NY 10011
Phone: 1+ (212) 727-2070

#452
Anthropologie
Women's Clothing, Home Decor
Average price: Expensive
District: Union Square, Flatiron
Address: 85 5th Ave
New York, NY 10003
Phone: 1+ (212) 627-5885

#453
Ben Sherman
Men's Clothing
Average price: Expensive
District: SoHo
Address: 96 Spring St
New York, NY 10012
Phone: 1+ (212) 680-0160

#454
Atlantis Attic
Used, Vintage
Average price: Inexpensive
District: East Williamsburg
Address: 771 Metropolitan Ave
Brooklyn, NY 11211
Phone: 1+ (718) 218-8670

#455
Cigar Inn
Tobacco Shop
Average price: Inexpensive
District: Yorkville, Upper East Side
Address: 334 E 73rd St
New York, NY 10021
Phone: 1+ (212) 717-7403

#456
Treehouse Brooklyn
Women's Clothing
Average price: Moderate
District: East Williamsburg
Address: 430 Graham Ave
Brooklyn, NY 11226
Phone: 1+ (718) 482-8733

#457
Manolo Blahnik Boutique
Shoe Store
Average price: Exclusive
District: Midtown West
Address: 31 W 54th St
New York, NY 10019
Phone: 1+ (212) 582-3007

#458
Madewell
Women's Clothing, Accessories, Shoe Store
Average price: Expensive
District: Flatiron
Address: 115 5th Avenue
New York, NY 10003
Phone: 1+ (212) 228-5172

#459
Namaste Bookshop
Bookstore
Average price: Moderate
District: Greenwich Village, Union Square,
Flatiron
Address: 2 W 14th St
New York, NY 10011
Phone: 1+ (212) 645-0141

#460
6 Avenue Tailor
Sewing & Alterations, Formal Wear
Average price: Expensive
District: Midtown West
Address: 57 W 57 St
New York, NY 10019
Phone: 1+ (646) 416-7928

#461
Tokio 7
Used, Vintage
Average price: Expensive
District: East Village
Address: 83 E 7th St
New York, NY 10003
Phone: 1+ (212) 353-8443

#462
DaVinci Artist Supply
Art Supplies
Average price: Moderate
District: Chelsea
Address: 132 W 21st St
New York, NY 10011
Phone: 1+ (212) 871-0220

#463
Alaric Flower Design
Florist
Average price: Expensive
District: Midtown West
Address: 42 W 56th St
New York, NY 10019
Phone: 1+ (212) 308-3794

#464
Mandolin Brothers
Musical Instruments
Average price: Exclusive
District: West Brighton
Address: 629 Forest Ave
Staten Island, NY 10310
Phone: 1+ (718) 981-8585

#465
Homage
Sporting Goods
Average price: Moderate
District: Cobble Hill
Address: 64 Bergen St
Brooklyn, NY 11201
Phone: 1+ (718) 596-1511

#466
Century 21 Department Store
Department Store
Average price: Moderate
District: Financial District
Address: 22 Cortlandt St
New York, NY 10007
Phone: 1+ (212) 227-9092

#467
Balenciaga
Women's Clothing, Accessories,
Men's Clothing
Average price: Exclusive
District: Chelsea
Address: 542 W 22nd St
New York, NY 10184
Phone: 1+ (212) 206-0872

#468
POP
Women's Clothing
Average price: Moderate
District: Williamsburg - South Side,
Williamsburg - North Side
Address: 308 Grand St
Brooklyn, NY 11211
Phone: 1+ (718) 486-6001

#469
Elijah Peters Optique
Eyewear, Optician, Optometrist
Average price: Moderate
District: Upper East Side
Address: 1039 3rd Ave
New York, NY 10065
Phone: 1+ (212) 759-5050

#470
Bauman Rare Books
Bookstore
Average price: Exclusive
District: Midtown East
Address: 535 Madison Ave
New York, NY 10022
Phone: 1+ (212) 751-0011

#471
Old Hollywood
Jewelry, Accessories, Women's Clothing
Average price: Moderate
District: Greenpoint
Address: 99 Franklin St
Brooklyn, NY 11222
Phone: 1+ (718) 389-0837

#472
Minzer's Optical
Eyewear, Optician
Average price: Inexpensive
District: Borough Park
Address: 907 48th St
Brooklyn, NY 11219
Phone: 1+ (718) 436-6963

#473
Homebody Boutique
Jewelry, Cards, Stationery, Gift Shop
Average price: Moderate
District: South Slope
Address: 449 7th Ave
Brooklyn, NY 11215
Phone: 1+ (718) 369-8980

#474
Chopin Chemists
Drugstore
Average price: Moderate
District: Greenpoint
Address: 911 Manhattan Ave
Brooklyn, NY 11222
Phone: 1+ (718) 383-7822

#475
Crossroads Trading
Men's Clothing, Women's Clothing,
Used, Vintage
Average price: Moderate
District: Williamsburg - North Side
Address: 135 N 7th St
Brooklyn, NY 11211
Phone: 1+ (347) 549-4005

#476
Bobby Berk Home
Furniture Store, Home Decor
Average price: Moderate
District: SoHo
Address: 59 Crosby St
New York, NY 10012
Phone: 1+ (212) 925-3635

#477
King Kog
Bikes
Average price: Moderate
District: East Williamsburg,
Williamsburg - North Side
Address: 455 Graham Ave
Brooklyn, NY 11222
Phone: 1+ (347) 689-2299

#478
Heaven Street
Vinyl Records
Average price: Moderate
District: East Williamsburg, Bushwick
Address: 184 Noll St
Brooklyn, NY 11237
Phone: 1+ (718) 381-5703

#479
Azena's Jewelry
Jewelry, Watch Repair
Average price: Inexpensive
District: South Slope, Park Slope
Address: 500 5th Ave
Brooklyn, NY 11215
Phone: 1+ (718) 788-4900

#480
The Dressing Room
Bar, Used, Vintage
Average price: Moderate
District: Lower East Side
Address: 75A Orchard St
New York, NY 10002
Phone: 1+ (212) 966-7330

#481
Better Than Jam
Women's Clothing, Jewelry, Arts & Crafts
Average price: Moderate
District: East Williamsburg, Bushwick
Address: 123 Knickerbocker Ave
Brooklyn, NY 11237
Phone: 1+ (631) 377-2500

#482
Grand Bicycle Center
Bikes
Average price: Moderate
District: Maspeth
Address: 70-13 Grand Ave
Maspeth, NY 11378
Phone: 1+ (718) 779-4691

#483
Columbus Art Gallery
Art Gallery, Framing
Average price: Moderate
District: Upper West Side
Address: 588 Columbus Ave
New York, NY 10024
Phone: 1+ (212) 875-1678

#484
Bronx Museum of the Arts
Museum, Art Gallery
Average price: Inexpensive
District: Concourse
Address: 1040 Grand Concourse
Bronx, NY 10456
Phone: 1+ (718) 681-6000

#485
Michael Kors
Accessories, Women's Clothing
Average price: Expensive
District: SoHo
Address: 101 Prince St
New York, NY 10012
Phone: 1+ (212) 965-0401

#486
The Face Shop
Cosmetics, Beauty Supply, Skin Care
Average price: Moderate
District: Chinatown
Address: 6-B Elizabeth St
New York, NY 10013
Phone: 1+ (212) 608-1988

#487
Catbird
Jewelry
Average price: Expensive
District: Williamsburg - North Side
Address: 219 Bedford Ave
Brooklyn, NY 11211
Phone: 1+ (718) 599-3457

#488
Pacific Trimmings
Fabric Store
Average price: Moderate
District: Midtown West
Address: 218 W 38 St
New York, NY 10018
Phone: 1+ (212) 279-9310

#489
H Brickman & Sons
Hardware Store, Shades & Blinds
Average price: Moderate
District: East Village
Address: 55 1st Ave
New York, NY 10003
Phone: 1+ (212) 674-3213

#490
Paper Source
Cards, Stationery, Art Supplies
Average price: Moderate
District: Upper West Side
Address: 309 Columbus Ave
New York, NY 10023
Phone: 1+ (646) 861-2879

#491
Mud Sweat & Tears Pottery
Arts & Crafts
Average price: Moderate
District: Hell's Kitchen, Midtown West
Address: 654 10th Ave
New York, NY 10036
Phone: 1+ (212) 974-9121

#492
Jeffrey
Shoe Store, Women's Clothing
Average price: Exclusive
District: Chelsea, West Village,
Meatpacking District
Address: 449 W 14th St
New York, NY 10014
Phone: 1+ (212) 206-1272

#493
**1:46 Watch Repair & Designer
Collective**
Watch Repair, Jewelry, Watches
Average price: Inexpensive
District: Williamsburg - North Side
Address: 146 N 7th St
Brooklyn, NY 11249
Phone: 1+ (718) 599-0347

#494
Crawford Doyle Booksellers
Average price: Bookstore
District: Upper East Side
Address: 1082 Madison Ave
New York, NY 10028
Phone: 1+ (212) 288-6300

#495
Goldy & Mac
Women's Clothing, Accessories
Average price: Moderate
District: South Slope, Park Slope
Address: 396 7th Ave
Brooklyn, NY 11215
Phone: 1+ (718) 832-4868

#496
Edith Machinist
Women's Clothing, Vintage
Average price: Expensive
District: Lower East Side
Address: 104 Rivington St
New York, NY 10002
Phone: 1+ (212) 979-9992

#497
Patagonia
Sports Wear, Outdoor Gear, Hats
Average price: Expensive
District: Upper West Side
Address: 426 Columbus Ave
New York, NY 10024
Phone: 1+ (917) 441-0011

#498
DQM New York
Sporting Goods, Shoe Store
Average price: Moderate
District: East Village
Address: 7 E 3rd St
New York, NY 10003
Phone: 1+ (212) 505-7551

#499
Lauren B Jewelry
Jewelry
Average price: Expensive
District: Midtown West
Address: 580 5th Ave
New York, NY 10036
Phone: +1 (212) 391-0633

#500
The Sock Man
Accessories
Average price: Moderate
District: East Village
Address: 27 St. Marks Pl
New York, NY 10003
Phone: +1 (212) 529-0300

TOP 500 RESTAURANTS

Most Recommended by Locals & Trevelers
Ranking (from #1 to #500)

#1
The Cinnamon Snail
Cuisines: Vegan, Food Truck
Average price: Under $10
District: Chelsea, Midtown West
Address: Location Varies.
New York, NY 10001
Phone: +1 (862) 246-6431

#2
Chef's Table
Cuisines: American
Average price: Above $61
District: Downtown
Brooklyn, Boerum Hill
Address: 212 Schermerhorn St
Brooklyn, NY 11217
Phone: +1 (718) 243-0050

#3
Le Bernardin
Cuisines: Seafood, French
Average price: Above $61
District: Midtown West, Theater
Address: 155 W 51st St
New York, NY 10019
Phone: +1 (212) 554-1515

#4
Gramercy Tavern
Cuisines: American
Average price: Above $61
District: Flatiron
Address: 42 E 20th St
New York, NY 10003
Phone: +1 (212) 477-0777

#5
Upstate
Cuisines: American, Seafood
Average price: $11-30
District: East Village
Address: 95 1st Ave
New York, NY 10003
Phone: +1 (917) 408-3395

#6
Taim
Cuisines: Middle Eastern,
Juice Bar, Vegetarian
Average price: Under $10
District: West Village
Address: 222 Waverly Pl
New York, NY 10014
Phone: +1 (212) 691-1287

#7
Gaia Italian Café
Cuisines: Italian
Average price: Under $10
District: Lower East Side
Address: 251 E Houston St
New York, NY 10002
Phone: +1 (646) 350-3977

#8
Breakroom
Cuisines: Burgers, Mexican
Average price: Under $10
District: Chinatown
Address: 83 Baxter St
New York, NY 10013
Phone: +1 (212) 227-2802

#9
Los Tacos No.1
Cuisines: Mexican
Average price: Under $10
District: Chelsea, Meatpacking
Address: 75 9th Ave
New York, NY 10011
Phone: +1 (212) 256-0343

#10
Prosperity Dumpling
Cuisines: Chinese
Average price: Under $10
District: Chinatown, Lower East Side
Address: 46 Eldridge St
New York, NY 10002
Phone: +1 (212) 343-0683

#11
Traif
Cuisines: American
Average price: $11-30
District: Williamsburg - South Side
Address: 229 S 4th St
Brooklyn, NY 11211
Phone: +1 (347) 844-9578

#12
Café Katja
Cuisines: German, Austrian
Average price: $11-30
District: Lower East Side
Address: 79 Orchard St
New York, NY 10002
Phone: +1 (212) 219-9545

#13
Gotham Bar And Grill
Cuisines: American, Bar
Average price: Above $61
District: Greenwich Village, Union Square
Address: 12 E 12th St
New York, NY 10003
Phone: +1 (212) 620-4020

#14
Pates Et Traditions
Cuisines: French
Average price: $11-30
District: Williamsburg - North Side
Address: 52 Havemeyer St
Brooklyn, NY 11211
Phone: +1 (718) 302-1878

#15
Il Bambino
Cuisines: Italian, Sandwiches
Average price: $11-30
District: Astoria
Address: 34-08 31st Ave
Astoria, NY 11106
Phone: +1 (718) 626-0087

#16
Despaña
Cuisines: Spanish, Basque, Grocery
Average price: $11-30
District: SoHo
Address: 408 Broome St
New York, NY 10013
Phone: +1 (212) 219-5050

#17
Café Mogador
Cuisines: Moroccan, Middle Eastern
Average price: $11-30
District: Williamsburg - North Side
Address: 133 Wythe Ave
Brooklyn, NY 11211
Phone: +1 (718) 486-9222

#18
Sweet & Sara
Cuisines: Desserts, Vegan, Specialty Food
Average price: $11-30
District: Sunnyside
Address: 43-31 33rd St
Long Island City, NY 11101
Phone: +1 (718) 707-2808

#19
L'Artusi
Cuisines: Italian
Average price: $31-60
District: West Village
Address: 228 W 10th St
New York, NY 10014
Phone: +1 (212) 255-5757

#20
Kaz An Nou
Cuisines: Caribbean, French
Average price: $11-30
District: Prospect Heights
Address: 53 6th Ave
Brooklyn, NY 11217
Phone: +1 (718) 938-3235

#21
Cocoron
Cuisines: Japanese
Average price: $11-30
District: Lower East Side
Address: 61 Delancey St
New York, NY 10002
Phone: +1 (212) 925-5220

#22
Trattoria L'incontro
Cuisines: Italian, Pizza
Average price: $31-60
District: Astoria
Address: 21-76 31st St
Astoria, NY 11105
Phone: +1 (718) 721-3532

#23
Ba Xuyen
Cuisines: Vietnamese, Sandwiches
Average price: Under $10
District: Borough Park
Address: 4222 8th Ave
Brooklyn, NY 11232
Phone: +1 (718) 633-6601

#24
Sakagura
Cuisines: Japanese, Seafood
Average price: $31-60
District: Midtown East
Address: 211 E 43rd St
New York, NY 10017
Phone: +1 (212) 953-7253

#25
House of Small Wonder
Cuisines: Sandwiches,
Breakfast & Brunch, Café
Average price: Under $10
District: Williamsburg - North Side
Address: 77 N 6th St
Brooklyn, NY 11211
Phone: +1 (718) 388-6160

#26
Caracas Arepa Bar
Cuisines: Venezuelan
Average price: $11-30
District: East Village
Address: 93 1/2 E 7th St
New York, NY 10009
Phone: +1 (212) 529-2314

#27
Taverna Kyclades East Village
Cuisines: Greek, Seafood
Average price: $11-30
District: East Village
Address: 228 1st Ave
New York, NY 10009
Phone: +1 (212) 432-0011

#28
The Saint Austere
Cuisines: Tapas Bar
Average price: $11-30
District: Williamsburg - North Side
Address: 613 Grand St
Brooklyn, NY 11211
Phone: +1 (718) 388-0012

#29
Ameslie
Cuisines: French, Wine Bar
Average price: $11-30
District: Greenwich Village
Address: 22 W 8th St
New York, NY 10011
Phone: +1 (212) 533-2962

#30
Pommes Frites
Cuisines: Belgian
Average price: Under $10
District: East Village
Address: 123 2nd Ave
New York, NY 10003
Phone: +1 (212) 674-1234

#31
Luke's Lobster
Cuisines: Seafood
Average price: $11-30
District: Financial
Address: 26 S William St
New York, NY 10004
Phone: +1 (212) 747-1700

#32
Scarpetta
Cuisines: Italian
Average price: $31-60
District: Chelsea, West Village,
Meatpacking
Address: 355 W 14th St
New York, NY 10014
Phone: +1 (212) 691-0555

#33
ABC Kitchen
Cuisines: American, French
Average price: $31-60
District: Union Square, Flatiron
Address: 35 E 18th St
New York, NY 10003
Phone: +1 (212) 475-5829

#34
Brooklyn Ice House
Cuisines: Barbeque, Pub
Average price: Under $10
District: Red Hook
Address: 318 Van Brunt St
Brooklyn, NY 11231
Phone: +1 (718) 222-1865

#35
Sergimmo Salumeria
Cuisines: Italian
Average price: $11-30
District: Hell's Kitchen, Midtown West
Address: 456 9th Ave
New York, NY 10018
Phone: +1 (212) 967-4212

#36
Siggy's Good Food
Cuisines: Mediterranean,
Vegan, Comfort Food
Average price: $11-30
District: NoHo
Address: 292 Elizabeth St
New York, NY 10012
Phone: +1 (212) 226-5775

#37
Pippali
Cuisines: Indian
Average price: $11-30
District: Flatiron
Address: 129 E 27th St
New York, NY 10016
Phone: +1 (212) 689-1999

#38
Mountain Province
Cuisines: Café, Bakery, Coffee & Tea
Average price: Under $10
District: East Williamsburg
Address: 1 Meserole St
Brooklyn, NY 11211
Phone: +1 (718) 387-7030

#39
Fresca La Crêpe
Cuisines: Crêperie
Average price: Under $10
District: Woodside
Address: 39-82 61st St
Woodside, NY 11377
Phone: +1 (347) 768-1488

#40
Perilla Restaurant
Cuisines: American
Average price: $31-60
District: West Village
Address: 9 Jones St
New York, NY 10014
Phone: +1 (212) 929-6868

#41
Lomzynianka
Cuisines: Polish
Average price: Under $10
District: Greenpoint
Address: 646 Manhattan Ave
Brooklyn, NY 11222
Phone: +1 (718) 389-9439

#42
Café Ollin
Cuisines: Mexican, Latin American
Average price: Under $10
District: East Harlem
Address: 339 E 108th St
New York, NY 10029
Phone: +1 (212) 828-3644

#43
Luke's Lobster
Cuisines: Seafood
Average price: $11-30
District: Yorkville, Upper East Side
Address: 242 E 81st St
New York, NY 10028
Phone: +1 (212) 249-4241

#44
Ootoya
Cuisines: Japanese
Average price: $11-30
District: Flatiron
Address: 8 W 18th St
New York, NY 10011
Phone: +1 (212) 255-0018

#45
Little Collins
Cuisines: Café
Average price: $11-30
District: Midtown East
Address: 667 Lexington Ave
New York, NY 10022
Phone: +1 (212) 308-1969

#46
Casellula
Cuisines: Wine Bar, American
Average price: $31-60
District: Hell's Kitchen, Midtown West
Address: 401 W 52nd St
New York, NY 10019
Phone: +1 (212) 247-8137

#47
JoJu
Cuisines: Vietnamese,
Sandwiches, Bubble Tea
Average price: Under $10
District: Elmhurst
Address: 83-25 Broadway
Elmhurst, NY 11373
Phone: +1 (347) 808-0887

#48
Ippudo Ny
Cuisines: Ramen, Desserts
Average price: $11-30
District: East Village
Address: 65 4th Ave
New York, NY 10003
Phone: +1 (212) 388-0088

#49
Bianca Restaurant
Cuisines: Italian
Average price: $11-30
District: NoHo
Address: 5 Bleecker St
New York, NY 10012
Phone: +1 (212) 260-4666

#50
Heidi's House
Cuisines: Comfort Food
Average price: $11-30
District: Yorkville, Upper East Side
Address: 308 E 78th St
New York, NY 10075
Phone: +1 (212) 249-0069

#51
The Islands
Cuisines: Caribbean
Average price: $11-30
District: Crown Heights, Prospect Heights
Address: 803 Washington Ave
Brooklyn, NY 11238
Phone: +1 (718) 398-3575

#52
The Dead Rabbit
Cuisines: Grocery, Bar, American
Average price: $31-60
District: Financial
Address: 30 Water St
New York, NY 10004
Phone: +1 (646) 422-7906

#53
Minetta Tavern
Cuisines: French, American,
Breakfast & Brunch
Average price: $31-60
District: Greenwich Village
Address: 113 Macdougal St
New York, NY 10012
Phone: +1 (212) 475-3850

#54
Xixa
Cuisines: Mexican
Average price: $31-60
District: Williamsburg - South Side
Address: 241 S 4th St
Brooklyn, NY 11211
Phone: +1 (718) 388-8860

#55
Tacos El Bronco
Cuisines: Mexican
Average price: Under $10
District: Sunset Park
Address: 4324 4th Ave
Brooklyn, NY 11220
Phone: +1 (718) 788-2229

#56
Degustation
Cuisines: French, American, Spanish
Average price: $31-60
District: East Village
Address: 239 E 5th St
New York, NY 10003
Phone: +1 (212) 979-1012

#57
Momo Sushi Shack
Cuisines: Japanese, Sushi Bar,
Asian Fusion
Average price: $11-30
District: East Williamsburg, Bushwick
Address: 43 Bogart St
Brooklyn, NY 11206
Phone: +1 (718) 418-6666

#58
Bergen Hill
Cuisines: Cocktail Bar, Seafood
Average price: $31-60
District: Carroll Gardens
Address: 387 Court St
Brooklyn, NY 11231
Phone: +1 (718) 858-5483

#59
Post Office
Cuisines: Bar, American
Average price: $11-30
District: Williamsburg - South Side
Address: 188 Havemeyer St
Brooklyn, NY 11211
Phone: +1 (718) 963-2574

#60
Momofuku Ko
Cuisines: American, Asian Fusion, Korean
Average price: Above $61
District: East Village
Address: 163 1st Ave
New York, NY 10003
Phone: +1 (212) 500-0831

#61
Mighty Quinn's Barbeque
Cuisines: Barbeque
Average price: $11-30
District: East Village
Address: 103 2nd Ave
New York, NY 10003
Phone: +1 (212) 677-3733

#62
Lot 2
Cuisines: American
Average price: $11-30
District: South Slope
Address: 687 6th Ave
Brooklyn, NY 11215
Phone: +1 (718) 499-5623

#63
The Little Owl
Cuisines: American
Average price: $31-60
District: West Village
Address: 90 Bedford St
New York, NY 10014
Phone: +1 (212) 741-4695

#64
Family Corner Restaurant
Cuisines: Diner, Greek, Italian
Average price: Under $10
District: Steinway
Address: 2102 31st St
Astoria, NY 11105
Phone: +1 (718) 204-7915

#65
Lamazou
Cuisines: Cheese Shop, Sandwiches
Average price: Under $10
District: Kips Bay
Address: 370 3rd Ave
New York, NY 10016
Phone: +1 (212) 532-2009

#66
Dar 525
Cuisines: Mediterranean, Middle Eastern
Average price: $11-30
District: Williamsburg - North Side
Address: 525 Grand St
Brooklyn, NY 11211
Phone: +1 (347) 422-0401

#67
David's Brisket House
Cuisines: Deli, Sandwiches
Average price: Under $10
District: Bedford Stuyvesant, Crown Heights
Address: 533 Nostrand Ave
Brooklyn, NY 11216
Phone: +1 (718) 789-1155

#68
La Taqueria Kermes
Cuisines: Mexican
Average price: $11-30
District: Ridgewood
Address: 66-36 Fresh Pond Rd
Ridgewood, NY 11385
Phone: +1 (347) 463-9263

#69
Café Habana
Cuisines: Cuban, Mexican
Average price: $11-30
District: Nolita
Address: 17 Prince St
New York, NY 10012
Phone: +1 (212) 625-2001

#70
Mu Ramen
Cuisines: Japanese
Average price: $11-30
District: Hunters Point, Long Island City
Address: 5106 Vernon Blvd
Long Island City, NY 11101
Phone: +1 (917) 868-8903

#71
La Goulette
Cuisines: Mediterranean, Middle Eastern
Average price: Under $10
District: Williamsburg - North Side
Address: 159 Grand St
Brooklyn, NY 11249
Phone: +1 (347) 689-4126

#72
Saro Bistro
Cuisines: Modern European,
Breakfast & Brunch, Comfort Food
Average price: $11-30
District: Lower East Side
Address: 102 Norfolk St
New York, NY 10002
Phone: +1 (212) 505-7276

#73
Porteno Restaurant
Cuisines: Argentine
Average price: $31-60
District: Chelsea
Address: 299 10th Ave
New York, NY 10001
Phone: +1 (212) 695-9694

#74
Yerba Buena
Cuisines: Latin American
Average price: $31-60
District: East Village, Alphabet City
Address: 23 Ave A
New York, NY 10009
Phone: +1 (212) 529-2919

#75
Taverna Kyclades
Cuisines: Seafood, Greek, Mediterranean
Average price: $11-30
District: Astoria
Address: 3307 Ditmars Blvd
Astoria, NY 11105
Phone: +1 (718) 545-8666

#76
Bogota Latin Bistro
Cuisines: Latin American, Gluten-Free
Average price: $11-30
District: Park Slope
Address: 141 5th Ave
Brooklyn, NY 11217
Phone: +1 (718) 230-3805

#77
The Meatball Shop
Cuisines: Italian, American
Average price: $11-30
District: Lower East Side
Address: 84 Stanton St
New York, NY 10002
Phone: +1 (212) 982-8895

#78
Café Triskell
Cuisines: French, Crêperie
Average price: $11-30
District: Astoria
Address: 33-04 36th Ave
Astoria, NY 11106
Phone: +1 (718) 472-0612

#79
Buddakan
Cuisines: Chinese, Asian Fusion
Average price: $31-60
District: Chelsea, Meatpacking
Address: 75 9th Ave
New York, NY 10011
Phone: +1 (212) 989-6699

#80
Market Table
Cuisines: American
Average price: $31-60
District: West Village
Address: 54 Carmine St
New York, NY 10014
Phone: +1 (212) 255-2100

#81
Battersby
Cuisines: American
Average price: $31-60
District: Cobble Hill, Gowanus
Address: 255 Smith St
Brooklyn, NY 11231
Phone: +1 (718) 852-8321

#82
Bite
Cuisines: Sandwiches
Average price: Under $10
District: Gramercy
Address: 211 E 14th St
New York, NY 10003
Phone: +1 (212) 677-3123

#83
Bistro Petit
Cuisines: French
Average price: $11-30
District: Williamsburg - South Side
Address: 170 S 3rd St
Brooklyn, NY 11211
Phone: +1 (718) 782-2582

#84
Parmys Persian Fusion
Cuisines: Barbeque, Persian/Iranian
Average price: $11-30
District: East Village
Address: 125 1st Ave
New York, NY 10003
Phone: +1 (212) 335-0207

#85
Manousheh
Cuisines: Lebanese
Average price: $11-30
District: Little Italy, Nolita
Address: 10 Kenmare St
New York, NY 10012
Phone: +1 (347) 971-5778

#86
Wechslers
Cuisines: German
Average price: Under $10
District: East Village
Address: 120 1st Ave
New York, NY 10009
Phone: +1 (212) 253-2222

#87
Olea
Cuisines: Mediterranean
Average price: $11-30
District: Fort Greene
Address: 171 Lafayette Ave
Brooklyn, NY 11238
Phone: +1 (718) 643-7003

#88
Distilled
Cuisines: American, Cocktail Bar
Average price: $31-60
District: TriBeCa
Address: 211 W Broadway
New York, NY 10013
Phone: +1 (212) 601-9514

#89
Petite Crevette
Cuisines: Seafood, French
Average price: $11-30
District: Carroll Gardens, Columbia Street
Waterfront
Address: 144 Union St
Brooklyn, NY 11231
Phone: +1 (718) 855-2632

#90
Eagle Trading
Cuisines: Café
Average price: Under $10
District: Greenpoint
Address: 258 Franklin St
Brooklyn, NY 11222
Phone: +1 (718) 576-3217

#91
Barboncino
Cuisines: Pizza, Bar
Average price: $11-30
District: Crown Heights
Address: 781 Franklin Ave
Brooklyn, NY 11238
Phone: +1 (718) 483-8834

#92
Colicchio & Sons Tap Room
Cuisines: American
Average price: $31-60
District: Chelsea, Meatpacking
Address: 85 10th Ave
New York, NY 10011
Phone: +1 (212) 400-6699

#93
Westville
Cuisines: Salad, Burgers, Sandwiches
Average price: $11-30
District: West Village
Address: 210 W 10th St
New York, NY 10014
Phone: +1 (212) 741-7971

#94
Il Triangolo Restaurant
Cuisines: Italian
Average price: $11-30
District: Elmhurst
Address: 96-01 Corona Ave
Corona, NY 11368
Phone: +1 (718) 271-1250

#95
PT Restaurant
Cuisines: Italian
Average price: $11-30
District: Williamsburg - South Side
Address: 331 Bedford Ave
Brooklyn, NY 11211
Phone: +1 (718) 388-7438

#96
Falanghina Pizza Bar
Cuisines: Italian
Average price: $11-30
District: East Village, Alphabet City
Address: 130 St Marks Pl
New York, NY 10009
Phone: +1 (212) 466-4686

#97
Piora
Cuisines: American
Average price: $31-60
District: West Village
Address: 430 Hudson St
New York, NY 10014
Phone: +1 (212) 960-3801

#98
The Jeffrey Craft Beer & Bites
Cuisines: Bar, Café
Average price: $11-30
District: Upper East Side
Address: 311 East 60th St
New York, NY 10022
Phone: +1 (212) 355-2337

#99
The Pickle Shack
Cuisines: Bar, Vegetarian
Average price: $11-30
District: Park Slope, Gowanus
Address: 256 4th Ave
Brooklyn, NY 11215
Phone: +1 (347) 763-2127

#100
Up Thai
Cuisines: Thai
Average price: $11-30
District: Yorkville, Upper East Side
Address: 1411 2nd Ave
New York, NY 10021
Phone: +1 (212) 256-1188

#101
Graffiti Food & Wine Bar
Cuisines: American, Wine Bar
Average price: $31-60
District: East Village
Address: 224 E 10th St
New York, NY 10003
Phone: +1 (212) 677-0695

#102
Café Mogador
Cuisines: Moroccan
Average price: $11-30
District: East Village, Alphabet City
Address: 101 St Marks Pl
New York, NY 10009
Phone: +1 (212) 677-2226

#103
Lali Restaurant
Cuisines: Dominican
Average price: Under $10
District: Hell's Kitchen, Midtown West
Address: 630 10th Ave
New York, NY 10036
Phone: +1 (212) 664-1507

#104
home/made
Cuisines: American,
Breakfast & Brunch, Pizza
Average price: $11-30
District: Red Hook
Address: 293 Van Brunt St
Brooklyn, NY 11231
Phone: +1 (347) 223-4135

#105
Nai Tapas Bar
Cuisines: Tapas Bar
Average price: $11-30
District: East Village
Address: 174 1st Ave
New York, NY 10009
Phone: +1 (212) 677-1030

#106
Vitae
Cuisines: American
Average price: $31-60
District: Midtown East
Address: 4 E 46th St
New York, NY 10017
Phone: +1 (212) 682-3562

#107
Tabares
Cuisines: Latin American
Average price: $11-30
District: Williamsburg - South Side
Address: 221 S 1st St
Brooklyn, NY 11211
Phone: +1 (347) 335-0187

#108
Purbird
Cuisines: American
Average price: $11-30
District: Park Slope, Prospect Heights
Address: 82 Sixth Ave
Brooklyn, NY 11217
Phone: +1 (718) 857-2473

#109
Juniper
Cuisines: Burgers, American
Average price: $11-30
District: Williamsburg - North Side
Address: 112 Berry St
Brooklyn, NY 11211
Phone: +1 (718) 782-8777

#110
Totto Ramen
Cuisines: Japanese
Average price: $11-30
District: Hell's Kitchen, Midtown West,
Theater
Address: 366 W 52nd St
New York, NY 10019
Phone: +1 (212) 582-0052

#111
Nam Nam
Cuisines: Vietnamese, Coffee & Tea
Average price: Under $10
District: East Williamsburg
Address: 109 Montrose Ave
Brooklyn, NY 11206
Phone: +1 (718) 302-9200

#112
Rubirosa
Cuisines: Italian, Pizza
Average price: $11-30
District: Nolita
Address: 235 Mulberry St
New York, NY 10012
Phone: +1 (212) 965-0500

#113
Bunna Café
Cuisines: Ethiopian
Average price: $11-30
District: East Williamsburg, Bushwick
Address: 1084 Flushing Ave
Brooklyn, NY 11237
Phone: +1 (347) 295-2227

#114
Lulu's
Cuisines: Pizza, Dive Bar
Average price: Under $10
District: Greenpoint
Address: 113 Franklin St
Brooklyn, NY 11222
Phone: +1 (718) 383-6000

#115
Arepas Café
Cuisines: Venezuelan, Spanish
Average price: Under $10
District: Astoria
Address: 33-07 36th Ave
Astoria, NY 11106
Phone: +1 (718) 937-3835

#116
Vesta
Cuisines: Italian, Breakfast & Brunch
Average price: $11-30
District: Astoria
Address: 21-02 30th Ave
Astoria, NY 11102
Phone: +1 (718) 545-5550

#117
Balthazar Restaurant
Cuisines: French
Average price: $31-60
District: SoHo
Address: 80 Spring St
New York, NY 10012
Phone: +1 (212) 965-1414

#118
The Greek
Cuisines: Greek
Average price: $11-30
District: TriBeCa
Address: 458 Greenwich St
New York, NY 10013
Phone: +1 (646) 476-3941

#119
Malatesta Trattoria
Cuisines: Italian
Average price: $11-30
District: West Village
Address: 649 Washington St
New York, NY 10014
Phone: +1 (212) 741-1207

#120
St. Anselm
Cuisines: American
Average price: $31-60
District: Williamsburg - North Side
Address: 355 Metropolitan Ave
Brooklyn, NY 11211
Phone: +1 (718) 384-5054

#121
Rye
Cuisines: American
Average price: $31-60
District: Williamsburg - South Side
Address: 247 S 1st St
Brooklyn, NY 11211
Phone: +1 (718) 218-8047

#122
Uva
Cuisines: Italian
Average price: $11-30
District: Yorkville, Upper East Side
Address: 1486 2nd Ave
New York, NY 10075
Phone: +1 (212) 472-4552

#123
Desnuda
Cuisines: Seafood, Peruvian, Cocktail Bar
Average price: $31-60
District: Williamsburg - South Side
Address: 221 S 1st St
Brooklyn, NY 11211
Phone: +1 (718) 387-0563

#124
ilili
Cuisines: Greek, Middle Eastern,
Mediterranean
Average price: $31-60
District: Flatiron
Address: 236 5th Ave
New York, NY 10001
Phone: +1 (212) 683-2929

#125
Der Kommissar
Cuisines: Bar, Austrian
Average price: $11-30
District: South Slope, Park Slope
Address: 559 5th Ave
Brooklyn, NY 11215
Phone: +1 (718) 788-0789

#126
Taqueria Lower East Side
Cuisines: Mexican, Bar
Average price: Under $10
District: Lower East Side
Address: 198 Orchard St
New York, NY 10002
Phone: +1 (212) 677-3910

#127
Taqueria Diana
Cuisines: Mexican
Average price: Under $10
District: East Village
Address: 129 2nd Ave
New York, NY 10003
Phone: +1 (646) 422-7871

#128
The Heath
Cuisines: American
Average price: $31-60
District: Chelsea
Address: 542 W 27th St
New York, NY 10001
Phone: +1 (212) 564-1662

#129
Jadis
Cuisines: French, Wine Bar
Average price: $11-30
District: Lower East Side
Address: 42 Rivington St
New York, NY 10002
Phone: +1 (212) 254-1675

#130
Forno Pizzeria E Trattoria
Cuisines: Italian, Pizza
Average price: $11-30
District: Maspeth
Address: 52-27 69th St
Maspeth, NY 11378
Phone: +1 (718) 424-1200

#131
Rincon Criollo
Cuisines: Cuban
Average price: $11-30
District: Elmhurst
Address: 40-09 Junction Blvd
Corona, NY 11368
Phone: +1 (718) 639-8158

#132
Buvette
Cuisines: French
Average price: $11-30
District: West Village
Address: 42 Grove St
New York, NY 10014
Phone: +1 (212) 255-3590

#133
Apiary
Cuisines: American, Italian
Average price: $31-60
District: East Village
Address: 60 3rd Ave
New York, NY 10003
Phone: +1 (212) 254-0888

#134
Pisillo Italian Panini
Cuisines: Italian, Sandwiches
Average price: $11-30
District: Financial
Address: 97 Nassau St
New York, NY 10038
Phone: +1 (212) 227-3104

#135
Wafa's
Cuisines: Mediterranean, Middle Eastern
Average price: $11-30
District: Forest Hills
Address: 100-05 Metropolitan Ave
Forest Hills, NY 11375
Phone: +1 (718) 880-2055

#136
Saigon Shack
Cuisines: Vietnamese
Average price: Under $10
District: Greenwich Village
Address: 114 Macdougal St
New York, NY 10012
Phone: +1 (212) 228-0588

#137
Earl's Beer & Cheese
Cuisines: Bar, Comfort Food, Beer,
Wine & Spirits
Average price: $11-30
District: East Harlem
Address: 1259 Park Ave
New York, NY 10029
Phone: +1 (212) 289-1581

#138
Westville
Cuisines: American
Average price: $11-30
District: East Village, Alphabet City
Address: 173 Ave A
New York, NY 10009
Phone: +1 (212) 677-2033

#139
Lam Zhou Handmade Noodle
Cuisines: Chinese
Average price: Under $10
District: Chinatown, Lower East Side
Address: 144 E Broadway
New York, NY 10002
Phone: +1 (212) 566-6933

#140
Kashkaval
Cuisines: Mediterranean, Cheese Shop
Average price: $11-30
District: Hell's Kitchen, Midtown West
Address: 856 9th Ave
New York, NY 10019
Phone: +1 (212) 581-8282

#141
Alta
Cuisines: Tapas Bar,
Mediterranean, Spanish
Average price: $31-60
District: Greenwich Village
Address: 64 W 10th St
New York, NY 10011
Phone: +1 (212) 505-7777

#142
Café Orlin
Cuisines: Middle Eastern,
Breakfast & Brunch, Café
Average price: $11-30
District: East Village
Address: 41 St. Marks Pl
New York, NY 10003
Phone: +1 (212) 777-1447

#143
Kelso Bistro Bar & Restaurant
Cuisines: Caribbean, Spanish,
Latin American
Average price: Under $10
District: Crown Heights
Address: 648 Franklin Ave
Brooklyn, NY 11238
Phone: +1 (718) 857-4137

#144
La Tarte Flambee
Cuisines: French, Breakfast & Brunch
Average price: $11-30
District: Yorkville, Upper East Side
Address: 1750 2nd Ave
New York, NY 10128
Phone: +1 (212) 860-0826

#145
Brooklyn Taco
Cuisines: Mexican
Average price: Under $10
District: Lower East Side
Address: 120 Essex St
New York, NY 10002
Phone: +1 (646) 820-8226

#146
Lupa
Cuisines: Italian, American
Average price: $31-60
District: Greenwich Village
Address: 170 Thompson St
New York, NY 10012
Phone: +1 (212) 982-5089

#147
The Farm On Adderley
Cuisines: American, Breakfast & Brunch
Average price: $11-30
District: Flatbush
Address: 1108 Cortelyou Rd
Brooklyn, NY 11218
Phone: +1 (718) 287-3101

#148
Pepolino Restaurant
Cuisines: Italian
Average price: $31-60
District: TriBeCa
Address: 281 W Broadway
New York, NY 10013
Phone: +1 (212) 966-9983

#149
Bistango
Cuisines: Italian, Gluten-Free
Average price: $11-30
District: Midtown East, Kips Bay
Address: 415 3rd Ave
New York, NY 10016
Phone: +1 (212) 725-8484

#150
Diner
Cuisines: American, Breakfast & Brunch
Average price: $31-60
District: South Williamsburg
Address: 85 Broadway
Brooklyn, NY 11211
Phone: +1 (718) 486-3077

#151
Mark
Cuisines: Burgers
Average price: Under $10
District: East Village
Address: 33 St Marks Pl
New York, NY 10003
Phone: +1 (212) 677-3132

#152
Maialino
Cuisines: Italian
Average price: $31-60
District: Gramercy, Flatiron
Address: 2 Lexington Ave
New York, NY 10010
Phone: +1 (212) 777-2410

#153
Mighty Quinn's
Cuisines: Barbeque
Average price: Under $10
District: Williamsburg - North Side
Address: 27 N 6th St
Brooklyn, NY 11211
Phone: +1 (718) 928-6603

#154
Bunker Vietnamese
Cuisines: Vietnamese
Average price: $11-30
District: Ridgewood
Address: 46-63 Metropolitan Ave
Ridgewood, NY 11385
Phone: +1 (718) 386-4282

#155
Butcher Block
Cuisines: Meat Shop, Grocery, Irish
Average price: Under $10
District: Sunnyside
Address: 43-46 41st St
Sunnyside, NY 11104
Phone: +1 (718) 784-1078

#156
Boubouki
Cuisines: Greek, Food Stands
Average price: Under $10
District: Lower East Side
Address: 120 Essex St
New York, NY 10002
Phone: +1 (718) 344-4202

#157
Employees Only
Cuisines: American, Lounge
Average price: $31-60
District: West Village
Address: 510 Hudson St
New York, NY 10014
Phone: +1 (212) 242-3021

#158
Rouge Tomate
Cuisines: American
Average price: $31-60
District: Upper East Side
Address: 10 E 60th St
New York, NY 10022
Phone: +1 (646) 237-8977

#159
Piacere
Cuisines: Pizza, Italian
Average price: $11-30
District: Little Italy, Nolita
Address: 351 Broome St
New York, NY 10013
Phone: +1 (212) 219-4080

#160
Salt & Fat
Cuisines: American, Asian Fusion
Average price: $11-30
District: Sunnyside
Address: 41-16 Queens Blvd
Sunnyside, NY 11104
Phone: +1 (718) 433-3702

#161
The Shakespeare
Cuisines: Pub, British
Average price: $31-60
District: Midtown East, Murray Hill
Address: 24 E 39th St
New York, NY 10016
Phone: +1 (646) 837-6779

#162
Tia Pol
Cuisines: Tapas Bar, Spanish
Average price: $31-60
District: Chelsea
Address: 205 10th Ave
New York, NY 10011
Phone: +1 (212) 675-8805

#163
LIC Market
Cuisines: Breakfast & Brunch, American
Average price: $11-30
District: Long Island City
Address: 21-52 44th Dr
Long Island City, NY 11101
Phone: +1 (718) 361-0013

#164
Astoria Bier and Cheese
Cuisines: American
Average price: $11-30
District: Astoria
Address: 34-14 Broadway
Astoria, NY 11106
Phone: +1 (718) 545-5588

#165
Ayada Thai
Cuisines: Thai
Average price: $11-30
District: Elmhurst
Address: 77-08 Woodside Ave
Elmhurst, NY 11373
Phone: +1 (718) 424-0844

#166
Xe May Sandwich Shop
Cuisines: Sandwiches, Vietnamese
Average price: Under $10
District: East Village
Address: 96 Saint Marks Pl
New York, NY 10009
Phone: +1 (212) 388-1688

#167
Siggy's Good Food
Cuisines: American, Mediterranean
Average price: $11-30
District: Brooklyn Heights
Address: 76 Henry St
Brooklyn, NY 11201
Phone: +1 (718) 237-3199

#168
L&B Spumoni Gardens
Cuisines: Pizza
Average price: Under $10
District: Gravesend
Address: 2725 86th St
Brooklyn, NY 11223
Phone: +1 (718) 449-1230

#169
La Lanterna di Vittorio
Cuisines: Italian
Average price: $11-30
District: Greenwich Village
Address: 129 MacDougal St
New York, NY 10012
Phone: +1 (212) 529-5945

#170
Marlow & Sons
Cuisines: American
Average price: $31-60
District: South Williamsburg
Address: 81 Broadway
Brooklyn, NY 11249
Phone: +1 (718) 384-1441

#171
Enthaice Thai Kitchen
Cuisines: Thai
Average price: $11-30
District: Astoria
Address: 33-20 31st Ave
Astoria, NY 11106
Phone: +1 (718) 932-1111

#172
Atera
Cuisines: American, Lounge
Average price: Above $61
District: Civic Center, TriBeCa
Address: 77 Worth St
New York, NY 10013
Phone: +1 (212) 226-1444

#173
Fette Sau
Cuisines: Barbeque
Average price: $11-30
District: Williamsburg - North Side
Address: 354 Metropolitan Ave
Brooklyn, NY 11211
Phone: +1 (718) 963-3404

#174
Salinas
Cuisines: Mediterranean, Spanish
Average price: $31-60
District: Chelsea
Address: 136 9th Avenue
New York, NY 10011
Phone: +1 (212) 776-1990

#175
Taste of Persia NYC
Cuisines: Persian/Iranian
Average price: $11-30
District: Flatiron
Address: 12 W 18th St
New York, NY 10011
Phone: +1 (917) 592-3467

#176
The Grocery
Cuisines: American
Average price: $31-60
District: Carroll Gardens, Gowanus
Address: 288 Smith St
Brooklyn, NY 11231
Phone: +1 (718) 596-3335

#177
Patacon Pisao
Cuisines: Latin American
Average price: Under $10
District: Elmhurst
Address: 85-22 Grand Ave
Elmhurst, NY 11373
Phone: +1 (718) 899-8922

#178
Piccolo Angolo
Cuisines: Italian
Average price: $11-30
District: West Village
Address: 621 Hudson St
New York, NY 10014
Phone: +1 (212) 229-9177

#179
Tanoreen
Cuisines: Middle Eastern, Mediterranean
Average price: $11-30
District: Bay Ridge
Address: 7523 3rd Ave
Brooklyn, NY 11209
Phone: +1 (718) 748-5600

#180
Café Moto
Cuisines: Café, Bar
Average price: $11-30
District: Williamsburg - South Side,
South Williamsburg
Address: 394 Broadway
Brooklyn, NY 11211
Phone: +1 (718) 599-6895

#181
Woorijip Authentic Korean Food
Cuisines: Korean
Average price: Under $10
District: Midtown West, Koreatown
Address: 12 W 32nd St
New York, NY 10001
Phone: +1 (212) 244-1115

#182
The Picnic Basket
Cuisines: Café, Sandwiches
Average price: Under $10
District: Midtown West
Address: 65 W 37th St
New York, NY 10018
Phone: +1 (212) 382-2627

#183
Danny Brown Wine Bar & Kitchen
Cuisines: American, Wine Bar, Tapas Bar
Average price: $31-60
District: Forest Hills
Address: 10402 Metropolitan Ave
Forest Hills, NY 11375
Phone: +1 (718) 261-2144

#184
Go! Go! Curry!
Cuisines: Japanese, Korean
Average price: Under $10
District: Midtown West
Address: 273 W 38th St
New York, NY 10018
Phone: +1 (212) 730-5555

#185
A Café New York
Cuisines: French
Average price: $11-30
District: Manhattan Valley
Address: 973 Columbus Ave
New York, NY 10025
Phone: +1 (212) 222-2033

#186
Jack the Horse Tavern
Cuisines: American
Average price: $31-60
District: Brooklyn Heights
Address: 66 Hicks St
Brooklyn, NY 11201
Phone: +1 (718) 852-5084

#187
Piccoli Trattoria
Cuisines: Italian
Average price: $11-30
District: South Slope, Park Slope
Address: 522 6th Ave
Brooklyn, NY 11215
Phone: +1 (718) 788-0066

#188
Joseph Leonard
Cuisines: American, French
Average price: $31-60
District: West Village
Address: 170 Waverly Pl
New York, NY 10014
Phone: +1 (646) 429-8383

#189
Tchoup Shop
Cuisines: Cajun/Creole, Southern, Caterer
Average price: $11-30
District: Bushwick
Address: 50 Wyckoff Ave
Brooklyn, NY 11237
Phone: +1 (347) 223-2710

#190
Sottocasa
Cuisines: Pizza, Italian
Average price: $11-30
District: Cobble Hill, Boerum Hill
Address: 298 Atlantic Ave
Brooklyn, NY 11201
Phone: +1 (718) 852-8758

#191
Otto's Tacos
Cuisines: Mexican
Average price: Under $10
District: East Village
Address: 141 2nd Ave
New York, NY 10003
Phone: +1 (646) 678-4018

#192
Roberta's
Cuisines: Pizza, American
Average price: $11-30
District: East Williamsburg, Bushwick
Address: 261 Moore St
Brooklyn, NY 11206
Phone: +1 (718) 417-1118

#193
Lulu & Po
Cuisines: American
Average price: $31-60
District: Fort Greene
Address: 154 Carlton Ave
Brooklyn, NY 11205
Phone: +1 (917) 435-3745

#194
Red Hook Lobster Pound
Cuisines: Seafood Markets, Seafood
Average price: $11-30
District: Red Hook
Address: 284 Van Brunt St
Brooklyn, NY 11231
Phone: +1 (718) 858-7650

#195
Defontes
Cuisines: Sandwiches
Average price: Under $10
District: Red Hook
Address: 379 Columbia St
Brooklyn, NY 11231
Phone: +1 (718) 625-8052

#196
Rex
Cuisines: Coffee & Tea, Sandwiches
Average price: Under $10
District: Hell's Kitchen, Midtown West
Address: 864 10th Ave
New York, NY 10019
Phone: +1 (212) 757-0580

#197
Five Leaves
Cuisines: American, Coffee & Tea
Average price: $11-30
District: Greenpoint
Address: 18 Bedford Ave
Brooklyn, NY 11222
Phone: +1 (718) 383-5345

#198
Mimi's Hummus
Cuisines: Mediterranean, Specialty Food
Average price: $11-30
District: Flatbush
Address: 1209 Cortelyou Rd
Brooklyn, NY 11218
Phone: +1 (718) 284-4444

#199
Giovanni's Brooklyn Eats
Cuisines: Italian
Average price: $11-30
District: South Slope
Address: 1657 8th Ave
Brooklyn, NY 11215
Phone: +1 (718) 788-8001

#200
The Meatball Shop
Cuisines: Italian, American
Average price: $11-30
District: West Village
Address: 64 Greenwich Ave
New York, NY 10011
Phone: +1 (212) 982-7815

#201
Taste Good Malaysian Cuisine
Cuisines: Malaysian
Average price: Under $10
District: Elmhurst
Address: 8218 45th Ave
Elmhurst, NY 11373
Phone: +1 (718) 898-8001

#202
Lamarca Cheese Shop
Cuisines: Cheese Shop, Comfort Food
Average price: Under $10
District: Gramercy
Address: 161 E 22nd St
New York, NY 10010
Phone: +1 (212) 673-7920

#203
Lobster Joint
Cuisines: Sports Bar, Seafood
Average price: $11-30
District: Lower East Side
Address: 201 E Houston St
New York, NY 10002
Phone: +1 (646) 896-1110

#204
Onya
Cuisines: Japanese, Soup
Average price: $11-30
District: Midtown East
Address: 143 E 47th St
New York, NY 10017
Phone: +1 (212) 715-0460

#205
Caracas Arepa Bar
Cuisines: Latin American
Average price: $11-30
District: Williamsburg - North Side
Address: 291 Grand St
Brooklyn, NY 11211
Phone: +1 (718) 218-6050

#206
BrisketTown
Cuisines: American, Barbeque
Average price: $11-30
District: Williamsburg - South Side
Address: 359 Bedford Ave
Brooklyn, NY 11211
Phone: +1 (718) 701-8909

#207
Rao's
Cuisines: Italian
Average price: Above $61
District: East Harlem
Address: 455 E 114th St
New York, NY 10029
Phone: +1 (212) 722-6709

#208
Prima
Cuisines: Seafood, Bar
Average price: $31-60
District: East Village
Address: 58 East 1 St
New York, NY 10003
Phone: +1 (646) 559-4823

#209
Da Mikele
Cuisines: Italian
Average price: $11-30
District: TriBeCa
Address: 275 Church St
New York, NY 10013
Phone: +1 (212) 925-8800

#210
Margon
Cuisines: Cuban
Average price: Under $10
District: Midtown West, Theater
Address: 136 W 46th St
New York, NY 10036
Phone: +1 (212) 354-5013

#211
Locanda Verde
Cuisines: Italian
Average price: $31-60
District: TriBeCa
Address: 377 Greenwich St
New York, NY 10013
Phone: +1 (212) 925-3797

#212
Testo
Cuisines: Italian, Gluten-Free
Average price: $11-30
District: East Williamsburg
Address: 141 Leonard St
Brooklyn, NY 11206
Phone: +1 (718) 388-4810

#213
Brooklyn Star
Cuisines: Southern, Bar
Average price: $11-30
District: Williamsburg - North Side
Address: 593 Lorimer St
Brooklyn, NY 11211
Phone: +1 (718) 599-9899

#214
The Mermaid Inn
Cuisines: Seafood
Average price: $31-60
District: Upper West Side
Address: 568 Amsterdam Ave
New York, NY 10024
Phone: +1 (212) 799-7400

#215
Zutto Japanese American Pub
Cuisines: Asian Fusion,
Japanese, Sushi Bar
Average price: $11-30
District: TriBeCa
Address: 77 Hudson St
New York, NY 10013
Phone: +1 (212) 233-3287

#216
The Levee
Cuisines: American, Bar
Average price: Under $10
District: Williamsburg - North Side
Address: 212 Berry St
Brooklyn, NY 11211
Phone: +1 (718) 218-8787

#217
Grill 212
Cuisines: Kosher, Middle Eastern,
Barbeque
Average price: $11-30
District: Upper West Side
Address: 212 W 80th St
New York, NY 10024
Phone: +1 (212) 724-7455

#218
Buttermilk Channel
Cuisines: American, Breakfast & Brunch
Average price: $31-60
District: Carroll Gardens
Address: 524 Ct St
Brooklyn, NY 11231
Phone: +1 (718) 852-8490

#219
Vin et Fleurs
Cuisines: French
Average price: $11-30
District: South Village
Address: 69 Thompson St
New York, NY 10012
Phone: +1 (212) 431-3335

#220
La Panineria
Cuisines: Sandwiches
Average price: $11-30
District: Greenwich Village
Address: 1 W 8th St
New York, NY 11001
Phone: +1 (917) 388-3257

#221
Sik Gaek
Cuisines: Korean, Seafood
Average price: $11-30
District: Woodside
Address: 49-11 Roosevelt Ave
Woodside, NY 11377
Phone: +1 (718) 205-4555

#222
Carmine's
Cuisines: Italian
Average price: $11-30
District: Midtown West, Theater
Address: 200 W 44th St
New York, NY 10036
Phone: +1 (212) 221-3800

#223
Ovest Pizzoteca
Cuisines: Pizza
Average price: $11-30
District: Chelsea
Address: 513 W 27th St
New York, NY 10001
Phone: +1 (212) 967-4392

#224
Casablanca Restaurant
Cuisines: Moroccan
Average price: $11-30
District: Bay Ridge
Address: 484 77th St
Brooklyn, NY 11209
Phone: +1 (718) 748-2077

#225
Pio Pio
Cuisines: Latin American, Peruvian
Average price: $11-30
District: Yorkville, Upper East Side
Address: 1746 1st Ave
New York, NY 10128
Phone: +1 (212) 426-5800

#226
La Pulperia
Cuisines: Latin American,
Seafood, Cocktail Bar
Average price: $31-60
District: Midtown West
Address: 371 W 46 St
New York, NY 10036
Phone: +1 (212) 956-3055

#227
Pata Negra
Cuisines: Tapas Bar, Wine Bar, Spanish
Average price: $11-30
District: East Village
Address: 345 E 12th St
New York, NY 10003
Phone: +1 (212) 228-1696

#228
Bedouin Tent Restaurant
Cuisines: Middle Eastern
Average price: Under $10
District: Downtown
Brooklyn, Boerum Hill
Address: 405 Atlantic Ave
Brooklyn, NY 11217
Phone: +1 (718) 852-5555

#229
Shake Shack
Cuisines: Burgers, Fast Food
Average price: $11-30
District: Battery Park
Address: 215 Murray St
New York, NY 10282
Phone: +1 (646) 545-4600

#230
Panino Rustico
Cuisines: Italian, Sandwiches
Average price: $11-30
District: Bensonhurst
Address: 8222 17th Ave
Brooklyn, NY 11214
Phone: +1 (718) 236-6343

#231
Sweet Afton
Cuisines: Bar, American
Average price: $11-30
District: Astoria
Address: 30-09 34th St
Astoria, NY 11103
Phone: +1 (718) 777-2570

#232
Verlaine
Cuisines: Tapas, Lounge
Average price: $11-30
District: Lower East Side
Address: 110 Rivington St
New York, NY 10002
Phone: +1 (212) 614-2494

#233
Royale
Cuisines: Burgers, Bar
Average price: Under $10
District: East Village, Alphabet City
Address: 157 Ave C
New York, NY 10009
Phone: +1 (212) 254-6600

#234
Samurai Mama
Cuisines: Japanese
Average price: $11-30
District: Williamsburg - South Side,
Williamsburg - North Side
Address: 205 Grand St
Brooklyn, NY 11211
Phone: +1 (718) 599-6161

#235
Puerto Viejo
Cuisines: Spanish, Caribbean,
Latin American
Average price: $11-30
District: Crown Heights
Address: 564 Grand Ave
Brooklyn, NY 11238
Phone: +1 (718) 398-3758

#236
Rustic L.E.S
Cuisines: Moroccan, Halal
Average price: $11-30
District: Lower East Side
Address: 124 Ridge St
New York, NY 10002
Phone: +1 (646) 833-0848

#237
Banhmigos
Cuisines: Bubble Tea,
Vietnamese, Sandwiches
Average price: Under $10
District: Park Slope
Address: 178 Lincoln Pl
Brooklyn, NY 11217
Phone: +1 (718) 399-3812

#238
Arepera Guacuco Restaurant
Cuisines: Latin American
Average price: $11-30
District: Bushwick
Address: 44 Irving Ave
Brooklyn, NY 11237
Phone: +1 (347) 305-3300

#239
Lobster Joint
Cuisines: Seafood
Average price: $11-30
District: Greenpoint
Address: 1073 Manhattan Ave
Brooklyn, NY 11222
Phone: +1 (718) 389-8990

#240
Freemans Restaurant
Cuisines: Breakfast & Brunch,
American, Lounge
Average price: $31-60
District: Lower East Side
Address: 8 Rivington St
New York, NY 10002
Phone: +1 (212) 420-0012

#241
Tito Rad's Grill & Restaurant
Cuisines: Barbeque, Filipino
Average price: $11-30
District: Woodside
Address: 49-12 Queens Blvd
Sunnyside, NY 11377
Phone: +1 (718) 205-7299

#242
Rucola
Cuisines: Italian, Desserts, Diner
Average price: $11-30
District: Boerum Hill
Address: 190 Dean St
Brooklyn, NY 11217
Phone: +1 (718) 576-3209

#243
Luke's Lobster
Cuisines: Seafood
Average price: $11-30
District: Upper West Side
Address: 426 Amsterdam Ave
New York, NY 10024
Phone: +1 (212) 877-8800

#244
V-Nam Café
Cuisines: Vietnamese, Sandwiches
Average price: Under $10
District: East Village
Address: 20 1st Ave
New York, NY 10003
Phone: +1 (212) 780-6020

#245
Petit Oven
Cuisines: French, American
Average price: $31-60
District: Bay Ridge
Address: 276 Bay Ridge Ave
Brooklyn, NY 11220
Phone: +1 (718) 833-3443

#246
Bayou
Cuisines: Cajun/Creole, Southern
Average price: $11-30
District: Clifton
Address: 1072 Bay St
Staten Island, NY 10305
Phone: +1 (718) 273-4383

#247
Pinto
Cuisines: Thai
Average price: $11-30
District: West Village
Address: 118 Christopher St
New York, NY 10014
Phone: +1 (212) 366-5455

#248
Kafana
Cuisines: Ethnic Food, Modern European
Average price: $11-30
District: East Village, Alphabet City
Address: 116 Ave C
New York, NY 10009
Phone: +1 (212) 353-8000

#249
Shanghai Asian Manor
Cuisines: Shanghainese
Average price: $11-30
District: Chinatown, Civic Center
Address: 21 Mott St
New York, NY 10013
Phone: +1 (212) 766-6311

#250
Il Buco
Cuisines: Italian, American
Average price: $31-60
District: NoHo
Address: 47 Bond St
New York, NY 10012
Phone: +1 (212) 533-1932

#251
The Stanton Social
Cuisines: Tapas, Bar
Average price: $31-60
District: Lower East Side
Address: 99 Stanton St
New York, NY 10002
Phone: +1 (212) 995-0099

#252
Hospoda
Cuisines: American
Average price: $31-60
District: Yorkville, Upper East Side
Address: 321 E 73rd St
New York, NY 10021
Phone: +1 (212) 861-1038

#253
SriPraPhai Thai Restaurant
Cuisines: Thai, Bar
Average price: $11-30
District: Woodside
Address: 6413 39th Ave
Woodside, NY 11377
Phone: +1 (718) 899-9599

#254
Yuca Bar & Restaurant
Cuisines: Latin American, Tapas Bar
Average price: $11-30
District: East Village, Alphabet City
Address: 111 Ave A
New York, NY 10009
Phone: +1 (212) 982-9533

#255
Mayfield
Cuisines: American
Average price: $11-30
District: Crown Heights
Address: 688 Franklin Ave
Brooklyn, NY 11238
Phone: +1 (347) 318-3643

#256
Cask Bar + Kitchen
Cuisines: Bar, American, Seafood
Average price: $11-30
District: Midtown East, Murray Hill, Kips Bay
Address: 167 E 33rd St
New York, NY 10016
Phone: +1 (212) 300-4924

#257
Freda's Caribbean & Soul Cuisine
Cuisines: Caribbean, Soul Food
Average price: Under $10
District: Manhattan Valley
Address: 993 Columbus Ave
New York, NY 10025
Phone: +1 (646) 438-9832

#258
Ellary's Greens
Cuisines: American, Vegan,
Juice Bar
Average price: $11-30
District: West Village
Address: 33 Carmine St
New York, NY 10014
Phone: +1 (212) 920-5072

#259
Las Ramblas
Cuisines: Tapas
Average price: $11-30
District: West Village
Address: 170 W 4th St
New York, NY 10014
Phone: +1 (646) 415-7924

#260
Mogu Sushi
Cuisines: Sushi Bar, Japanese
Average price: $11-30
District: Downtown Flushing, Flushing
Address: 13322 39th Ave
Flushing, NY 11354
Phone: +1 (718) 886-2618

#261
Pio Pio
Cuisines: Peruvian
Average price: $11-30
District: Hell's Kitchen, Midtown West
Address: 604 10th Ave
New York, NY 10036
Phone: +1 (212) 459-2929

#262
Trattoria Trecolori
Cuisines: Italian
Average price: $11-30
District: Midtown West, Theater
Address: 254 W 47th St
New York, NY 10036
Phone: +1 (212) 997-4540

#263
Hudson Clearwater
Cuisines: American
Average price: $31-60
District: West Village
Address: 447 Hudson St
New York, NY 10014
Phone: +1 (212) 989-3255

#264
Umami Burger
Cuisines: Burgers
Average price: $11-30
District: Greenwich Village
Address: 432 6th Ave
New York, NY 10011
Phone: +1 (212) 677-8626

#265
Jane
Cuisines: Breakfast & Brunch, American
Average price: $11-30
District: Greenwich Village
Address: 100 W Houston St
New York, NY 10012
Phone: +1 (212) 254-7000

#266
Le Barricou
Cuisines: Breakfast & Brunch, French
Average price: $11-30
District: Williamsburg - North Side
Address: 533 Grand St
Brooklyn, NY 11211
Phone: +1 (718) 782-7372

#267
Barrio Chino
Cuisines: Mexican, Bar
Average price: $11-30
District: Lower East Side
Address: 253 Broome St
New York, NY 10002
Phone: +1 (212) 228-6710

#268
Villa Brazil Café Grill
Cuisines: Brazilian
Average price: Under $10
District: Astoria
Address: 4316 34th Ave
Long Island City, NY 11101
Phone: +1 (347) 670-4202

#269
Papa Pasquale Ravoli Pasta
Cuisines: Specialty Food, Italian, Deli
Average price: $11-30
District: Bensonhurst
Address: 7813 15th Avenue
Brooklyn, NY 11228
Phone: +1 (718) 232-1798

#270
Beco
Cuisines: Brazilian, Bar
Average price: $11-30
District: Williamsburg - North Side
Address: 45 Richardson St
Brooklyn, NY 11211
Phone: +1 (718) 599-1645

#271
Mountain Bird
Cuisines: French
Average price: $31-60
District: Harlem
Address: 231 W 145th St
New York, NY 10039
Phone: +1 (212) 281-5752

#272
Kimchi Grill
Cuisines: Mexican, Korean, Barbeque
Average price: Under $10
District: Crown Heights, Prospect Heights
Address: 766 Washington Ave
Brooklyn, NY 11238
Phone: +1 (718) 360-1839

#273
Anthi's Greek Food
Cuisines: Greek, Ethnic Food
Average price: Under $10
District: Upper West Side
Address: 614 Amsterdam Ave
New York, NY 10024
Phone: +1 (212) 787-1007

#274
Momofuku Ssam Bar
Cuisines: Korean, American
Average price: $31-60
District: East Village
Address: 207 2nd Ave
New York, NY 10003
Phone: +1 (212) 254-3500

#275
Harlem Public
Cuisines: American, Pub
Average price: $11-30
District: Harlem
Address: 3612 Broadway
New York, NY 10031
Phone: +1 (212) 939-9404

#276
Maharlika
Cuisines: Filipino
Average price: $11-30
District: East Village
Address: 111 1st Ave
New York, NY 10003
Phone: +1 (646) 392-7880

#277
Le Parisien
Cuisines: French
Average price: $11-30
District: Midtown East, Murray Hill, Kips Bay
Address: 163 E 33rd St
New York, NY 10016
Phone: +1 (212) 889-5489

#278
Houdini
Cuisines: Pizza
Average price: $11-30
District: Ridgewood, Bushwick
Address: 15-63 Decatur St
Ridgewood, NY 11385
Phone: +1 (718) 456-3770

#279
Ceetay
Cuisines: Sushi Bar, Asian Fusion, Thai
Average price: $11-30
District: Mott Haven
Address: 129 Alexander Ave
Bronx, NY 10454
Phone: +1 (718) 618-7020

#280
Cienfuegos
Cuisines: Cuban, American
Average price: $31-60
District: East Village, Alphabet City
Address: 95 Ave A
New York, NY 10009
Phone: +1 (212) 614-6818

#281
Kofte Piyaz
Cuisines: Ethnic Food, Turkish
Average price: Under $10
District: Sunset Park
Address: 881 5th Ave
Brooklyn, NY 11232
Phone: +1 (347) 227-7036

#282
Grimaldi's
Cuisines: Pizza
Average price: $11-30
District: DUMBO
Address: 1 Front St
Brooklyn, NY 11201
Phone: +1 (718) 858-4300

#283
Olla Wine Bar
Cuisines: Italian, French, Spanish
Average price: $31-60
District: Bay Ridge
Address: 7204 3rd Ave
Brooklyn, NY 11209
Phone: +1 (718) 238-1110

#284
Pó
Cuisines: Italian
Average price: $31-60
District: West Village
Address: 31 Cornelia St
New York, NY 10014
Phone: +1 (212) 645-2189

#285
Black Tree
Cuisines: American
Average price: $11-30
District: Lower East Side
Address: 131 Orchard St
New York, NY 10002
Phone: +1 (212) 533-4684

#286
Joe's Shanghai
Cuisines: Shanghainese, Dim Sum
Average price: $11-30
District: Chinatown, Civic Center
Address: 9 Pell St
New York, NY 10013
Phone: +1 (212) 233-8888

#287
Ippudo Westside
Cuisines: Ramen
Average price: $11-30
District: Hell's Kitchen, Midtown West
Address: 321 W 51st St
New York, NY 10019
Phone: +1 (212) 974-2500

#288
The Grey Dog
Cuisines: Coffee & Tea, Breakfast & Brunch
Average price: $11-30
District: Chelsea
Address: 242 W 16th St
New York, NY 10011
Phone: +1 (212) 229-2345

#289
Malagueta Restaurant
Cuisines: Brazilian
Average price: $11-30
District: Astoria
Address: 2535 36th Ave
Astoria, NY 11106
Phone: +1 (718) 937-4821

#290
Cuba
Cuisines: Cuban
Average price: $11-30
District: Greenwich Village
Address: 222 Thompson St
New York, NY 10012
Phone: +1 (212) 420-7878

#291
The Anchored Inn
Cuisines: Bar, American
Average price: $11-30
District: East Williamsburg
Address: 57 Waterbury St
Brooklyn, NY 11206
Phone: +1 (718) 576-3297

#292
The Grand Bar and Grill
Cuisines: Gastropub, American
Average price: $11-30
District: Williamsburg - North Side
Address: 647 Grand St
Brooklyn, NY 11211
Phone: +1 (718) 782-4726

#293
Tony's Di Napoli
Cuisines: Italian
Average price: $11-30
District: Midtown West, Theater
Address: 147 W 43rd St
New York, NY 10036
Phone: +1 (212) 221-0100

#294
Greenpoint Heights
Cuisines: Bar, American
Average price: $11-30
District: Greenpoint
Address: 278 Nassau Ave
Brooklyn, NY 11222
Phone: +1 (718) 389-0110

#295
Taci's Beyti
Cuisines: Turkish, Middle Eastern,
Mediterranean
Average price: $11-30
District: Gravesend, Midwood
Address: 1955 Coney Island Ave
Brooklyn, NY 11223
Phone: +1 (718) 627-5750

#296
Jacob's Pickles
Cuisines: American, Bar
Average price: $11-30
District: Upper West Side
Address: 509 Amsterdam Ave
New York, NY 10024
Phone: +1 (212) 470-5566

#297
DuMont
Cuisines: American, Burgers
Average price: $11-30
District: Williamsburg - North Side
Address: 432 Union Ave
Brooklyn, NY 11206
Phone: +1 (718) 486-7717

#298
Nish Nush
Cuisines: Middle Eastern,
Vegetarian, Kosher
Average price: Under $10
District: TriBeCa
Address: 88 Reade St
New York, NY 10013
Phone: +1 (212) 964-1318

#299
Ferdinando's
Cuisines: Italian
Average price: $11-30
District: Columbia Street Waterfront
Address: 151 Union St
Brooklyn, NY 11231
Phone: +1 (718) 855-1545

#300
Stone Park Café
Cuisines: Breakfast & Brunch
Average price: $11-30
District: Park Slope
Address: 324 5th Ave
Brooklyn, NY 11215
Phone: +1 (718) 369-0082

#301
Calle Ocho
Cuisines: Cuban, Latin American
Average price: $11-30
District: Upper West Side
Address: 45 W 81st St
New York, NY 10024
Phone: +1 (212) 873-5025

#302
Two 8 Two
Cuisines: Burgers, Bar
Average price: $11-30
District: Cobble Hill, Boerum Hill
Address: 282 Atlantic Ave
Brooklyn, NY 11201
Phone: +1 (718) 596-2282

#303
Ear Inn
Cuisines: Bar, American
Average price: $11-30
District: South Village
Address: 326 Spring St
New York, NY 10013
Phone: +1 (212) 226-9060

#304
Frankies 457
Cuisines: Italian
Average price: $11-30
District: Carroll Gardens
Address: 457 Court St
Brooklyn, NY 11231
Phone: +1 (718) 403-0033

#305
Dear Bushwick
Cuisines: British
Average price: $11-30
District: Bushwick
Address: 41 Wilson Ave
Brooklyn, NY 11237
Phone: +1 (929) 234-2344

#306
Tortas Neza
Cuisines: Mexican, Food Stands
Average price: Under $10
District: Elmhurst
Address: 11103 Roosevelt Ave
Corona, NY 11368
Phone: +1 (718) 505-2121

#307
Aroma Kitchen & Winebar
Cuisines: Italian, Wine Bar
Average price: $31-60
District: NoHo
Address: 36 E 4th St
New York, NY 10003
Phone: +1 (212) 375-0100

#308
Knife
Cuisines: Coffee & Tea, Sandwiches
Average price: Under $10
District: Williamsburg - South Side
Address: 330 S 3rd St
Brooklyn, NY 11211
Phone: +1 (718) 486-0008

#309
The Good Fork
Cuisines: American
Average price: $31-60
District: Red Hook
Address: 391 Van Brunt St
Brooklyn, NY 11231
Phone: +1 (718) 643-6636

#310
Print
Cuisines: American, Lounge
Average price: $31-60
District: Hell's Kitchen, Midtown West
Address: 653 11th Ave
New York, NY 10036
Phone: +1 (212) 757-2224

#311
Mesmes Mediterranean
Cuisines: Mediterranean
Average price: $11-30
District: West Village
Address: 581 Hudson Street
New York, NY 10014
Phone: +1 (646) 692-8450

#312
Fish
Cuisines: Seafood
Average price: $11-30
District: West Village
Address: 280 Bleecker St
New York, NY 10014
Phone: +1 (212) 727-2879

#313
Casa Adela
Cuisines: Latin American, Puerto Rican
Average price: Under $10
District: East Village, Alphabet City
Address: 66 Ave C
New York, NY 10009
Phone: +1 (212) 473-1882

#314
Don Nico's
Cuisines: Mexican
Average price: Under $10
District: Downtown Brooklyn
Address: 9-43 Dekalb Ave
Brooklyn, NY 11201
Phone: +1 (718) 288-0107

#315
Ward III
Cuisines: American, Lounge
Average price: $11-30
District: TriBeCa
Address: 111 Reade St
New York, NY 10013
Phone: +1 (212) 240-9194

#316
The Red Cat
Cuisines: American
Average price: $31-60
District: Chelsea
Address: 227 10th Ave
New York, NY 10011
Phone: +1 (212) 242-1122

#317
Ryan's Daughter
Cuisines: Pub, American
Average price: $11-30
District: Yorkville, Upper East Side
Address: 350 E 85th St
New York, NY 10028
Phone: +1 (212) 628-2613

#318
Gena's Grill
Cuisines: Dominican, Puerto Rican
Average price: Under $10
District: East Village
Address: 210 1st Ave
New York, NY 10009
Phone: +1 (212) 473-3700

#319
Supper
Cuisines: Italian
Average price: $11-30
District: East Village, Alphabet City
Address: 156 E 2nd St
New York, NY 10009
Phone: +1 (212) 477-7600

#320
Northern Spy Food Co.
Cuisines: American
Average price: $11-30
District: East Village, Alphabet City
Address: 511 E 12th St
New York, NY 10009
Phone: +1 (212) 228-5100

#321
Amy Ruth's
Cuisines: Southern, Soul Food
Average price: $11-30
District: Harlem
Address: 113 W 116th St
New York, NY 10026
Phone: +1 (212) 280-8779

#322
Henry's End
Cuisines: American
Average price: $31-60
District: Brooklyn Heights
Address: 44 Henry St
Brooklyn, NY 11201
Phone: +1 (718) 834-1776

#323
Huckleberry Bar
Cuisines: Bar, American
Average price: $11-30
District: East Williamsburg
Address: 588 Grand St
Brooklyn, NY 11211
Phone: +1 (718) 218-8555

#324
Fonda
Cuisines: Mexican
Average price: $11-30
District: East Village, Alphabet City
Address: 40 Avenue B
New York, NY 10009
Phone: +1 (212) 677-4096

#325
L'asso
Cuisines: Italian, Pizza, Gluten-Free
Average price: $11-30
District: Nolita
Address: 192 Mott St
New York, NY 10012
Phone: +1 (212) 219-2353

#326
Da Andrea
Cuisines: Italian
Average price: $11-30
District: Greenwich Village
Address: 35 W 13th St
New York, NY 10011
Phone: +1 (212) 367-1979

#327
East Harbor Seafood Palace
Cuisines: Dim Sum, Cantonese, Seafood
Average price: $11-30
District: Dyker Heights
Address: 714 65th St
Brooklyn, NY 11220
Phone: +1 (718) 765-0098

#328
Fong Inn Too
Cuisines: Desserts, Chinese
Average price: Under $10
District: Chinatown, Civic Center
Address: 46 Mott St
New York, NY 10013
Phone: +1 (212) 962-5196

#329
Westville
Cuisines: American
Average price: $11-30
District: Chelsea
Address: 246 W 18th St
New York, NY 10011
Phone: +1 (212) 924-2223

#330
Kristophe
Cuisines: Comfort Food, Bar, American
Average price: $11-30
District: Williamsburg - North Side
Address: 221 N 4th St
Brooklyn, NY 11211
Phone: +1 (718) 302-5100

#331
Yakitori Taisho
Cuisines: Japanese, Sushi Bar
Average price: $11-30
District: East Village
Address: 5 St Marks Pl
New York, NY 10003
Phone: +1 (212) 228-5086

#332
Giuseppina's
Cuisines: Pizza
Average price: $11-30
District: South Slope
Address: 691 6th Ave
Brooklyn, NY 11215
Phone: +1 (718) 499-5052

#333
Tink's Restaurant
Cuisines: American, Comfort Food,
Breakfast & Brunch
Average price: $11-30
District: East Village
Address: 102 E 7th St
New York, NY 10009
Phone: +1 (646) 833-7844

#334
The Spotted Pig
Cuisines: Burgers, Gastropub
Average price: $31-60
District: West Village
Address: 314 W 11th St
New York, NY 10014
Phone: +1 (212) 620-0393

#335
Ten Degrees Bar
Cuisines: Wine Bar, Gastropub
Average price: $11-30
District: East Village, Alphabet City
Address: 121 St. Marks Pl
New York, NY 10009
Phone: +1 (212) 358-8600

#336
The Cellar
Cuisines: Wine Bar, American
Average price: $11-30
District: Flatiron
Address: 900 Broadway
New York, NY 10003
Phone: +1 (212) 466-3340

#337
Iron Chef House
Cuisines: Sushi Bar
Average price: $11-30
District: Brooklyn Heights
Address: 92 Clark St
Brooklyn, NY 11201
Phone: +1 (718) 858-8517

#338
Stocked
Cuisines: American, Sandwiches
Average price: Under $10
District: Prospect Heights
Address: 635 Vanderbilt Ave
Brooklyn, NY 11238
Phone: +1 (929) 234-6554

#339
Luke's Lobster
Cuisines: Seafood
Average price: $11-30
District: Midtown West
Address: 1 W 59th St
New York, NY 10019
Phone: +1 (646) 755-3227

#340
Cipriani Le Specialita
Cuisines: Italian
Average price: $11-30
District: Midtown East, Murray Hill
Address: 110 E 42nd St
New York, NY 10017
Phone: +1 (212) 557-5088

#341
Barnyard
Cuisines: Cheese Shop, Sandwiches
Average price: $11-30
District: East Village, Alphabet City
Address: 149 Ave C
New York, NY 10009
Phone: +1 (212) 674-2276

#342
Bite
Cuisines: Food Stands, Sandwiches
Average price: Under $10
District: NoHo
Address: 333 Lafayette St
New York, NY 10012
Phone: +1 (212) 431-0301

#343
Boqueria
Cuisines: Spanish
Average price: $31-60
District: South Village
Address: 171 Spring St
New York, NY 10012
Phone: +1 (212) 343-4255

#344
Wafels & Dinges
Cuisines: Belgian
Average price: $11-30
District: East Village, Alphabet City
Address: 15 Ave B
New York, NY 10009
Phone: +1 (646) 257-2592

#345
Cafécito
Cuisines: Cuban
Average price: $11-30
District: East Village, Alphabet City
Address: 185 Ave C
New York, NY 10009
Phone: +1 (212) 253-9966

#346
Do or Dine
Cuisines: Bar, American,
Breakfast & Brunch
Average price: $11-30
District: Bedford Stuyvesant
Address: 1108 Bedford Ave
Brooklyn, NY 11216
Phone: +1 (718) 684-2290

#347
Luke's Lobster
Cuisines: Seafood, Food Stands
Average price: $11-30
District: Midtown West
Address:
New York, NY
Phone:

#348
The Marshal
Cuisines: American
Average price: $11-30
District: Hell's Kitchen, Midtown West
Address: 628 10th Ave
New York, NY 10036
Phone: +1 (212) 582-6300

#349
Polonica Restaurant
Cuisines: Polish
Average price: $11-30
District: Bay Ridge
Address: 7214 3rd Ave
Brooklyn, NY 11209
Phone: +1 (718) 630-5805

#350
Lock Yard
Cuisines: American, Hot Dogs, Pub
Average price: $11-30
District: Fort Hamilton, Bay Ridge
Address: 9221 5th Ave
Brooklyn, NY 11209
Phone: +1 (718) 333-5282

#351
Kiwiana
Cuisines: American
Average price: $11-30
District: Park Slope
Address: 847 Union St
Brooklyn, NY 11215
Phone: +1 (718) 230-3682

#352
Duzan Mediterranean Grill
Cuisines: Mediterranean
Average price: Under $10
District: Astoria
Address: 2411 Steinway St
Astoria, NY 11103
Phone: +1 (718) 204-7488

#353
Anella
Cuisines: American
Average price: $11-30
District: Greenpoint
Address: 222 Franklin St
Brooklyn, NY 11222
Phone: +1 (718) 389-8100

#354
Palma
Cuisines: Italian
Average price: $31-60
District: West Village
Address: 28 Cornelia St
New York, NY 10014
Phone: +1 (212) 691-2223

#355
The Otheroom
Cuisines: Lounge, Wine Bar, American
Average price: $11-30
District: West Village
Address: 143 Perry St
New York, NY 10014
Phone: +1 (212) 645-9758

#356
Osteria Morini
Cuisines: Italian
Average price: $31-60
District: SoHo
Address: 218 Lafayette St
New York, NY 10012
Phone: +1 (212) 965-8777

#357
Emporio
Cuisines: Italian
Average price: $11-30
District: Nolita
Address: 231 Mott St
New York, NY 10012
Phone: +1 (212) 966-1234

#358
Gato
Cuisines: Mediterranean, Spanish
Average price: $31-60
District: NoHo
Address: 324 Lafayette St
New York, NY 10012
Phone: +1 (212) 334-6400

#359
Wolfnights
Cuisines: Sandwiches
Average price: Under $10
District: Lower East Side
Address: 99 Rivington St
New York, NY 10002
Phone: +1 (646) 669-8070

#360
Han Dynasty
Cuisines: Szechuan, Soup
Average price: $11-30
District: East Village
Address: 90 3rd Ave
New York, NY 10003
Phone: +1 (212) 390-8685

#361
Bombay Duck
Cuisines: Indian
Average price: $11-30
District: Greenwich Village
Address: 190 Bleecker St
New York, NY 10012
Phone: +1 (212) 529-2900

#362
Habana Outpost
Cuisines: Cuban
Average price: $11-30
District: Fort Greene
Address: 757 Fulton St
Brooklyn, NY 11217
Phone: +1 (718) 858-9500

#363
Rose Water Restaurant
Cuisines: American, Breakfast & Brunch
Average price: $11-30
District: Park Slope
Address: 787 Union St
Brooklyn, NY 11215
Phone: +1 (718) 783-3800

#364
Minca
Cuisines: Japanese
Average price: $11-30
District: East Village, Alphabet City
Address: 536 E 5th St
New York, NY 10009
Phone: +1 (212) 505-8001

#365
Zum Stammtisch
Cuisines: German
Average price: $11-30
District: Glendale
Address: 6946 Myrtle Ave
Glendale, NY 11385
Phone: +1 (718) 386-3014

#366
Gueros
Cuisines: Tex-Mex, Mexican
Average price: Under $10
District: Crown Heights
Address: 605 Prospect Pl
Brooklyn, NY 11238
Phone: +1 (718) 230-4941

#367
Miriam
Cuisines: Wine Bar, Mediterranean,
Breakfast & Brunch
Average price: $11-30
District: Park Slope
Address: 79 5th Ave
Brooklyn, NY 11215
Phone: +1 (718) 622-2250

#368
Il Corallo Trattoria
Cuisines: Italian, Pizza
Average price: $11-30
District: South Village
Address: 172 Prince St
New York, NY 10012
Phone: +1 (212) 941-7119

#369
Ichabod's
Cuisines: American
Average price: $31-60
District: Union Square, Flatiron
Address: 15 Irving Pl
Manhattan, NY 10003
Phone: +1 (212) 777-5102

#370
Blue Ribbon Brasserie
Cuisines: Seafood, American
Average price: $31-60
District: South Village
Address: 97 Sullivan St
New York, NY 10012
Phone: +1 (212) 274-0404

#371
IL Passatore
Cuisines: Italian
Average price: $11-30
District: East Williamsburg
Address: 14 Bushwick Ave
Brooklyn, NY 11211
Phone: +1 (718) 963-3100

#372
Flor De Mayo
Cuisines: Latin American, Peruvian
Average price: $11-30
District: Upper West Side
Address: 484 Amsterdam Ave
New York, NY 10024
Phone: +1 (212) 787-3388

#373
Blue Hill
Cuisines: American
Average price: Above $61
District: Greenwich Village
Address: 75 Washington Pl
New York, NY 10011
Phone: +1 (212) 539-1776

#374
Casa Enrique
Cuisines: Mexican
Average price: $11-30
District: Hunters Point, Long Island City
Address: 5-48 49th Ave
Long Island City, NY 11101
Phone: +1 (347) 448-6040

#375
Casa Mono
Cuisines: Spanish, Tapas Bar, Basque
Average price: $31-60
District: Union Square, Gramercy, Flatiron
Address: 52 Irving Pl
New York, NY 10003
Phone: +1 (212) 253-2773

#376
Crescent Grill
Cuisines: American
Average price: $11-30
District: Long Island City
Address: 38-40 Crescent St
Long Island City, NY 11101
Phone: +1 (718) 729-4040

#377
Jimmy's Diner
Cuisines: Diner, Breakfast & Brunch,
Comfort Food
Average price: $11-30
District: Williamsburg - North Side
Address: 577 Union Ave
Brooklyn, NY 11211
Phone: +1 (718) 218-7174

#378
The Castello Plan
Cuisines: Bar, American
Average price: $11-30
District: Flatbush
Address: 1213 Cortelyou Rd
Brooklyn, NY 11218
Phone: +1 (718) 856-8888

#379
Gottino
Cuisines: Wine Bar, Italian
Average price: $11-30
District: West Village
Address: 52 Greenwich Ave
New York, NY 10011
Phone: +1 (212) 633-2590

#380
Risotteria
Cuisines: Italian, Gluten-Free, Vegetarian
Average price: $11-30
District: West Village
Address: 270 Bleecker St
New York, NY 10014
Phone: +1 (212) 924-6664

#381
Toby's Public House
Cuisines: Pizza, Bar
Average price: $11-30
District: South Slope
Address: 686 6th Ave
Brooklyn, NY 11215
Phone: +1 (718) 788-1186

#382
Cronin & Phelan's
Cuisines: Pub, American
Average price: $11-30
District: Astoria
Address: 38-14 Broadway
Astoria, NY 11102
Phone: +1 (718) 545-8999

#383
Chavela's
Cuisines: Mexican
Average price: $11-30
District: Crown Heights
Address: 736 Franklin Ave
Brooklyn, NY 11238
Phone: +1 (718) 622-3100

#384
China Express
Cuisines: Chinese
Average price: Under $10
District: East Williamsburg
Address: 192 Union Ave
Brooklyn, NY 11206
Phone: +1 (718) 218-7919

#385
The Harrison
Cuisines: American
Average price: $31-60
District: TriBeCa
Address: 355 Greenwich St
New York, NY 10013
Phone: +1 (212) 274-9310

#386
The Plaza Food Hall
Cuisines: American
Average price: $31-60
District: Midtown West
Address: 1 W 59th St
New York, NY 10019
Phone: +1 (212) 546-5499

#387
Spicy Village
Cuisines: Chinese
Average price: Under $10
District: Lower East Side
Address: 68 Forsyth St
New York, NY 10002
Phone: +1 (212) 625-8299

#388
Shabu-Tatsu East Village
Cuisines: Japanese
Average price: $11-30
District: East Village
Address: 216 E 10th St
New York, NY 10003
Phone: +1 (212) 477-2972

#389
Telepan
Cuisines: American
Average price: $31-60
District: Upper West Side
Address: 72 W 69th St
New York, NY 10023
Phone: +1 (212) 580-4300

#390
Joya
Cuisines: Thai
Average price: Under $10
District: Cobble Hill
Address: 215 Court St
Brooklyn, NY 11201
Phone: +1 (718) 222-3484

#391
Terri
Cuisines: American,
Sandwiches, Juice Bar
Average price: $11-30
District: Financial
Address: 100 Maiden Ln
New York, NY 10038
Phone: +1 (212) 742-7901

#392
The Thirsty Koala
Cuisines: Australian
Average price: $11-30
District: Astoria
Address: 35-12 Ditmars Blvd
Astoria, NY 11105
Phone: +1 (718) 626-5430

#393
Sorella
Cuisines: Italian, Wine Bar
Average price: $31-60
District: Lower East Side
Address: 95 Allen St
New York, NY 10002
Phone: +1 (212) 274-9595

#394
Hometown Bar-B-Que
Cuisines: Barbeque
Average price: $11-30
District: Red Hook
Address: 454 Van Brunt St
Brooklyn, NY 11231
Phone: +1 (347) 294-4644

#395
Café SaBarky
Cuisines: German, Café
Average price: $11-30
District: Upper East Side
Address: 1048 5th Ave
New York, NY 10028
Phone: +1 (212) 288-0665

#396
Parkside Restaurant
Cuisines: Italian
Average price: $31-60
District: Elmhurst
Address: 107-01 Corona Ave
Corona, NY 11368
Phone: +1 (718) 271-9871

#397
Buster's
Cuisines: American
Average price: $11-30
District: Manhattan Valley
Address: 892 Amsterdam Ave
New York, NY 10025
Phone: +1 (212) 665-5045

#398
Le Gigot
Cuisines: French
Average price: $31-60
District: West Village
Address: 18 Cornelia St
New York, NY 10014
Phone: +1 (212) 627-3737

#399
BZ Grill
Cuisines: Greek
Average price: Under $10
District: Astoria
Address: 2702 Astoria Blvd
Astoria, NY 11102
Phone: +1 (718) 932-7858

#400
Hillstone
Cuisines: American
Average price: $31-60
District: Midtown East
Address: 153 E 53rd St
New York, NY 10022
Phone: +1 (212) 888-3828

#401
Oregano
Cuisines: Italian, Pizza
Average price: $11-30
District: Williamsburg - North Side
Address: 102 Berry St
Brooklyn, NY 11211
Phone: +1 (718) 599-5988

#402
Café Condesa
Cuisines: American, Mexican
Average price: $11-30
District: West Village
Address: 183 W 10th St
New York, NY 10014
Phone: +1 (212) 352-0050

#403
Totonno's
Cuisines: Pizza
Average price: $11-30
District: Coney Island
Address: 1524 Neptune Ave
Brooklyn, NY 11224
Phone: +1 (718) 372-8606

#404
The Bodega
Cuisines: Pub, Breakfast & Brunch
Average price: $11-30
District: Bushwick
Address: 24 St. Nicholas Ave
Brooklyn, NY 11237
Phone: +1 (347) 305-3344

#405
Cedars Meat House
Cuisines: Middle Eastern, Halal
Average price: Under $10
District: Astoria
Address: 41-08 30th Ave
Astoria, NY 11102
Phone: +1 (718) 606-1244

#406
Windy City Ale House
Cuisines: Sports Bar, American
Average price: $11-30
District: Bay Ridge
Address: 7915 3rd Ave
Brooklyn, NY 11209
Phone: +1 (718) 630-5700

#407
Lure Fishbar
Cuisines: Seafood
Average price: $31-60
District: SoHo
Address: 142 Mercer St
New York, NY 10012
Phone: +1 (212) 431-7676

#408
Café Tibet
Cuisines: Chinese
Average price: Under $10
District: Flatbush
Address: 1510 Cortelyou Rd
Brooklyn, NY 11226
Phone: +1 (718) 941-2725

#409
I Am Thai
Cuisines: Thai
Average price: Under $10
District: Woodside
Address: 49-08 43rd Ave
Woodside, NY 11377
Phone: +1 (718) 457-7700

#410
Dillinger's
Cuisines: Coffee & Tea, Breakfast & Brunch
Average price: Under $10
District: Bushwick
Address: 146 Evergreen Ave
Brooklyn, NY 11206
Phone: +1 (347) 260-2123

#411
Dinosaur Bar-B-Que
Cuisines: Barbeque
Average price: $11-30
District: Harlem
Address: 700 W 125th St
New York, NY 10027
Phone: +1 (212) 694-1777

#412
Yefsi Estiatorio
Cuisines: Greek
Average price: $11-30
District: Yorkville, Upper East Side
Address: 1481 York Ave
New York, NY 10075
Phone: +1 (212) 535-0293

#413
Newtown
Cuisines: Vegetarian, Middle Eastern
Average price: Under $10
District: East Williamsburg
Address: 55 Waterbury St
Brooklyn, NY 11206
Phone: +1 (347) 984-6215

#414
Bijan's
Cuisines: Bar, American
Average price: $11-30
District: Downtown
Brooklyn, Boerum Hill
Address: 81 Hoyt St
Brooklyn, NY 11201
Phone: +1 (718) 855-5574

#415
Marietta
Cuisines: Southern, American
Average price: $11-30
District: Clinton Hill
Address: 285 Grand Ave
Brooklyn, NY 11238
Phone: +1 (718) 638-9500

#416
Ardesia
Cuisines: Wine Bar, Tapas
Average price: $11-30
District: Hell's Kitchen, Midtown West
Address: 510 W 52nd St
New York, NY 10019
Phone: +1 (212) 247-9191

#417
The Burger Bistro
Cuisines: Burgers, American, American
Average price: $11-30
District: Bay Ridge
Address: 7217 3rd Ave
Brooklyn, NY 11209
Phone: +1 (718) 833-5833

#418
J'eatjet?
Cuisines: Gastropub
Average price: $11-30
District: South Slope
Address: 685 5th Ave
Brooklyn, NY 11215
Phone: +1 (347) 227-7410

#419
Junior's Restaurant
Cuisines: Diner, American,
Breakfast & Brunch
Average price: $11-30
District: Midtown West, Theater
Address: 1515 Broadway
New York, NY 10036
Phone: +1 (212) 302-2000

#420
Boqueria
Cuisines: Spanish, Tapas Bar
Average price: $31-60
District: Flatiron
Address: 53 W 19th St
New York, NY 10011
Phone: +1 (212) 255-4160

#421
SoCo
Cuisines: Cajun/Creole,
Barbeque, Soul Food
Average price: $11-30
District: Clinton Hill
Address: 509 Myrtle Ave
Brooklyn, NY 11205
Phone: +1 (718) 783-1936

#422
Vbar
Cuisines: Wine Bar, American
Average price: $11-30
District: Greenwich Village
Address: 225 Sullivan St
New York, NY 10012
Phone: +1 (212) 253-5740

#423
Milk And Roses
Cuisines: Coffee & Tea, Wine Bar, Italian
Average price: $11-30
District: Greenpoint
Address: 1110 Manhattan Ave
Brooklyn, NY 11222
Phone: +1 (718) 389-0160

#424
Pisticci
Cuisines: Italian
Average price: $11-30
District: Harlem
Address: 125 La Salle St
New York, NY 10027
Phone: +1 (212) 932-3500

#425
Petite Abeille
Cuisines: Breakfast & Brunch, Belgian
Average price: $11-30
District: Flatiron
Address: 44 W 17th St
New York, NY 10011
Phone: +1 (212) 727-2989

#426
Black Iris
Cuisines: Middle Eastern
Average price: $11-30
District: Fort Greene
Address: 228 Dekalb Ave
Brooklyn, NY 11205
Phone: +1 (718) 852-9800

#427
Queens Comfort
Cuisines: Breakfast & Brunch,
American, Comfort Food
Average price: $11-30
District: Astoria
Address: 4009 30th Ave
Astoria, NY 11103
Phone: +1 (718) 728-2350

#428
Kotobuki Manhattan
Cuisines: Japanese, Sushi Bar, Seafood
Average price: $11-30
District: East Village
Address: 56 3rd Ave
New York, NY 10003
Phone: +1 (212) 353-5088

#429
Maison Kayser
Cuisines: Breakfast & Brunch,
Bakery, French
Average price: $11-30
District: Yorkville, Upper East Side
Address: 1294 3rd Ave 74th St
New York, NY 10021
Phone: +1 (212) 744-3100

#430
Gino's
Cuisines: Pizza, Italian
Average price: $11-30
District: Bay Ridge
Address: 7414 5th Ave
Brooklyn, NY 11209
Phone: +1 (718) 748-1698

#431
The Meatball Shop
Cuisines: American, Italian
Average price: $11-30
District: Williamsburg - North Side
Address: 170 Bedford Ave
Brooklyn, NY 11211
Phone: +1 (718) 551-0520

#432
Zampa
Cuisines: Italian, Wine Bar, Tapas Bar
Average price: $31-60
District: West Village
Address: 306 W 13th St
New York, NY 10014
Phone: +1 (212) 206-0601

#433
The Queens Kickshaw
Cuisines: Coffee & Tea, Gastropub,
Breakfast & Brunch
Average price: $11-30
District: Astoria
Address: 40-17 Broadway
Astoria, NY 11103
Phone: +1 (718) 777-0913

#434
Bar Jamón
Cuisines: Spanish, Tapas Bar
Average price: $31-60
District: Gramercy
Address: 125 E 17th St
New York, NY 10003
Phone: +1 (212) 253-2773

#435
M.O.B.
Cuisines: Vegetarian, Vegan
Average price: $11-30
District: Boerum Hill
Address: 525 Atlantic Ave
Brooklyn, NY 11217
Phone: +1 (718) 797-2555

#436
Quality Italian
Cuisines: Italian, Steakhouses
Average price: $31-60
District: Midtown West
Address: 57 W 57th St
New York, NY 10019
Phone: +1 (212) 390-1111

#437
Elim Deli Café
Cuisines: Deli
Average price: Under $10
District: Upper East Side
Address: 851 Lexington Ave
New York, NY 10065
Phone: +1 (212) 439-8320

#438
Sweet Chick
Cuisines: Southern
Average price: $11-30
District: Williamsburg - North Side
Address: 164 Bedford Avenue
Brooklyn, NY 11211
Phone: +1 (347) 725-4793

#439
Grape and Grain
Cuisines: Wine Bar, American
Average price: $11-30
District: East Village, Alphabet City
Address: 620 E 6th St
New York, NY 10009
Phone: +1 (212) 420-0002

#440
Perry St
Cuisines: American, French
Average price: $31-60
District: West Village
Address: 176 Perry St
New York, NY 10014
Phone: +1 (212) 352-1900

#441
DiWine
Cuisines: Wine Bar, Tapas, American
Average price: $11-30
District: Astoria
Address: 41-15 31st Ave
Astoria, NY 11103
Phone: +1 (718) 777-1355

#442
Vol de Nuit
Cuisines: Lounge, American
Average price: $11-30
District: Greenwich Village
Address: 148 W 4th St
New York, NY 10012
Phone: +1 (212) 982-3388

#443
Aurora Soho
Cuisines: Italian, Breakfast & Brunch
Average price: $31-60
District: South Village
Address: 510 Broome St
New York, NY 10013
Phone: +1 (212) 334-9020

#444
Extra Virgin
Cuisines: Seafood, Greek, Italian
Average price: $11-30
District: West Village
Address: 259 W 4th St
New York, NY 10014
Phone: +1 (212) 691-9359

#445
Shade
Cuisines: Bar, American, Crêperie
Average price: $11-30
District: Greenwich Village
Address: 241 Sullivan St
New York, NY 10012
Phone: +1 (212) 982-6275

#446
Café Luluc
Cuisines: French, Breakfast & Brunch, Café
Average price: $11-30
District: Cobble Hill, Gowanus
Address: 214 Smith St
Brooklyn, NY 11201
Phone: +1 (718) 625-3815

#447
Convivium Osteria
Cuisines: Spanish, Italian, Portuguese
Average price: $31-60
District: Park Slope
Address: 68 5th Ave
Brooklyn, NY 11217
Phone: +1 (718) 857-1833

#448
Joy Burger Bar
Cuisines: Burgers, Sandwiches
Average price: Under $10
District: East Harlem
Address: 1567 Lexington Ave
New York, NY 10029
Phone: +1 (212) 289-6222

#449
The Redhead
Cuisines: American, Bar
Average price: $11-30
District: East Village
Address: 349 E 13th St
New York, NY 10003
Phone: +1 (212) 533-6212

#450
Tiella
Cuisines: Italian
Average price: $31-60
District: Upper East Side
Address: 1109 1st Ave
New York, NY 10065
Phone: +1 (212) 588-0100

#451
Sotto 13
Cuisines: Italian, Pizza, Tapas
Average price: $11-30
District: West Village
Address: 140 W 13th St
New York, NY 10011
Phone: +1 (212) 647-1001

#452
Queen Italian Restaurant
Cuisines: Italian
Average price: $31-60
District: Brooklyn Heights
Address: 84 Court St
Brooklyn, NY 11201
Phone: +1 (718) 596-5955

#453
Hahm Ji Bach
Cuisines: Korean
Average price: $11-30
District: Murray Hill, Flushing
Address: 40-11 149th Pl
Flushing, NY 11355
Phone: +1 (718) 460-9289

#454
Riverpark
Cuisines: American, Breakfast & Brunch
Average price: $31-60
District: Midtown East, Stuyvesant Town
Address: 450 E 29th St
New York, NY 10016
Phone: +1 (212) 729-9790

#455
Norma's
Cuisines: Café, Coffee & Tea, Bakery
Average price: Under $10
District: Ridgewood
Address: 59-02 Catalpa Ave
Ridgewood, NY 11385
Phone: +1 (347) 294-0185

#456
Friedman's
Cuisines: American, Breakfast & Brunch
Average price: $11-30
District: Midtown West
Address: 132 W 31st St
New York, NY 10001
Phone: +1 (212) 971-9400

#457
Blue Ribbon Brasserie Brooklyn
Cuisines: American
Average price: $31-60
District: Park Slope
Address: 280 5th Ave
Brooklyn, NY 11215
Phone: +1 (718) 840-0404

#458
Bacaro
Cuisines: Italian
Average price: $31-60
District: Chinatown, Lower East Side
Address: 136 Division St
New York, NY 10002
Phone: +1 (212) 941-5060

#459
Brindle Room
Cuisines: American
Average price: $11-30
District: East Village, Alphabet City
Address: 277 E 10th St
New York, NY 10009
Phone: +1 (212) 529-9702

#460
Nyonya
Cuisines: Asian Fusion, Malaysian, Chinese
Average price: $11-30
District: Little Italy
Address: 199 Grand St
New York, NY 10013
Phone: +1 (212) 334-3669

#461
Snack
Cuisines: Sandwiches, Mediterranean
Average price: $11-30
District: South Village
Address: 105 Thompson St
New York, NY 10012
Phone: +1 (212) 925-1040

#462
Blue Ribbon Bakery &Café
Cuisines: Bakery, Breakfast & Brunch
Average price: $31-60
District: West Village
Address: 35 Downing St
New York, NY 10014
Phone: +1 (212) 337-0404

#463
Balaboosta
Cuisines: Mediterranean,
Breakfast & Brunch
Average price: $31-60
District: Nolita
Address: 214 Mulberry St
New York, NY 10012
Phone: +1 (212) 966-7366

#464
Char No. 4
Cuisines: Bar, Southern
Average price: $31-60
District: Cobble Hill, Gowanus
Address: 196 Smith St
Brooklyn, NY 11201
Phone: +1 (718) 643-2106

#465
Via Quadronno
Cuisines: Sandwiches, Italian
Average price: $11-30
District: Upper East Side
Address: 25 E 73rd St
New York, NY 10021
Phone: +1 (212) 650-9880

#466
Noodle Pudding
Cuisines: Italian
Average price: $11-30
District: Brooklyn Heights
Address: 38 Henry St
Brooklyn, NY 11201
Phone: +1 (718) 625-3737

#467
Sunny and Annie's
Cuisines: Sandwiches, Deli, Grocery
Average price: Under $10
District: East Village, Alphabet City
Address: 94 Ave B
New York, NY 10003
Phone: +1 (212) 677-3131

#468
Tartine
Cuisines: French, Breakfast & Brunch
Average price: $11-30
District: West Village
Address: 253 W 11th St
New York, NY 10014
Phone: +1 (212) 229-2611

#469
Beauty & Essex
Cuisines: Bar, American, Tapas
Average price: $31-60
District: Lower East Side
Address: 146 Essex St
New York, NY 10002
Phone: +1 (212) 614-0146

#470
George Keeley's
Cuisines: Pub, American, Sports Bar
Average price: $11-30
District: Upper West Side
Address: 485 Amsterdam Ave
New York, NY 10024
Phone: +1 (212) 873-0251

#471
Café Himalaya
Cuisines: Asian Fusion, Vegetarian,
Himalayan/Nepalese, Vegetarian
Average price: Under $10
District: East Village
Address: 78 E 1st St
New York, NY 10009
Phone: +1 (212) 358-0160

#472
Waldy's Wood Fired Pizza & Penne
Cuisines: Pizza
Average price: $11-30
District: Flatiron
Address: 800 6th Ave
New York, NY 10001
Phone: +1 (212) 213-5042

#473
Toloache
Cuisines: Mexican
Average price: $31-60
District: Midtown West, Theater
Address: 251 W 50th St
New York, NY 10019
Phone: +1 (212) 581-1818

#474
One If By Land Two If By Sea
Cuisines: American
Average price: Above $61
District: West Village
Address: 17 Barrow St
New York, NY 10014
Phone: +1 (212) 228-0822

#475
The Green Fig Bakery Café
Cuisines: Café, Bakery
Average price: Under $10
District: Sunset Park
Address: 462 36th St
Brooklyn, NY 11232
Phone: +1 (718) 369-8937

#476
Wine:30
Cuisines: Wine Bar, American
Average price: $11-30
District: Midtown East
Address: 41 E 30th St
New York, NY 10016
Phone: +1 (212) 481-0197

#477
Jin Ramen
Cuisines: Japanese
Average price: $11-30
District: Harlem
Address: 3183 Broadway
New York, NY 10027
Phone: +1 (646) 559-2862

#478
Ghenet Brooklyn
Cuisines: Ethiopian
Average price: $11-30
District: Park Slope, Gowanus
Address: 348 Douglass St
Brooklyn, NY 11217
Phone: +1 (718) 230-4475

#479
El Camion
Cuisines: Mexican
Average price: $11-30
District: East Village, Alphabet City
Address: 194 Ave A
New York, NY 10009
Phone: +1 (212) 533-5436

#480
Le Moulin a Café
Cuisines: French, Café, Desserts
Average price: $11-30
District: Yorkville, Upper East Side
Address: 1439 York Ave
New York, NY 10075
Phone: +1 (212) 288-5088

#481
H K Wonton Garden
Cuisines: Chinese
Average price: Under $10
District: Chinatown
Address: 79 Mulberry St
New York, NY 10013
Phone: +1 (212) 349-1495

#482
DTUT
Cuisines: Bar, Café
Average price: Under $10
District: Yorkville, Upper East Side
Address: 1744 2nd Ave
New York, NY 10128
Phone: +1 (212) 410-6449

#483
Great Jones Café
Cuisines: Southern, Cajun/Creole,
Breakfast & Brunch
Average price: $11-30
District: East Village, NoHo
Address: 54 Great Jones St
New York, NY 10012
Phone: +1 (212) 674-9304

#484
Soba-ya
Cuisines: Japanese
Average price: $11-30
District: East Village
Address: 229 E 9th St
New York, NY 10003
Phone: +1 (212) 533-6966

#485
Excellent Pork Chop House
Cuisines: Chinese, Taiwanese
Average price: Under $10
District: Chinatown, Civic Center
Address: 3 Doyers St
New York, NY 10013
Phone: +1 (212) 791-7007

#486
Seasonal
Cuisines: Austrian
Average price: $31-60
District: Midtown West
Address: 132 W 58th St
New York, NY 10019
Phone: +1 (212) 957-5550

#487
Sweet Science
Cuisines: Bar, Burgers, American
Average price: $11-30
District: East Williamsburg
Address: 135 Graham Ave
Brooklyn, NY 11206
Phone: +1 (347) 763-0872

#488
Hiroko's Place
Cuisines: Japanese
Average price: $11-30
District: South Village
Address: 75 Thompson St
New York, NY 10012
Phone: +1 (212) 625-1303

#489
Chayhana Salom
Cuisines: Middle Eastern, Russian,
Mediterranean
Average price: $11-30
District: Sheepshead Bay
Address: 1652 Sheepshead Bay Rd
Brooklyn, NY 11235
Phone: +1 (718) 332-2200

#490
Portalia
Cuisines: Italian
Average price: $11-30
District: Astoria
Address: 35-03 Broadway
Astoria, NY 11106
Phone: +1 (718) 545-3500

#491
BXL Zoute
Cuisines: Belgian
Average price: $11-30
District: Flatiron
Address: 50 W 22nd St
New York, NY 10010
Phone: +1 (646) 692-9282

#492
Hearth
Cuisines: American, Italian,
Breakfast & Brunch
Average price: $31-60
District: East Village
Address: 403 E 12th St
New York, NY 10009
Phone: +1 (646) 602-1300

#493
Mesa Coyoacan
Cuisines: Mexican
Average price: $11-30
District: East Williamsburg
Address: 372 Graham Ave
Brooklyn, NY 11211
Phone: +1 (718) 782-8171

#494
Feast
Cuisines: American, Breakfast & Brunch
Average price: $31-60
District: East Village
Address: 102 3rd Ave
New York, NY 10003
Phone: +1 (212) 529-8880

#495
Edi & the Wolf
Cuisines: German
Average price: $31-60
District: East Village, Alphabet City
Address: 102 Ave C
New York, NY 10009
Phone: +1 (212) 598-1040

#496
Tutt Café
Cuisines: Middle Eastern
Average price: Under $10
District: Brooklyn Heights
Address: 47 Hicks St
Brooklyn, NY 11201
Phone: +1 (718) 722-7777

#497
100 Montaditos
Cuisines: Tapas, Spanish
Average price: Under $10
District: Greenwich Village
Address: 176 Bleecker St
New York, NY 10012
Phone: +1 (646) 719-1713

#498
Cork 'n Fork
Cuisines: Tapas, Wine Bar
Average price: $11-30
District: East Village, Alphabet City
Address: 186 Ave A
New York, NY 10009
Phone: +1 (646) 707-0707

#499
Kefi
Cuisines: Greek, Mediterranean, Tapas
Average price: $11-30
District: Upper West Side
Address: 505 Columbus Ave
New York, NY 10024
Phone: +1 (212) 873-0200

#500
Dig Inn Seasonal Market
Cuisines: American
Average price: Under $10
District: Midtown West
Address: 40 W 55th St
New York, NY 10019
Phone: +1 (212) 246-6844

TOP 500 BARS & PUBS

Most Recommended by Locals & Trevelers
Ranking (from #1 to #500)

#1
Sunny's Bar
Bar
Average price: Inexpensive
District: Red Hook
Address: 253 Conover St
Brooklyn, NY 11231
Phone: +1 (718) 625-8211

#2
Bed-Vyne Wine
Beer, Wine & Spirits, Wine Bar,
Food Delivery
Average price: Moderate
District: Bedford Stuyvesant
Address: 370 Tompkins Ave
Brooklyn, NY 11216
Phone: +1 (347) 915-1080

#3
South
Bar
Average price: Inexpensive
District: South Slope
Address: 629 5th Ave
Brooklyn, NY 11215
Phone: +1 (718) 832-4720

#4
Angel's Share
Lounge, Cocktail Bar
Average price: Expensive
District: East Village
Address: 8 Stuyvesant St
New York, NY 10003
Phone: +1 (212) 777-5415

#5
Amor y Amargo
Cocktail Bar
Average price: Moderate
District: East Village, Alphabet City
Address: 443 E 6th St
New York, NY 10009
Phone: +1 (212) 614-6818

#6
Mosaic Cafe & Lounge
Wine Bar, Lounge, Venue & Event Space
Average price: Moderate
District: Astoria
Address: 25-19 24th Ave
Astoria, NY 11102
Phone: +1 (718) 728-0708

#7
The Pony Bar
Bar
Average price: Moderate
District: Hell's Kitchen, Midtown West
Address: 637 10th Ave
New York, NY 10036
Phone: +1 (212) 586-2707

#8
McSorley's Old Ale House
Dive Bar, Brewerie
Average price: Inexpensive
District: East Village
Address: 15 E 7th St
New York, NY 10003
Phone: +1 (212) 473-9148

#9
Brooklyn Ice House
Barbeque, Pub
Average price: Inexpensive
District: Red Hook
Address: 318 Van Brunt St
Brooklyn, NY 11231
Phone: +1 (718) 222-1865

#10
Whiskey Tavern
Pub
Average price: Moderate
District: Chinatown
Address: 79 Baxter St
New York, NY 10013
Phone: +1 (212) 374-9119

#11
Blue Ribbon Downing Street Bar
Lounge
Average price: Expensive
District: West Village
Address: 34 Downing St
New York, NY 10014
Phone: +1 (212) 691-0404

#12
4th Avenue Pub
Pub
Average price: Moderate
District: Park Slope, Boerum Hill, Gowanus
Address: 76 4th Ave
Brooklyn, NY 11217
Phone: +1 (718) 643-2273

#13
Flatiron Room
Lounge, Jazz & Blues
Average price: Expensive
District: Flatiron
Address: 37 W 26th St
New York, NY 10010
Phone: +1 (212) 725-3860

#14
Caledonia Scottish Pub
Pub, Scottish
Average price: Moderate
District: Yorkville, Upper East Side
Address: 1609 2nd Ave
New York, NY 10028
Phone: +1 (212) 879-0402

#15
The Dead Rabbit
Grocery, Bar, American
Average price: Expensive
District: Financial District
Address: 30 Water St
New York, NY 10004
Phone: +1 (646) 422-7906

#16
Bergen Hill
Cocktail Bar, Seafood
Average price: Expensive
District: Carroll Gardens
Address: 387 Court St
Brooklyn, NY 11231
Phone: +1 (718) 858-5483

#17
Post Office
Bar, American
Average price: Moderate
District: Williamsburg - South Side
Address: 188 Havemeyer St
Brooklyn, NY 11211
Phone: +1 (718) 963-2574

#18
The Wayland
Bar
Average price: Moderate
District: East Village, Alphabet City
Address: 700 E 9th St
New York, NY 10009
Phone: +1 (212) 777-7022

#19
Little Branch
Lounge, Cocktail Bar
Average price: Expensive
District: West Village
Address: 22 7th Ave S
New York, NY 10014
Phone: +1 (212) 929-4360

#20
Burning Waters Cantina
Cocktail Bar
Average price: Moderate
District: Greenwich Village
Address: 116 MacDougal St
New York, NY 10012
Phone: +1 (646) 707-0078

#21
Tip Top Bar & Grill
Dive Bar
Average price: Inexpensive
District: Bedford Stuyvesant, Clinton Hill
Address: 432 Franklin Ave
Brooklyn, NY 11238
Phone: +1 (718) 857-9744

#22
Distilled
American, Cocktail Bar
Average price: Expensive
District: TriBeCa
Address: 211 W Broadway
New York, NY 10013
Phone: +1 (212) 601-9514

#23
Spuyten Duyvil
Pub
Average price: Moderate
District: Williamsburg - North Side
Address: 359 Metropolitan Ave
Brooklyn, NY 11211
Phone: +1 (718) 963-4140

#24
The Jeffrey Craft Beer & Bites
Bar, Cafe
Average price: Moderate
District: Upper East Side
Address: 311 East 60th St
New York, NY 10022
Phone: +1 (212) 355-2337

#25
Vin Sur Vingt
Wine Bar, French
Average price: Expensive
District: West Village
Address: 201 W 11th St
New York, NY 10014
Phone: +1 (212) 924-4442

#26
Blueprint
Cocktail Bar
Average price: Moderate
District: Park Slope
Address: 196 5th Ave
Brooklyn, NY 11217
Phone: +1 (718) 622-6644

#27
The Quays Pub
Pub
Average price: Inexpensive
District: Astoria
Address: 45-02 30th Ave
Astoria, NY 11103
Phone: +1 (718) 204-8435

#28
2nd Floor on Clinton
Lounge
Average price: Expensive
District: Lower East Side
Address: 67 Clinton St
New York, NY 10002
Phone: +1 (212) 529-6900

#29
Lulu's
Pizza, Dive Bar
Average price: Inexpensive
District: Greenpoint
Address: 113 Franklin St
Brooklyn, NY 11222
Phone: +1 (718) 383-6000

#30
Black Mountain Wine House
Wine Bar
Average price: Moderate
District: Gowanus
Address: 415 Union St
Brooklyn, NY 11231
Phone: +1 (718) 522-4340

#31
Duff's Brooklyn
Dive Bar
Average price: Inexpensive
District: Williamsburg - South Side
Address: 168 Marcy Ave
Brooklyn, NY 11211
Phone: +1 (718) 599-2092

#32
South 4th Bar & Café
Coffee & Tea, Bar
Average price: Inexpensive
District: Williamsburg - South Side
Address: 90 S 4th St
Brooklyn, NY 11249
Phone: +1 (718) 218-7478

#33
The Winslow
Bar
Average price: Moderate
District: Gramercy
Address: 243 E 14th St
New York, NY 10003
Phone: +1 (212) 777-7717

#34
Bemelmans Bar
Lounge
Average price: Exclusive
District: Upper East Side
Address: 35 E 76th St
New York, NY 10021
Phone: +1 (212) 744-1600

#35
Desnuda
Seafood, Peruvian, Cocktail Bar
Average price: Expensive
District: Williamsburg - South Side
Address: 221 S 1st St
Brooklyn, NY 11211
Phone: +1 (718) 387-0563

#36
The Richardson
Bar
Average price: Moderate
District: Williamsburg - North Side
Address: 451 Graham Ave
Brooklyn, NY 11222
Phone: +1 (718) 389-0839

#37
Noorman's Kil
Bar, Sandwiches
Average price: Moderate
District: Williamsburg - North Side
Address: 609 Grand St
Brooklyn, NY 11211
Phone: +1 (347) 384-2526

#38
Freddy's Bar
Bar
Average price: Inexpensive
District: South Slope
Address: 627 5th Ave
Brooklyn, NY 11215
Phone: +1 (718) 768-0131

#39
Earl's Beer & Cheese
Bar, Comfort Food, Beer, Wine & Spirits
Average price: Moderate
District: East Harlem
Address: 1259 Park Ave
New York, NY 10029
Phone: +1 (212) 289-1581

#40
Sunita Bar
Lounge
Average price: Moderate
District: Lower East Side
Address: 106 Norfolk St
New York, NY 10002
Phone: +1 (212) 253-8860

#41
Elsa
Bar
Average price: Moderate
District: East Village, Alphabet City
Address: 217 E 3rd St
New York, NY 10009
Phone: +1 (917) 882-7395

#42
Clover Club
Lounge, American
Average price: Expensive
District: Cobble Hill, Gowanus
Address: 210 Smith St
Brooklyn, NY 11201
Phone: +1 (718) 855-7939

#43
Dutch Kills
Lounge, Cocktail Bar
Average price: Moderate
District: Long Island City
Address: 27-24 Jackson Ave
Long Island City, NY 11101
Phone: +1 (718) 383-2724

#44
The Bourgeois Pig
Lounge, Wine Bar
Average price: Moderate
District: East Village, Alphabet City
Address: 111 E 7th St
New York, NY 10009
Phone: +1 (212) 475-2246

#45
Proletariat
Bar
Average price: Moderate
District: East Village, Alphabet City
Address: 102 St Marks Pl
New York, NY 10009
Phone: +1 (212) 777-6707

#46
Irish Rover
Pub, Sport Bar
Average price: Inexpensive
District: Astoria
Address: 3718 28th Ave
Astoria, NY 11103
Phone: +1 (718) 278-9372

#47
Hotel Delmano
Lounge
Average price: Expensive
District: Williamsburg - North Side
Address: 82 Berry St
Brooklyn, NY 11211
Phone: +1 (718) 387-1945

#48
Brookvin
Wine Bar, Tapas Bar
Average price: Moderate
District: South Slope, Park Slope
Address: 381 7th Ave
Brooklyn, NY 11215
Phone: +1 (718) 768-9463

#49
Employees Only
American, Lounge
Average price: Expensive
District: West Village
Address: 510 Hudson St
New York, NY 10014
Phone: +1 (212) 242-3021

#50
Domaine Wine Bar
Wine Bar, Jazz & Blues
Average price: Moderate
District: Hunters Point, Long Island City
Address: 50-04 Vernon Blvd
Long Island City, NY 11101
Phone: +1 (718) 784-2350

#51
The Shakespeare
Pub, British
Average price: Expensive
District: Midtown East, Murray Hill
Address: 24 E 39th St
New York, NY 10016
Phone: +1 (646) 837-6779

#52
Brandy Library
American, Lounge, Wine Bar
Average price: Expensive
District: TriBeCa
Address: 25 N Moore St
New York, NY 10013
Phone: +1 (212) 226-5545

#53
The Immigrant
Wine Bar
Average price: Moderate
District: East Village
Address: 341 E 9th St
New York, NY 10003
Phone: +1 (646) 308-1724

#54
Black Crescent
Cocktail Bar
Average price: Moderate
District: Lower East Side
Address: 76 Clinton St
New York, NY 10002
Phone: +1 (212) 477-1771

#55
Manitoba's
Bar
Average price: Inexpensive
District: East Village, Alphabet City
Address: 99 Ave B
New York, NY 10009
Phone: +1 (212) 982-2511

#56
Pouring Ribbons
Lounge, Cocktail Bar
Average price: Expensive
District: East Village, Alphabet City
Address: 225 Ave B
New York, NY 10009
Phone: +1 (917) 656-6788

#57
Café Moto
Cafe, Bar
Average price: Moderate
District: Williamsburg - South Side,
South Williamsburg
Address: 394 Broadway
Brooklyn, NY 11211
Phone: +1 (718) 599-6895

#58
Pegu Club
Lounge
Average price: Expensive
District: SoHo
Address: 77 W Houston St
New York, NY 10012
Phone: +1 (212) 473-7348

#59
Death & Co
Lounge, Music Venue
Average price: Expensive
District: East Village, Alphabet City
Address: 433 E 6th St
New York, NY 10009
Phone: +1 (212) 388-0882

#60
124 Old Rabbit Club
Bar
Average price: Moderate
District: Greenwich Village
Address: 124 MacDougal St
New York, NY 10012
Phone: +1 (212) 254-0575

#61
Wine Escape
Wine Bar
Average price: Moderate
District: Hell's Kitchen, Midtown West
Address: 405 W 44th St
New York, NY 10036
Phone: +1 (212) 262-7000

#62
Corkbuzz Wine Studio
Wine Bar, American
Average price: Expensive
District: Greenwich Village, Union Square
Address: 13 E 13 St
New York, NY 10003
Phone: +1 (646) 873-6071

#63
The Diamond
Bar, Beer, Wine & Spirits
Average price: Moderate
District: Greenpoint
Address: 43 Franklin St
Brooklyn, NY 11222
Phone: +1 (718) 383-5030

#64
Brooklyn Star
Southern, Bar
Average price: Moderate
District: Williamsburg - North Side
Address: 593 Lorimer St
Brooklyn, NY 11211
Phone: +1 (718) 599-9899

#65
The Levee
American, Bar
Average price: Inexpensive
District: Williamsburg - North Side
Address: 212 Berry St
Brooklyn, NY 11211
Phone: +1 (718) 218-8787

#66
Barcade
Bar, Arcade
Average price: Moderate
District: Williamsburg - North Side
Address: 388 Union Ave
Brooklyn, NY 11224
Phone: +1 (718) 302-6464

#67
B Flat
Lounge, Jazz & Blues
Average price: Moderate
District: TriBeCa
Address: 277 Church St
New York, NY 10013
Phone: +1 (212) 219-2970

#68
Sweet Afton
Bar, American
Average price: Moderate
District: Astoria
Address: 30-09 34th St
Astoria, NY 11103
Phone: +1 (718) 777-2570

#69
Verlaine
Tapas, Lounge
Average price: Moderate
District: Lower East Side
Address: 110 Rivington St
New York, NY 10002
Phone: +1 (212) 614-2494

#70
The Owl's Head
Wine Bar
Average price: Moderate
District: Bay Ridge
Address: 479 74th St
Brooklyn, NY 11209
Phone: +1 (718) 680-2436

#71
The Habitat
Pub
Average price: Moderate
District: Greenpoint
Address: 988 Manhattan Ave
Brooklyn, NY 11222
Phone: +1 (718) 383-5615

#72
Cask Bar + Kitchen
Bar, American, Seafood
Average price: Moderate
District: Midtown East, Murray Hill
Address: 167 E 33rd St
New York, NY 10016
Phone: +1 (212) 300-4924

#73
Sycamore
Bar, Florist, Music Venue
Average price: Moderate
District: Flatbush
Address: 1118 Cortelyou Rd
Brooklyn, NY 11218
Phone: +1 (347) 240-5850

#74
The Shanty
Bar
Average price: Moderate
District: Williamsburg - North Side
Address: 79 Richardson St
Brooklyn, NY 11211
Phone: +1 (718) 412-0874

#75
Beer Culture
Beer, Wine & Spirits, Bar
Average price: Moderate
District: Hell's Kitchen, Midtown West,
Theater District
Address: 328 W 45th St
New York, NY 10036
Phone: +1 (646) 590-2139

#76
TØRST
Pub
Average price: Expensive
District: Greenpoint
Address: 615 Manhattan Ave
Brooklyn, NY 11222
Phone: +1 (718) 389-6034

#77
Lelabar
Wine Bar, Lounge
Average price: Moderate
District: West Village
Address: 422 Hudson St
New York, NY 10014
Phone: +1 (212) 206-0594

#78
Keybar
Lounge, Pub
Average price: Inexpensive
District: East Village, Alphabet City
Address: 432 E 13th St
New York, NY 10009
Phone: +1 (212) 478-3021

#79
Harlem Public
American, Pub
Average price: Moderate
District: Harlem
Address: 3612 Broadway
New York, NY 10031
Phone: +1 (212) 939-9404

#80
The Bar Room at The Modern
Lounge, French
Average price: Expensive
District: Midtown West
Address: 9 W 53rd St
New York, NY 10019
Phone: +1 (212) 333-1220

#81
Circa Tabac
Lounge, Cocktail Bar, Tobacco Shop
Average price: Moderate
District: South Village
Address: 32 Watts St
New York, NY 10013
Phone: +1 (212) 941-1781

#82
The Anchored Inn
Bar, American
Average price: Moderate
District: East Williamsburg
Address: 57 Waterbury St
Brooklyn, NY 11206
Phone: +1 (718) 576-3297

#83
Two 8 Two
Burgers, Bar
Average price: Moderate
District: Cobble Hill, Boerum Hill
Address: 282 Atlantic Ave
Brooklyn, NY 11201
Phone: +1 (718) 596-2282

#84
Ear Inn
Bar, American
Average price: Moderate
District: South Village
Address: 326 Spring St
New York, NY 10013
Phone: +1 (212) 226-9060

#85
Pete's Candy Store
Music Venue, Dive Bar, Pub
Average price: Inexpensive
District: Williamsburg - North Side
Address: 709 Lorimer St
Brooklyn, NY 11211
Phone: +1 (718) 302-3770

#86
The Room
Lounge, Wine Bar
Average price: Moderate
District: South Village
Address: 144 Sullivan St
New York, NY 10012
Phone: +1 (212) 477-2102

#87
Ward III
American, Lounge
Average price: Moderate
District: TriBeCa
Address: 111 Reade St
New York, NY 10013
Phone: +1 (212) 240-9194

#88
Flatiron Lounge
Lounge
Average price: Expensive
District: Flatiron
Address: 37 W 19th St
New York, NY 10011
Phone: +1 (212) 727-7741

#89
Ryan's Daughter
Pub, American
Average price: Moderate
District: Yorkville, Upper East Side
Address: 350 E 85th St
New York, NY 10028
Phone: +1 (212) 628-2613

#90
Huckleberry Bar
Bar, American
Average price: Moderate
District: East Williamsburg
Address: 588 Grand St
Brooklyn, NY 11211
Phone: +1 (718) 218-8555

#91
Pravda
Lounge, Cocktail Bar
Average price: Expensive
District: Nolita
Address: 281 Lafayette St
New York, NY 10012
Phone: +1 (212) 226-4944

#92
Bua
Bar
Average price: Moderate
District: East Village, Alphabet City
Address: 122 St Marks Pl
New York, NY 10009
Phone: +1 (212) 979-6276

#93
The Sackett
Bar
Average price: Moderate
District: Park Slope, Gowanus
Address: 661 Sackett St
Brooklyn, NY 11217
Phone: +1 (718) 622-0437

#94
Apothéke
Lounge, Cocktail Bar
Average price: Expensive
District: Chinatown, Civic Center
Address: 9 Doyers St
New York, NY 10013
Phone: +1 (212) 406-0400

#95
Ten Degrees Bar
Wine Bar, Gastropub
Average price: Moderate
District: East Village, Alphabet City
Address: 121 St. Marks Pl
New York, NY 10009
Phone: +1 (212) 358-8600

#96
The Cellar
Wine Bar, American, American
Average price: Moderate
District: Flatiron
Address: 900 Broadway
New York, NY 10003
Phone: +1 (212) 466-3340

#97
Brooklyn Winery
Wineries, Wine Bar, Venue & Event Space
Average price: Moderate
District: Williamsburg - North Side
Address: 213 N 8th St
Brooklyn, NY 11211
Phone: +1 (347) 763-1506

#98
Dram
Cocktail Bar
Average price: Moderate
District: Williamsburg - South Side
Address: 177 S 4th St
Brooklyn, NY 11211
Phone: +1 (718) 486-3726

#99
Lucky 13 Saloon
Bar
Average price: Inexpensive
District: South Slope, Park Slope
Address: 273 13th St
Brooklyn, NY 11215
Phone: +1 (718) 499-7553

#100
The Bell House
Music Venue, Lounge
Average price: Moderate
District: Gowanus
Address: 149 7th St
Brooklyn, NY 11215
Phone: +1 (718) 643-6510

#101
Matt Torrey's
Bar
Average price: Moderate
District: East Williamsburg
Address: 46 Bushwick Ave
Brooklyn, NY 11211
Phone: +1 (718) 218-7646

#102
Lock Yard
American, Hot Dogs, Pub
Average price: Moderate
District: Fort Hamilton, Bay Ridge
Address: 9221 5th Ave
Brooklyn, NY 11209
Phone: +1 (718) 333-5282

#103
Russian Vodka Room
Lounge, Russian, Jazz & Blues
Average price: Moderate
District: Midtown West, Theater District
Address: 265 W 52nd St
New York, NY 10019
Phone: +1 (212) 307-5835

#104
Middle Branch
Bar
Average price: Moderate
District: Midtown East, Murray Hill, Kips Bay
Address: 154 E 33rd St
New York, NY 10016
Phone: +1 (212) 213-1350

#105
The Otheroom
Lounge, Wine Bar, American
Average price: Moderate
District: West Village
Address: 143 Perry St
New York, NY 10014
Phone: +1 (212) 645-9758

#106
Pacific Standard Brooklyn
Bar
Average price: Inexpensive
District: Park Slope, Gowanus
Address: 82 4th Ave
Brooklyn, NY 11217
Phone: +1 (718) 858-1951

#107
The Owl Farm
Pub
Average price: Moderate
District: Park Slope, Gowanus
Address: 297 9th St
Brooklyn, NY 11215
Phone: +1 (718) 499-4988

#108
Shoolbred's
Lounge
Average price: Moderate
District: East Village
Address: 197 2nd Ave
New York, NY 10003
Phone: +1 (212) 529-0340

#109
The Ginger Man
Bar, Brewerie
Average price: Moderate
District: Midtown East
Address: 11 E 36th St
New York, NY 10016
Phone: +1 (212) 532-3740

#110
The Castello Plan
Bar, American
Average price: Moderate
District: Flatbush
Address: 1213 Cortelyou Rd
Brooklyn, NY 11218
Phone: +1 (718) 856-8888

#111
Gottino
Wine Bar, Italian
Average price: Moderate
District: West Village
Address: 52 Greenwich Ave
New York, NY 10011
Phone: +1 (212) 633-2590

#112
Toby's Public House
Pizza, Bar
Average price: Moderate
District: South Slope
Address: 686 6th Ave
Brooklyn, NY 11215
Phone: +1 (718) 788-1186

#113
Minibar
Wine Bar, Lounge
Average price: Moderate
District: Carroll Gardens
Address: 482 Court St
Brooklyn, NY 11231
Phone: +1 (718) 569-2321

#114
Cronin & Phelan's
Pub, American
Average price: Moderate
District: Astoria
Address: 38-14 Broadway
Astoria, NY 11102
Phone: +1 (718) 545-8999

#115
Idle Hands Bar
Bar, American
Average price: Moderate
District: East Village, Alphabet City
Address: 25 Ave B
New York, NY 10009
Phone: +1 (917) 338-7090

#116
The Campbell Apartment
Lounge
Average price: Expensive
District: Midtown East
Address: 15 Vanderbilt Ave
New York, NY 10017
Phone: +1 (212) 953-0409

#117
Kaia Wine Bar
Wine Bar
Average price: Moderate
District: Yorkville, Upper East Side
Address: 1614 3rd Ave
New York, NY 10128
Phone: +1 (212) 722-0490

#118
Weather Up
Bar
Average price: Moderate
District: Prospect Heights
Address: 589 Vanderbilt Ave
Brooklyn, NY 11226
Phone: +1 (212) 766-3202

#119
The Bodega
Pub, Breakfast & Brunch
Average price: Moderate
District: Bushwick
Address: 24 St. Nicholas Ave
Brooklyn, NY 11237
Phone: +1 (347) 305-3344

#120
Windy City Ale House
Sport Bar, American
Average price: Moderate
District: Bay Ridge
Address: 7915 3rd Ave
Brooklyn, NY 11209
Phone: +1 (718) 630-5700

#121
Bijan's
Bar, American
Average price: Moderate
District: Downtown Brooklyn, Boerum Hill
Address: 81 Hoyt St
Brooklyn, NY 11201
Phone: +1 (718) 855-5574

#122
Beloved
Cocktail Bar
Average price: Moderate
District: Greenpoint
Address: 674 Manhattan Ave
Brooklyn, NY 11222
Phone: +1 (347) 457-5448

#123
The Pony Bar
Bar
Average price: Moderate
District: Yorkville, Upper East Side
Address: 1444 1st Ave
New York, NY 10021
Phone: +1 (212) 288-0090

#124
Zampa
Italian, Wine Bar, Tapas Bar
Average price: Expensive
District: West Village
Address: 306 W 13th St
New York, NY 10014
Phone: +1 (212) 206-0601

#125
Ardesia
Wine Bar, Tapas
Average price: Moderate
District: Hell's Kitchen, Midtown West
Address: 510 W 52nd St
New York, NY 10019
Phone: +1 (212) 247-9191

#126
The Jakewalk
Wine Bar, Fondue
Average price: Moderate
District: Carroll Gardens, Gowanus
Address: 282 Smith St
Brooklyn, NY 11231
Phone: +1 (347) 599-0294

#127
The Village Underground
Dance Club, Lounge
Average price: Moderate
District: Greenwich Village
Address: 130 W 3rd St
New York, NY 10012
Phone: +1 (212) 777-7745

#128
Vbar
Wine Bar, American
Average price: Moderate
District: Greenwich Village
Address: 225 Sullivan St
New York, NY 10012
Phone: +1 (212) 253-5740

#129
Maracuja Bar & Grill
Lounge
Average price: Inexpensive
District: Williamsburg - North Side
Address: 279 Grand St
Brooklyn, NY 11211
Phone: +1 (718) 302-9023

#130
Harefield Road
Bar, Breakfast & Brunch
Average price: Moderate
District: East Williamsburg
Address: 769 Metropolitan Ave
Brooklyn, NY 11211
Phone: +1 (718) 388-6870

#131
Subject
Cocktail Bar
Average price: Moderate
District: Lower East Side
Address: 188 Suffolk St
New York, NY 10002
Phone: +1 (646) 422-7898

#132
DiWine
Wine Bar, Tapas Bar, American
Average price: Moderate
District: Astoria
Address: 41-15 31st Ave
Astoria, NY 11103
Phone: +1 (718) 777-1355

#133
Vol de Nuit
Lounge, American
Average price: Moderate
District: Greenwich Village
Address: 148 W 4th St
New York, NY 10012
Phone: +1 (212) 982-3388

#134
The Way Station
Bar, Music Venue
Average price: Moderate
District: Crown Heights, Prospect Heights
Address: 683 Washington Ave
Brooklyn, NY 11238
Phone: +1 (347) 627-4949

#135
Mission Dolores Bar
Bar
Average price: Moderate
District: Park Slope, Gowanus
Address: 249 4th Ave
Brooklyn, NY 11215
Phone: +1 (347) 457-5606

#136
The Redhead
American, Bar
Average price: Moderate
District: East Village
Address: 349 E 13th St
New York, NY 10003
Phone: +1 (212) 533-6212

#137
George Keeley's
Pub, American, Sport Bar
Average price: Moderate
District: Upper West Side
Address: 485 Amsterdam Ave
New York, NY 10024
Phone: +1 (212) 873-0251

#138
Clandestino
Wine Bar
Average price: Moderate
District: Chinatown, Lower East Side
Address: 35 Canal St
New York, NY 10002
Phone: +1 (212) 475-5505

#139
Red Hook Bait & Tackle
Dive Bar
Average price: Inexpensive
District: Red Hook
Address: 320 Van Brunt St
Brooklyn, NY 11231
Phone: +1 (718) 797-4892

#140
Alphabet City Beer Company
Bar, Beer, Wine & Spirits
Average price: Moderate
District: East Village, Alphabet City
Address: 96 Ave C
New York, NY 10009
Phone: +1 (646) 422-7103

#141
Char No. 4
Bar, Southern
Average price: Expensive
District: Cobble Hill, Gowanus
Address: 196 Smith St
Brooklyn, NY 11201
Phone: +1 (718) 643-2106

#142
The Whiskey Ward
Bar
Average price: Moderate
District: Lower East Side
Address: 121 Essex St
New York, NY 10002
Phone: +1 (212) 477-2998

#143
Beauty & Essex
Bar, American, Tapas
Average price: Expensive
District: Lower East Side
Address: 146 Essex St
New York, NY 10002
Phone: +1 (212) 614-0146

#144
DTUT
Bar, Cafe
Average price: Inexpensive
District: Yorkville, Upper East Side
Address: 1744 2nd Ave
New York, NY 10128
Phone: +1 (212) 410-6449

#145
Jimmy's Corner
Pub, Sport Bar, Dive Bar
Average price: Inexpensive
District: Midtown West, Theater District
Address: 140 W 44th St
New York, NY 10036
Phone: +1 (212) 221-9510

#146
Radegast Hall and Biergarten
Pub, German
Average price: Moderate
District: Williamsburg - North Side
Address: 113 N 3rd St
Brooklyn, NY 11249
Phone: +1 (718) 963-3973

#147
Bar Great Harry
Pub
Average price: Moderate
District: Carroll Gardens, Gowanus
Address: 280 Smith St
Brooklyn, NY 11231
Phone: +1 (718) 222-1103

#148
Louis 649
Jazz & Blues, Cocktail Bar
Average price: Moderate
District: East Village, Alphabet City
Address: 649 East 9th Street
New York, NY 10009
Phone: +1 (212) 673-1190

#149
The Bar Downstairs
Lounge
Average price: Expensive
District: Midtown East
Address: 485 5th Ave
New York, NY 10017
Phone: +1 (212) 601-1234

#150
Cork 'n Fork
Tapas, Wine Bar
Average price: Moderate
District: East Village, Alphabet City
Address: 186 Ave A
New York, NY 10009
Phone: +1 (646) 707-0707

#151
Lighthouse
Bar, Modern European, American
Average price: Moderate
District: Williamsburg - South Side
Address: 145 Borinquen Pl
Brooklyn, NY 11211
Phone: +1 (347) 789-7742

#152
Woodwork
Sport Bar, Gastropub, Beer, Wine & Spirits
Average price: Moderate
District: Prospect Heights
Address: 583 Vanderbilt Ave
Brooklyn, NY 11238
Phone: +1 (718) 857-5777

#153
Old Man Hustle
Wine Bar, Dive Bar, Music Venue
Average price: Inexpensive
District: Lower East Side
Address: 39 Essex St
New York, NY 10002
Phone: +1 (212) 253-7747

#154
**Onieal's Grand St. Bar
& Restaurant**
Bar, American
Average price: Moderate
District: Little Italy
Address: 174 Grand St
New York, NY 10013
Phone: +1 (212) 941-9119

#155
Skinny Dennis
Bar
Average price: Inexpensive
District: Williamsburg - North Side
Address: 152 Metropolitan Ave
Brooklyn, NY 11249
Phone: +1 (212) 555-1212

#156
Wheated
Pizza, Vegan, Cocktail Bar
Average price: Moderate
District: Flatbush
Address: 905 Church Ave
Brooklyn, NY 11218
Phone: +1 (347) 240-2813

#157
Banter
Bar
Average price: Moderate
District: Williamsburg - South Side
Address: 132 Havemeyer St
Brooklyn, NY 11211
Phone: +1 (718) 599-5200

#158
Five Points
American, Mediterranean, Bar
Average price: Moderate
District: NoHo
Address: 31 Great Jones St
New York, NY 10012
Phone: +1 (212) 253-5700

#159
Bushwick Country Club
Bar, Mini Golf
Average price: Inexpensive
District: East Williamsburg
Address: 618 Grand St
Brooklyn, NY 11211
Phone: +1 (718) 388-2114

#160
Shalel Lounge
Lounge, Moroccan
Average price: Moderate
District: Upper West Side
Address: 65 W 70th St
New York, NY 10023
Phone: +1 (212) 873-2300

#161
B Side
Dive Bar
Average price: Inexpensive
District: East Village, Alphabet City
Address: 204 Ave B
New York, NY 10009
Phone: +1 (212) 475-4600

#162
The Royal Palms Shuffleboard Club
Social Club, Bar, Recreation Center
Average price: Moderate
District: Gowanus
Address: 514 Union St
Brooklyn, NY 11215
Phone: +1 (347) 223-4410

#163
The Narrows
Bar, American
Average price: Moderate
District: East Williamsburg, Bushwick
Address: 1037 Flushing Ave
Brooklyn, NY 11237
Phone: +1 (281) 827-1800

#164
The Double Windsor
Pub, Gastropub
Average price: Moderate
District: South Slope, Windsor Terrace
Address: 210 Prospect Park W
Brooklyn, NY 11215
Phone: +1 (347) 725-3479

#165
Bondurants
Cocktail Bar, American, Gastropub
Average price: Moderate
District: Yorkville, Upper East Side
Address: 303 E 85th St
New York, NY 10028
Phone: +1 (212) 249-1509

#166
Valhalla
Pub
Average price: Moderate
District: Hell's Kitchen, Midtown West
Address: 815 9th Ave
New York, NY 10019
Phone: +1 (212) 757-2747

#167
Doris
Bar
Average price: Moderate
District: Bedford Stuyvesant, Clinton Hill
Address: 1088 Fulton St
Brooklyn, NY 11238
Phone: +1 (347) 240-3350

#168
Sunswick
Bar, American
Average price: Moderate
District: Astoria
Address: 3502 35th St
Astoria, NY 11106
Phone: +1 (718) 752-0620

#169
Sweet Science
Bar, Burgers, American
Average price: Moderate
District: East Williamsburg
Address: 135 Graham Ave
Brooklyn, NY 11206
Phone: +1 (347) 763-0872

#170
International Bar
Dive Bar, Lounge
Average price: Inexpensive
District: East Village
Address: 120 1/2 1st Ave
New York, NY 10009
Phone: +1 (212) 777-1643

#171
The Whiskey Brooklyn
Bar, American
Average price: Moderate
District: Williamsburg - North Side
Address: 44 Berry St
Brooklyn, NY 11211
Phone: +1 (718) 387-8444

#172
Canal Bar
Dive Bar, Cocktail Bar
Average price: Inexpensive
District: Gowanus
Address: 270 3rd Ave
Brooklyn, NY 11215
Phone: +1 (718) 246-0011

#173
Maysville
American, Wine Bar
Average price: Expensive
District: Flatiron
Address: 17 W 26th St
New York, NY 10010
Phone: +1 (646) 490-8240

#174
Botanica Bar
Bar
Average price: Inexpensive
District: Nolita
Address: 47 E Houston St
New York, NY 10012
Phone: +1 (212) 343-7251

#175
Iron Horse NYC
Dive Bar, Pub
Average price: Inexpensive
District: Financial District
Address: 32 Cliff St
New York, NY 10038
Phone: +1 (646) 546-5426

#176
Trinity Pub
Pub
Average price: Moderate
District: Yorkville, Upper East Side
Address: 229 E 84th St
New York, NY 10028
Phone: +1 (212) 327-4450

#177
The Tippler
Bar
Average price: Moderate
District: Chelsea, Meatpacking District
Address: 425 W 15th St
New York, NY 10011
Phone: +1 (212) 206-0000

#178
Swift
Restaurant, Bar
Average price: Moderate
District: NoHo
Address: 34 E 4th St
New York, NY 10003
Phone: +1 (212) 227-9438

#179
Jones Wood Foundry
British, Pub, Gastropub
Average price: Moderate
District: Yorkville, Upper East Side
Address: 401 E 76th St
New York, NY 10021
Phone: +1 (212) 249-2700

#180
Molly Blooms
Irish, Pub
Average price: Moderate
District: Sunnyside
Address: 43-13 Queens Blvd
Sunnyside, NY 11104
Phone: +1 (718) 433-1916

#181
Pinkerton Wine Bar
Wine Bar
Average price: Moderate
District: Williamsburg - North Side
Address: 263 N 6th St
Brooklyn, NY 11211
Phone: +1 (718) 782-7171

#182
The Auction House
Lounge
Average price: Moderate
District: Yorkville, Upper East Side
Address: 300 E 89th St
New York, NY 10128
Phone: +1 (212) 427-4458

#183
The Rum House
Lounge, Cocktail Bar
Average price: Expensive
District: Midtown West, Theater District
Address: 228 W 47th St
New York, NY 10036
Phone: +1 (646) 490-6924

#184
Session House
Irish, Pub
Average price: Moderate
District: Midtown East
Address: 1009 2nd Ave
New York, NY 10022
Phone: +1 (646) 559-4404

#185
Analogue
Cocktail Bar, Jazz & Blues, Lounge
Average price: Expensive
District: Greenwich Village
Address: 19 W 8th St
New York, NY 10011
Phone: +1 (212) 432-0200

#186
Burp Castle
Pub, Lounge
Average price: Moderate
District: East Village
Address: 41 E 7th St
New York, NY 10003
Phone: +1 (212) 982-4576

#187
Sharlene's
Bar
Average price: Inexpensive
District: Prospect Heights
Address: 353 Flatbush Ave
Brooklyn, NY 11238
Phone: +1 (347) 350-8225

#188
Sanford's Restaurant
American, Breakfast & Brunch, Bar
Average price: Moderate
District: Astoria
Address: 30-13 Broadway
Astoria, NY 11106
Phone: +1 (718) 932-9569

#189
Fresh Salt
Bar, American
Average price: Moderate
District: South Street Seaport
Address: 146 Beekman St
New York, NY 10038
Phone: +1 (212) 962-0053

#190
Two Bit's Retro Arcade
Arcade, Dive Bar
Average price: Inexpensive
District: Lower East Side
Address: 153 Essex St
New York, NY 10002
Phone: +1 (212) 477-8161

#191
Upright Brew House
American, Bar
Average price: Moderate
District: West Village
Address: 547 Hudson St
New York, NY 10014
Phone: +1 (212) 810-9944

#192
Johnny's Bar
Dive Bar
Average price: Inexpensive
District: West Village
Address: 90 Greenwich Ave
New York, NY 10011
Phone: +1 (212) 741-5279

#193
Dram Shop
Burgers, Bar
Average price: Moderate
District: South Slope, Park Slope
Address: 339 9th St
Brooklyn, NY 11215
Phone: +1 (718) 788-1444

#194
Ba'sik
Cocktail Bar, Salad, Sandwiches
Average price: Moderate
District: Williamsburg - North Side
Address: 323 Graham Ave
Brooklyn, NY 11211
Phone: +1 (347) 889-7597

#195
Iona
Bar
Average price: Moderate
District: Williamsburg - South Side
Address: 180 Grand St
Brooklyn, NY 11211
Phone: +1 (718) 384-5008

#196
Parkside Lounge
Music Venue, Lounge
Average price: Inexpensive
District: Lower East Side
Address: 317 E Houston St
New York, NY 10002
Phone: +1 (212) 673-6270

#197
Double Wide
Southern, Bar, Breakfast & Brunch
Average price: Moderate
District: East Village, Alphabet City
Address: 505 E 12th St
New York, NY 10009
Phone: +1 (917) 261-6461

#198
The Fulton Grand
Bar
Average price: Moderate
District: Clinton Hill
Address: 1011 Fulton St
Brooklyn, NY 11238
Phone: +1 (718) 399-2240

#199
Destination Bar & Grill
American, Cocktail Bar
Average price: Inexpensive
District: East Village, Alphabet City
Address: 211 Ave A
New York, NY 10009
Phone: +1 (212) 388-9844

#200
Anotheroom
Lounge
Average price: Moderate
District: TriBeCa
Address: 249 W Broadway
New York, NY 10013
Phone: +1 (212) 226-1418

#201
reBar
Bar, American, Venue & Event Space
Average price: Moderate
District: DUMBO
Address: 147 Front St.
Brooklyn, NY 11201
Phone: +1 (718) 766-9110

#202
Palace Cafe
Bar
Average price: Inexpensive
District: Greenpoint
Address: 206 Nassau Ave
Brooklyn, NY 11222
Phone: +1 (718) 383-9848

#203
Black Rabbit
Pub
Average price: Moderate
District: Greenpoint
Address: 91 Greenpoint Ave
Brooklyn, NY 11222
Phone: +1 (718) 349-1595

#204
Ugly Kitchen
Bar, Asian Fusion, Filipino
Average price: Moderate
District: East Village
Address: 103 1st Ave
New York, NY 10003
Phone: +1 (212) 777-6677

#205
Standings
Sport Bar, Pub
Average price: Moderate
District: East Village
Address: 43 E 7th St
New York, NY 10003
Phone: +1 (212) 420-0671

#206
Alligator Lounge
Lounge, Dive Bar, Karaoke
Average price: Inexpensive
District: Williamsburg - North Side
Address: 600 Metropolitan Ave
Brooklyn, NY 11211
Phone: +1 (718) 599-4440

#207
The Monro Pub
Pub
Average price: Inexpensive
District: South Slope, Park Slope
Address: 481 5th Ave
Brooklyn, NY 11215
Phone: +1 (718) 499-2005

#208
Shade
Bar, American, Crêperie
Average price: Moderate
District: Greenwich Village
Address: 241 Sullivan St
New York, NY 10012
Phone: +1 (212) 982-6275

#209
Barramundi
Venue & Event Space, Lounge
Average price: Inexpensive
District: Lower East Side
Address: 67 Clinton St
New York, NY 10002
Phone: +1 (212) 529-6999

#210
Commonwealth
Bar
Average price: Moderate
District: South Slope, Park Slope
Address: 497 5th Ave
Brooklyn, NY 11215
Phone: +1 (718) 768-2040

#211
Briciola
Italian, Wine Bar
Average price: Moderate
District: Hell's Kitchen, Midtown West,
Theater District
Address: 370 W 51 St
New York, NY 10019
Phone: +1 (646) 678-5763

#212
The Stag's Head
Pub
Average price: Moderate
District: Midtown East
Address: 252 E 51st St
New York, NY 10022
Phone: +1 (212) 888-2453

#213
Molly's
American, Irish, Pub
Average price: Moderate
District: Gramercy
Address: 287 3rd Ave
New York, NY 10010
Phone: +1 (212) 889-3361

#214
Réunion
Cocktail Bar
Average price: Moderate
District: Hell's Kitchen, Midtown West,
Theater District
Address: 357 W 44th St
New York, NY 10036
Phone: +1 (212) 582-3200

#215
Lillie's Victorian Bar & Restaurant
Irish, Pub
Average price: Moderate
District: Union Square, Flatiron
Address: 13 E 17th St
New York, NY 10003
Phone: +1 (212) 337-1970

#216
Mother's Ruin
Bar, American, Breakfast & Brunch
Average price: Moderate
District: Nolita
Address: 18 Spring St
New York, NY 10012
Phone: +1 (212) 219-0942

#217
11th Street Bar
Pub
Average price: Inexpensive
District: East Village, Alphabet City
Address: 510 E 11th St
New York, NY 10009
Phone: +1 (212) 982-3929

#218
61 Local
Pub, Venue & Event Space, Coffee & Tea
Average price: Moderate
District: Cobble Hill
Address: 61 Bergen St
Brooklyn, NY 11201
Phone: +1 (718) 875-1150

#219
Hibernia
Bar, American
Average price: Moderate
District: Hell's Kitchen, Midtown West
Address: 401 W 50th St
New York, NY 10019
Phone: +1 (212) 969-9703

#220
Greenpoint Tavern
Dive Bar
Average price: Inexpensive
District: Williamsburg - North Side
Address: 188 Bedford Ave
Brooklyn, NY 11211
Phone: +1 (718) 384-9539

#221
Bohemian Hall & Beer Garden
Pub, Music Venue, Czech
Average price: Moderate
District: Astoria
Address: 2919 24th Ave
Astoria, NY 11102
Phone: +1 (718) 274-4925

#222
The Library
Dive Bar, Jazz & Blues
Average price: Inexpensive
District: East Village, Alphabet City
Address: 7 Ave A
New York, NY 10009
Phone: +1 (212) 375-1352

#223
Tom & Jerry's
Bar
Average price: Moderate
District: NoHo
Address: 288 Elizabeth St
New York, NY 10012
Phone: +1 (212) 260-5045

#224
On The Rocks
Lounge
Average price: Moderate
District: Hell's Kitchen, Midtown West
Address: 696 10th Ave
New York, NY 10019
Phone: +1 (212) 247-2055

#225
Station House
Pub, American, Gastropub
Average price: Moderate
District: Forest Hills
Address: 106-11 71st Ave
Forest Hills, NY 11375
Phone: +1 (718) 544-5000

#226
Otto's Shrunken Head
Dive Bar
Average price: Moderate
District: East Village, Alphabet City
Address: 538 E 14th St
New York, NY 10009
Phone: +1 (212) 228-2240

#227
Hourglass Tavern
American, Lounge, American
Average price: Moderate
District: Hell's Kitchen, Midtown West,
Theater District
Address: 373 W 46th St
New York, NY 10036
Phone: +1 (212) 265-2060

#228
Barbes
Bar, Jazz & Blues
Average price: Moderate
District: South Slope, Park Slope
Address: 376 9th St
Brooklyn, NY 11215
Phone: +1 (347) 422-0248

#229
Black Swan
Pub, Gastropub
Average price: Moderate
District: Bedford Stuyvesant
Address: 1048 Bedford Ave
Brooklyn, NY 11205
Phone: +1 (718) 783-4744

#230
Lantern's Keep
Cocktail Bar
Average price: Expensive
District: Midtown West
Address: 49 W 44th St
New York, NY 10036
Phone: +1 (212) 453-4287

#231
Drop Off Service
Bar
Average price: Inexpensive
District: East Village, Alphabet City
Address: 211 Ave A
New York, NY 10009
Phone: +1 (212) 260-2914

#232
Bathtub Gin
Bar
Average price: Expensive
District: Chelsea
Address: 132 9th Ave
New York, NY 10011
Phone: +1 (646) 559-1671

#233
Good Co.
Bar
Average price: Inexpensive
District: Williamsburg - North Side
Address: 10 Hope St
Brooklyn, NY 11211
Phone: +1 (718) 218-7191

#234
Rattle 'N' Hum
Pub, American
Average price: Moderate
District: Midtown East
Address: 14 E 33rd St
New York, NY 10016
Phone: +1 (212) 481-1586

#235
Wolf and Deer
Wine Bar, American
Average price: Moderate
District: Park Slope
Address: 74 5th Ave
Brooklyn, NY 11217
Phone: +1 (718) 398-3181

#236
Barcelona Bar
Dive Bar
Average price: Moderate
District: Hell's Kitchen, Midtown West
Address: 923 8th Ave
New York, NY 10019
Phone: +1 (212) 245-3212

#237
Gottscheer Hall
Caterers, German, Pub
Average price: Inexpensive
District: Ridgewood
Address: 657 Fairview Ave
Ridgewood, NY 11385
Phone: +1 (718) 366-3030

#238
Union Hall
Pub, Music Venue
Average price: Moderate
District: Park Slope
Address: 702 Union St
Brooklyn, NY 11215
Phone: +1 (718) 638-4400

#239
Common Ground
Bar, American
Average price: Moderate
District: East Village, Alphabet City
Address: 206 Ave A
New York, NY 10009
Phone: +1 (212) 228-6231

#240
Boat Bar
Dive Bar
Average price: Inexpensive
District: Cobble Hill, Boerum Hill
Address: 175 Smith St
Brooklyn, NY 11201
Phone: +1 (718) 254-0607

#241
Vintry Wine and Whiskey
Bar
Average price: Expensive
District: Financial District
Address: 57 Stone St
New York, NY 10004
Phone: +1 (212) 480-9800

#242
Terroir Tribeca
Wine Bar, American
Average price: Moderate
District: TriBeCa
Address: 24 Harrison St
New York, NY 10013
Phone: +1 (212) 625-9463

#243
Wogies
Bar, American
Average price: Moderate
District: West Village
Address: 39 Greenwich Ave
New York, NY 10014
Phone: +1 (212) 229-2171

#244
The Wren
Bar, Breakfast & Brunch
Average price: Moderate
District: East Village
Address: 344 Bowery
New York, NY 10012
Phone: +1 (212) 388-0148

#245
Washington Commons
Pub
Average price: Inexpensive
District: Crown Heights, Prospect Heights
Address: 748 Washington Ave
Brooklyn, NY 11238
Phone: +1 (718) 230-3666

#246
Draught 55
Bar
Average price: Moderate
District: Midtown East
Address: 245 E 55th St
New York, NY 10022
Phone: +1 (212) 300-4096

#247
bOb Bar
Lounge, Dance Club
Average price: Moderate
District: Lower East Side
Address: 235 Eldridge St
New York, NY 10002
Phone: +1 (212) 529-1807

#248
Lansdowne Road
Pub, Sport Bar
Average price: Moderate
District: Hell's Kitchen, Midtown West
Address: 599 10th Ave
New York, NY 10036
Phone: +1 (212) 239-8020

#249
Kilo
Tapas Bar, Wine Bar
Average price: Moderate
District: Hell's Kitchen, Midtown West
Address: 857 9th Ave
New York, NY 10019
Phone: +1 (212) 707-8770

#250
Uvarara
Italian, Wine Bar
Average price: Expensive
District: Middle Village
Address: 79-28 Metropolitan Ave
Middle Village, NY 11379
Phone: +1 (718) 894-0052

#251
Catfish
Cajun/Creole, Cocktail Bar,
Breakfast & Brunch
Average price: Moderate
District: Crown Heights
Address: 1433 Bedford Ave
Brooklyn, NY 11216
Phone: +1 (347) 305-3233

#252
Mercury Lounge
Dive Bar
Average price: Moderate
District: Lower East Side
Address: 217 East Houston St.
New York, NY 10002
Phone: +1 (212) 260-4700

#253
Uncorked Wine & Tapas
Wine Bar, Lounge, Tapas
Average price: Moderate
District: Midtown East
Address: 344 E 59th St
New York, NY 10022
Phone: +1 (646) 429-8365

#254
The Four-Faced Liar
Pub
Average price: Inexpensive
District: West Village
Address: 165 W 4th St
New York, NY 10014
Phone: +1 (212) 206-8959

#255
Bearded Lady
Bar
Average price: Moderate
District: Prospect Heights
Address: 686A Washington Ave
Brooklyn, NY 11238
Phone: +1 (469) 232-7333

#256
Piccolo Cafe
Coffee & Tea, Italian, Wine Bar
Average price: Moderate
District: Midtown West, Theater District
Address: 274 W 40th St
New York, NY 10018
Phone: +1 (212) 302-0143

#257
Paddy Reilly's Music Bar
Pub, Music Venue
Average price: Inexpensive
District: Midtown East, Kips Bay
Address: 519 2nd Ave
New York, NY 10016
Phone: +1 (212) 686-1210

#258
Dirty Pierre's
Pub, Burgers
Average price: Moderate
District: Forest Hills
Address: 13 Station Sq
Forest Hills, NY 11375
Phone: +1 (718) 830-9698

#259
BXL East
Belgian, Pub
Average price: Moderate
District: Midtown East
Address: 210 E 51st St
New York, NY 10022
Phone: +1 (212) 888-7782

#260
Tiny's & the Bar Upstairs
Bar, American
Average price: Expensive
District: TriBeCa
Address: 135 W Broadway
New York, NY 10013
Phone: +1 (212) 374-1135

#261
The Gutter
Bowling, Dive Bar
Average price: Moderate
District: Williamsburg - North Side
Address: 200 N 14th St
Brooklyn, NY 11222
Phone: +1 (718) 387-3585

#262
Aria Wine Bar
Wine Bar, Tapas
Average price: Moderate
District: West Village
Address: 117 Perry St
New York, NY 10014
Phone: +1 (212) 242-4233

#263
Brandy's Piano Bar
Bar, Music Venue
Average price: Moderate
District: Yorkville, Upper East Side
Address: 235 E 84th St
New York, NY 10028
Phone: +1 (212) 744-4949

#264
Sample
Bar
Average price: Moderate
District: Cobble Hill
Address: 152 Smith St
Brooklyn, NY 11201
Phone: +1 (718) 643-6622

#265
Ayza Wine & Chocolate Bar
Desserts, Wine Bar, Mediterranean
Average price: Moderate
District: West Village
Address: 1 7th Ave S
New York, NY 10014
Phone: +1 (212) 365-2992

#266
Double Down Saloon
Dive Bar
Average price: Inexpensive
District: East Village, Alphabet City
Address: 14 Ave A
New York, NY 10009
Phone: +1 (212) 982-0543

#267
The NoMad Library
Gastropub, Lounge
Average price: Expensive
District: Flatiron
Address: 1170 Broadway & 28th St
New York, NY 10001
Phone: +1 (347) 472-5660

#268
Mary's Bar
Pub
Average price: Moderate
District: South Slope
Address: 708 5th Ave
Brooklyn, NY 11215
Phone: +1 (718) 499-2175

#269
Pearl's Social & Billy Club
Dive Bar, Cocktail Bar
Average price: Moderate
District: Bushwick
Address: 40 Saint Nicholas Ave
Brooklyn, NY 11237
Phone: +1 (347) 627-9985

#270
Heavy Woods
Bar, Cafe, Cajun/Creole
Average price: Moderate
District: Bushwick
Address: 50 Wyckoff Ave
New York, NY 11237
Phone: +1 (929) 234-3500

#271
Hell Gate Social
Lounge, Pub
Average price: Inexpensive
District: Astoria
Address: 1221 Astoria Blvd
Astoria, NY 11102
Phone: +1 (718) 204-8313

#272
The Belfry
Bar
Average price: Moderate
District: East Village
Address: 222 E 14th St
New York, NY 10003
Phone: +1 (212) 473-6590

#273
Lillie's Victorian Bar & Restaurant
Lounge, American
Average price: Moderate
District: Midtown West, Theater District
Address: 249 W 49th St
New York, NY 10019
Phone: +1 (212) 957-4530

#274
The Crown Inn
Bar
Average price: Moderate
District: Crown Heights
Address: 724 Franklin Ave
Brooklyn, NY 11238
Phone: +1 (347) 915-1131

#275
Daddy-O
Bar
Average price: Moderate
District: West Village
Address: 44 Bedford St
New York, NY 10014
Phone: +1 (212) 414-8884

#276
Booker and Dax
Lounge
Average price: Expensive
District: East Village
Address: 207 2nd Ave
New York, NY 10003
Phone: +1 (212) 254-3500

#277
One Mile House
Bar, American
Average price: Moderate
District: Lower East Side
Address: 10 Delancey St
New York, NY 10012
Phone: +1 (646) 559-0702

#278
Lucien
French, Wine Bar
Average price: Expensive
District: East Village
Address: 14 1st Ave
New York, NY 10009
Phone: +1 (212) 260-6481

#279
Deacon Brodie's
Pub
Average price: Inexpensive
District: Hell's Kitchen, Midtown West,
Theater District
Address: 370 W 46th St
New York, NY 10036
Phone: +1 (212) 262-1452

#280
Kazuza
Hookah Bar, Middle Eastern
Average price: Moderate
District: East Village, Alphabet City
Address: 107 Ave A
New York, NY 10009
Phone: +1 (212) 505-9300

#281
Juke Bar
Bar
Average price: Moderate
District: East Village
Address: 196 2nd Ave
New York, NY 10003
Phone: +1 (212) 228-7464

#282
Rose Bar
Lounge
Average price: Exclusive
District: Gramercy, Flatiron
Address: 2 Lexington Ave
New York, NY 10010
Phone: +1 (212) 920-3300

#283
Epistrophy
Wine Bar, Italian
Average price: Moderate
District: Nolita
Address: 200 Mott St
New York, NY 10012
Phone: +1 (212) 966-0904

#284
Measure
Lounge, Jazz & Blues, Tapas
Average price: Expensive
District: Midtown West
Address: 400 5th Ave
New York, NY 10018
Phone: +1 (212) 695-4005

#285
Mad Donkey Beer Bar & Grill
Dive Bar
Average price: Inexpensive
District: Astoria
Address: 3207 36th Ave
Astoria, NY 11106
Phone: +1 (718) 204-2070

#286
Montero's Bar & Grill
Dive Bar, American
Average price: Inexpensive
District: Brooklyn Heights, Cobble Hill
Address: 73 Atlantic Ave
Brooklyn, NY 11201
Phone: +1 (646) 729-4129

#287
est. 1986 Wine Bar/Lounge
Wine Bar, Lounge
Average price: Moderate
District: Midtown West, Koreatown
Address: 43 W 32nd St
New York, NY 10001
Phone: +1 (212) 563-1500

#288
Boulton & Watt
Bar, American, Gastropub
Average price: Moderate
District: Lower East Side, Alphabet City
Address: 5 Ave A
New York, NY 10009
Phone: +1 (646) 490-6004

#289
Billymark's West
Dive Bar
Average price: Inexpensive
District: Chelsea, Midtown West
Address: 332 9th Ave
New York, NY 10001
Phone: +1 (212) 629-0118

#290
Landmark Tavern
Pub, American
Average price: Moderate
District: Hell's Kitchen, Midtown West
Address: 626 11th Ave
New York, NY 10036
Phone: +1 (212) 247-2562

#291
St. Andrews
Pub, Seafood, Scottish
Average price: Moderate
District: Midtown West, Theater District
Address: 140 W 46th St
New York, NY 10036
Phone: +1 (212) 840-8413

#292
Rue B
Bar, Jazz & Blues, Brasserie
Average price: Moderate
District: East Village, Alphabet City
Address: 188 Ave B
New York, NY 10009
Phone: +1 (212) 358-1700

#293
ReSette
Bar, American, Italian
Average price: Expensive
District: Midtown West
Address: 7 W 45th St
New York, NY 10036
Phone: +1 (212) 221-7530

#294
Turks & Frogs
Wine Bar, Turkish
Average price: Moderate
District: West Village
Address: 323 W 11th St #2
New York, NY 10014
Phone: +1 (212) 691-8875

#295
Barcibo Enoteca
Wine Bar
Average price: Moderate
District: Upper West Side
Address: 2020 Broadway
New York, NY 10023
Phone: +1 (212) 595-2805

#296
B Cafe
Bar, Belgian
Average price: Moderate
District: Yorkville, Upper East Side
Address: 240 E 75th St
New York, NY 10021
Phone: +1 (212) 249-3300

#297
The Three Monkeys
Bar, American, Gastropub
Average price: Moderate
District: Midtown West, Theater District
Address: 236 W 54th St
New York, NY 10019
Phone: +1 (212) 586-2080

#298
Tutu's
Pub, American, Breakfast & Brunch
Average price: Moderate
District: East Williamsburg, Bushwick
Address: 25 Bogart St
Brooklyn, NY 11206
Phone: +1 (718) 456-7898

#299
Littlefield
Performing Arts, Art Gallery, Bar
Average price: Moderate
District: Gowanus
Address: 622 Degraw St
Brooklyn, NY 11217
Phone: +1 (718) 855-3388

#300
Cake Shop
Coffee & Tea, Bar, Music Venue
Average price: Inexpensive
District: Lower East Side
Address: 152 Ludlow St
New York, NY 10002
Phone: +1 (212) 253-0036

#301
The Sparrow Tavern
Bar, Breakfast & Brunch, American
Average price: Moderate
District: Astoria
Address: 24-01 29th St
Astoria, NY 11102
Phone: +1 (718) 606-2260

#302
V Bar
Wine Bar, Italian
Average price: Moderate
District: East Village
Address: 132 1st Ave
New York, NY 10009
Phone: +1 (212) 473-7200

#303
ViV
Thai, Bar
Average price: Moderate
District: Hell's Kitchen, Midtown West,
Theater District
Address: 717 9th Ave
New York, NY 10019
Phone: +1 (212) 581-5999

#304
Lion's Head Tavern
Bar
Average price: Inexpensive
District: Manhattan Valley
Address: 995 Amsterdam Ave
New York, NY 10025
Phone: +1 (212) 866-1030

#305
Hollow Nickel
Pub
Average price: Moderate
District: Boerum Hill
Address: 494 Atlantic Ave
New York, NY 11217
Phone: +1 (347) 236-3417

#306
Franklin Park
Bar
Average price: Moderate
District: Crown Heights
Address: 618 St John's Pl
Brooklyn, NY 11238
Phone: +1 (718) 975-0196

#307
Jack & Nellie's
American, Wine Bar, Breakfast & Brunch
Average price: Moderate
District: Forest Hills
Address: 108-25 Ascan Ave
Forest Hills, NY 11375
Phone: +1 (718) 268-2696

#308
L.I.C. Bar
Bar, Music Venue
Average price: Moderate
District: Hunters Point, Long Island City
Address: 4558 Vernon Blvd
Long Island City, NY 11101
Phone: +1 (718) 786-5400

#309
The Brooklyn Inn
Bar
Average price: Inexpensive
District: Boerum Hill
Address: 138 Bergen St
Brooklyn, NY 11217
Phone: +1 (718) 522-2525

#310
Local 138
Bar
Average price: Inexpensive
District: Lower East Side
Address: 138 Ludlow St
New York, NY 10002
Phone: +1 (212) 477-0280

#311
Pencil Factory Bar
Bar
Average price: Moderate
District: Greenpoint
Address: 142 Franklin St
Brooklyn, NY 11222
Phone: +1 (718) 609-5858

#312
Scratcher
Pub, American
Average price: Inexpensive
District: East Village
Address: 209 E 5th St
New York, NY 10003
Phone: +1 (212) 477-0030

#313
Press Lounge
Lounge
Average price: Expensive
District: Hell's Kitchen, Midtown West
Address: 653 11th Ave
New York, NY 10036
Phone: +1 (212) 757-2224

#314
Amsterdam Tavern
Bar
Average price: Moderate
District: Manhattan Valley
Address: 938 Amsterdam Ave
New York, NY 10025
Phone: +1 (212) 280-8070

#315
Miles
Wine Bar, American, Cocktail Bar
Average price: Moderate
District: Bushwick
Address: 101 Wilson Ave
Brooklyn, NY 11237
Phone: +1 (718) 483-9172

#316
Lucey's Lounge
Lounge
Average price: Moderate
District: Gowanus
Address: 475 3rd Ave
Brooklyn, NY 11231
Phone: +1 (718) 877-1075

#317
Pine Box Rock Shop
Bar, Vegan, Karaoke, Shopping
Average price: Moderate
District: East Williamsburg, Bushwick
Address: 12 Grattan St
Brooklyn, NY 11206
Phone: +1 (718) 366-6311

#318
Gotham City Lounge
Dive Bar
Average price: Inexpensive
District: Bushwick
Address: 1293 Myrtle Ave
Brooklyn, NY 11221
Phone: +1 (718) 387-4182

#319
La Sultana Cafe
Hookah Bar
Average price: Moderate
District: East Village
Address: 124 E 4th St
New York, NY 10003
Phone: +1 (212) 228-7678

#320
Bar Reis
Bar
Average price: Moderate
District: Park Slope
Address: 375 5th Ave
Brooklyn, NY 11215
Phone: +1 (718) 974-2412

#321
The Sampler Bushwick
Bar
Average price: Moderate
District: Bushwick
Address: 234 Starr St
Brooklyn, NY 11237
Phone: +1 (718) 484-3560

#322
Sea Witch
Lounge, Gastropub
Average price: Inexpensive
District: South Slope
Address: 703 5th Ave
Brooklyn, NY 11215
Phone: +1 (347) 227-7166

#323
The Dead Poet
Bar
Average price: Moderate
District: Upper West Side
Address: 450 Amsterdam Ave
New York, NY 10024
Phone: +1 (212) 595-5670

#324
G.Lee's Smokin BBQ
Cocktail Bar, Barbeque
Average price: Moderate
District: Crown Heights
Address: 813 Nostrand Ave
Brooklyn, NY 11225
Phone: +1 (347) 413-8680

#325
Whitman and Bloom
American, Seafood, Cocktail Bar
Average price: Moderate
District: Kips Bay
Address: 384 3rd Ave
New York, NY 10016
Phone: +1 (212) 725-4110

#326
Bar Tano
Bar, Italian
Average price: Moderate
District: Gowanus
Address: 457 3rd Ave
Brooklyn, NY 11215
Phone: +1 (718) 499-3400

#327
Alfie's
Bar
Average price: Moderate
District: Hell's Kitchen, Midtown West,
Theater District
Address: 800 9th Ave
New York, NY 10019
Phone: +1 (212) 757-2390

#328
Cibar
Lounge
Average price: Expensive
District: Gramercy
Address: 56 Irving Pl
New York, NY 10003
Phone: +1 (212) 460-5656

#329
Lederhosen
German, Bar
Average price: Moderate
District: West Village
Address: 39 Grove St
New York, NY 10014
Phone: +1 (212) 206-7691

#330
Rocky Sullivan's
Irish, Pub
Average price: Moderate
District: Red Hook
Address: 34 Van Dyke St
Brooklyn, NY 11231
Phone: +1 (718) 246-8050

#331
Therapy
Gay Bar
Average price: Moderate
District: Hell's Kitchen, Midtown West,
Theater District
Address: 348 W 52nd St
New York, NY 10019
Phone: +1 (212) 397-1700

#332
Fraunces Tavern
American, Bar
Average price: Moderate
District: Financial District
Address: 54 Pearl St
New York, NY 10004
Phone: +1 (212) 968-1776

#333
Doc Holliday's
Bar, American
Average price: Inexpensive
District: East Village, Alphabet City
Address: 141 Ave A
New York, NY 10009
Phone: +1 (212) 979-0312

#334
Night of Joy
Lounge
Average price: Moderate
District: Williamsburg - North Side
Address: 667 Lorimer St
Brooklyn, NY 11211
Phone: +1 (718) 388-8693

#335
Village Pisco
Cocktail Bar, Peruvian, American
Average price: Moderate
District: Greenwich Village
Address: 45 W 8th St
New York, NY 10011
Phone: +1 (212) 995-2700

#336
The Carnegie Club
Lounge
Average price: Expensive
District: Midtown West
Address: 156 West 56th St
New York, NY 10019
Phone: +1 (212) 957-9676

#337
Shrine
Bar, Music Venue
Average price: Moderate
District: Harlem
Address: 2271 Adam Clayton Powell Blvd
New York, NY 10030
Phone: +1 (212) 690-7807

#338
Dominie's Hoek
Bar, American
Average price: Moderate
District: Hunters Point, Long Island City
Address: 4817 Vernon Blvd
Long Island City, NY 11356
Phone: +1 (718) 706-6531

#339
Lowlands Bar
Bar
Average price: Inexpensive
District: Gowanus
Address: 543 3rd Ave
Brooklyn, NY 11215
Phone: +1 (347) 463-9458

#340
B Cafe West
Belgian, Bar
Average price: Moderate
District: Upper West Side
Address: 566 Amsterdam Ave
New York, NY 10024
Phone: +1 (212) 873-1800

#341
Art Bar
Lounge, American
Average price: Moderate
District: West Village
Address: 52 8th Ave
New York, NY 10014
Phone: +1 (212) 727-0244

#342
Vetro by Russo's on the Bay
Italian, Lounge
Average price: Expensive
District: Howard Beach
Address: 164-49 Crossbay Blvd
Howard Beach, NY 11414
Phone: +1 (718) 843-8387

#343
Against the Grain
Bar
Average price: Moderate
District: East Village, Alphabet City
Address: 620 E 6th St
New York, NY 10009
Phone: +1 (212) 358-7065

#344
Madam Geneva
Lounge
Average price: Moderate
District: NoHo
Address: 4 Bleecker St
New York, NY 10012
Phone: +1 (212) 254-0350

#345
The Counting Room
American, Bar
Average price: Moderate
District: Williamsburg - North Side
Address: 44 Berry St
Brooklyn, NY 11211
Phone: +1 (718) 599-1860

#346
Soho House
Restaurant, Lounge
Average price: Exclusive
District: West Village, Meatpacking
Address: 29 9th Ave
New York, NY 10014
Phone: +1 (212) 627-3647

#347
Trophy Bar
Dance Club, Cocktail Bar
Average price: Moderate
District: Williamsburg - South Side,
South Williamsburg
Address: 351 Broadway
Brooklyn, NY 11211
Phone: +1 (347) 227-8515

#348
Sidecar
American, Cocktail Bar
Average price: Moderate
District: South Slope, Park Slope
Address: 560 5th Ave
Brooklyn, NY 11215
Phone: +1 (718) 369-0077

#349
Cafe Rue Dix
African, French, Cocktail Bar
Average price: Moderate
District: Crown Heights
Address: 1451 Bedford Ave
Brooklyn, NY 11216
Phone: +1 (929) 234-2543

#350
Malbec and Tango House
Wine Bar, American
Average price: Exclusive
District: NoHo
Address: 428 Lafayette St
New York, NY 10003
Phone: +1 (212) 419-4645

#351
Tandem
Bar, Breakfast & Brunch, American
Average price: Moderate
District: Bushwick
Address: 236 Troutman St
Brooklyn, NY 11237
Phone: +1 (718) 386-2369

#352
Dylan's Candy Bar
Chocolatier& Shops, Cocktail Bar
Average price: Moderate
District: Upper East Side
Address: 1011 3rd Ave
New York, NY 10065
Phone: +1 (646) 735-0078

#353
Halyards
Lounge
Average price: Moderate
District: Gowanus
Address: 406 3rd Ave
Brooklyn, NY 11215
Phone: +1 (718) 532-8787

#354
One Stop Beer Shop
Bar, Gastropub
Average price: Moderate
District: East Williamsburg
Address: 134 Kingsland Ave
Brooklyn, NY 11222
Phone: +1 (718) 599-0128

#355
Manhattan Proper
Sport Bar, American, Lounge
Average price: Moderate
District: Civic Center, TriBeCa
Address: 6 Murray St
New York, NY 10007
Phone: +1 (646) 559-4445

#356
Biddy's Pub
Pub
Average price: Inexpensive
District: Yorkville, Upper East Side
Address: 301 E 91st St
New York, NY 10128
Phone: +1 (212) 534-4785

#357
St. Mazie
Bar, Comfort Food, Music Venue
Average price: Moderate
District: Williamsburg - North Side
Address: 345 Grand St Williamsburg
Brooklyn, NY 11211
Phone: +1 (718) 384-4807

#358
54 Below
Jazz & Blues, Lounge
Average price: Expensive
District: Midtown West, Theater District
Address: 254 W 54th St
New York, NY 10019
Phone: +1 (866) 468-7619

#359
Soigne Restaurant & Wine Bar
Wine Bar, American
Average price: Expensive
District: South Slope, Park Slope
Address: 486 6th Ave
Brooklyn, NY 11215
Phone: +1 (718) 369-4814

#360
Terraza 7
Bar, Music Venue, Jazz & Blues
Average price: Moderate
District: Elmhurst
Address: 40-19 Gleane St
Elmhurst, NY 11373
Phone: +1 (718) 803-9602

#361
Battery Harris
Bar, Caribbean
Average price: Moderate
District: Williamsburg - North Side
Address: 64 Frost St
Brooklyn, NY 11211
Phone: +1 (718) 384-8900

#362
Greenwich Treehouse
Lounge, Pub
Average price: Inexpensive
District: West Village
Address: 46 Greenwich Ave
New York, NY 10011
Phone: +1 (212) 675-0395

#363
Sel Rrose
Cocktail Bar, Seafood
Average price: Moderate
District: Lower East Side
Address: 1 Delancey St
New York, NY 10002
Phone: +1 (212) 226-2510

#364
Abilene
Dive Bar, Lounge, American
Average price: Moderate
District: Carroll Gardens
Address: 442 Court St
Brooklyn, NY 11231
Phone: +1 (718) 522-6900

#365
Spitzer's Corner
Pub
Average price: Moderate
District: Lower East Side
Address: 101 Rivington St
New York, NY 10002
Phone: +1 (212) 228-0027

#366
Bar Sepia
Bar
Average price: Moderate
District: Prospect Heights
Address: 234 Underhill Ave
Brooklyn, NY 11238
Phone: +1 (718) 399-6680

#367
The Malt House
Pub, Gastropub
Average price: Moderate
District: Greenwich Village
Address: 206 Thompson St
New York, NY 10012
Phone: +1 (212) 228-7713

#368
Molasses Books
Cafe, Bookstore, Bar
Average price: Inexpensive
District: Bushwick
Address: 770 Hart St
Brooklyn, NY 11237
Phone: +1 (631) 882-5188

#369
Biblio
Bar, American, Gastropub
Average price: Moderate
District: Williamsburg - North Side
Address: 149 N 6th St
Brooklyn, NY 11211
Phone: +1 (718) 384-8200

#370
Oxcart Tavern
American, Pub, Gastropub
Average price: Moderate
District: Flatbush
Address: 1301 Newkirk Ave
Brooklyn, NY 11230
Phone: +1 (718) 284-0005

#371
Trading Post
American, Bar, Seafood
Average price: Expensive
District: South Street Seaport
Address: 170 John St
New York, NY 10038
Phone: +1 (646) 370-3337

#372
Blue Bar
Bar
Average price: Expensive
District: Midtown West
Address: 59 W 44th St
New York, NY 10036
Phone: +1 (212) 840-6800

#373
Jimmy's No. 43
Bar
Average price: Moderate
District: East Village
Address: 43 E 7th St
New York, NY 10003
Phone: +1 (212) 982-3006

#374
Milano's Bar
Dive Bar
Average price: Inexpensive
District: Nolita
Address: 51 E Houston St
New York, NY 10012
Phone: +1 (212) 226-8844

#375
Brooklyn Social
Lounge
Average price: Moderate
District: Gowanus
Address: 335 Smith St
Brooklyn, NY 11231
Phone: +1 (718) 858-7758

#376
Ivy
American, Lounge, Cocktail Bar
Average price: Moderate
District: Hell's Kitchen, Midtown West
Address: 944 8th Ave
New York, NY 10019
Phone: +1 (212) 459-9444

#377
The Spring Lounge
Lounge, Dive Bar
Average price: Moderate
District: Nolita
Address: 48 Spring St
New York, NY 10012
Phone: +1 (212) 965-1774

#378
Saxon + Parole
American, Bar
Average price: Expensive
District: NoHo
Address: 316 Bowery
New York, NY 10012
Phone: +1 (212) 254-0350

#379
Rapture Lounge
Lounge, American
Average price: Moderate
District: Astoria
Address: 3427 28th Ave
Astoria, NY 11103
Phone: +1 (718) 626-8044

#380
Little Zelda
Coffee & Tea, Wine Bar
Average price: Moderate
District: Crown Heights
Address: 728 Franklin Ave
New York, NY 11238
Phone: +1 (917) 499-3244

#381
Donovan's Pub
Burgers, Pub
Average price: Moderate
District: Woodside
Address: 57-24 Roosevelt Ave
Woodside, NY 11377
Phone: +1 (718) 429-9339

#382
Ciccio
Italian, Bar
Average price: Moderate
District: South Village
Address: 190 6th Ave
New York, NY 10012
Phone: +1 (646) 476-9498

#383
Big Bar
Bar
Average price: Moderate
District: East Village
Address: 75 E 7th St
New York, NY 10003
Phone: +1 (212) 777-6969

#384
Lone Wolf
Bar, Music Venue
Average price: Inexpensive
District: Bedford Stuyvesant, Bushwick
Address: 1089 Broadway
Brooklyn, NY 11221
Phone: +1 (718) 455-2028

#385
Legends Bar & Grill
Bar, Barbeque
Average price: Moderate
District: Jackson Heights
Address: 7104 35th Ave
Jackson Heights, NY 11372
Phone: +1 (718) 899-9553

#386
Cock & Bull
British, Pub
Average price: Moderate
District: Midtown West
Address: 23 W 45th St
New York, NY 10036
Phone: +1 (212) 819-1900

#387
The 'Dam
American, Pub
Average price: Moderate
District: Manhattan Valley
Address: 998 Amsterdam Ave
New York, NY 10025
Phone: +1 (212) 257-4998

#388
Videology
Cinema, Bar
Average price: Inexpensive
District: Williamsburg - South Side
Address: 308 Bedford Ave
Brooklyn, NY 11249
Phone: +1 (718) 782-3468

#389
Dublin 6
Irish, Pub, American
Average price: Moderate
District: West Village
Address: 575 Hudson St
New York, NY 10014
Phone: +1 (646) 638-2900

#390
O'hanlons
Pub, Irish
Average price: Inexpensive
District: Stuyvesant Town, Gramercy,
East Village
Address: 349 E 14th St
New York, NY 10003
Phone: +1 (212) 533-7333

#391
Last Exit Bar & Lounge
Lounge, Dive Bar
Average price: Inexpensive
District: Cobble Hill
Address: 136 Atlantic Ave
Brooklyn, NY 11201
Phone: +1 (718) 222-9198

#392
Peter Dillon's
Pub
Average price: Inexpensive
District: Midtown East, Murray Hill
Address: 130 E 40th St
New York, NY 10016
Phone: +1 (212) 213-3998

#393
Library Bar at Hudson
Lounge
Average price: Expensive
District: Hell's Kitchen, Midtown West
Address: 356 W 58th St
New York, NY 10019
Phone: +1 (212) 554-6000

#394
Winebar
Wine Bar, Tapas Bar
Average price: Moderate
District: East Village
Address: 65 2nd Ave
New York, NY 10003
Phone: +1 (212) 777-1608

#395
The West
Coffee & Tea, Bagels, Bar
Average price: Moderate
District: Williamsburg - North Side
Address: 379 Union Ave
Brooklyn, NY 11211
Phone: +1 (718) 599-1704

#396
Hill and Dale
Bar, American
Average price: Moderate
District: Lower East Side
Address: 115 Allen St
New York, NY 10002
Phone: +1 (212) 420-1115

#397
Loreley
German, Pub
Average price: Moderate
District: Lower East Side
Address: 7 Rivington St
New York, NY 10002
Phone: +1 (212) 253-7077

#398
The Ding-Dong Lounge
Dive Bar
Average price: Inexpensive
District: Manhattan Valley
Address: 929 Columbus Ave
New York, NY 10025
Phone: +1 (212) 663-2600

#399
Grace
Wine Bar, Gastropub, Cocktail Bar
Average price: Moderate
District: Kips Bay
Address: 365 3rd Ave
New York, NY 10016
Phone: +1 (646) 918-6553

#400
Lavender Lake
Gastropub, Pub, Cocktail Bar
Average price: Moderate
District: Gowanus
Address: 383 Carroll St
Brooklyn, NY 11231
Phone: +1 (347) 799-2154

#401
Walker's
American, Bar
Average price: Moderate
District: TriBeCa
Address: 16 N Moore St
New York, NY 10013
Phone: +1 (212) 941-0142

#402
Veslo
Lounge, Mediterranean
Average price: Moderate
District: Astoria
Address: 32-11 Broadway
Astoria, NY 11106
Phone: +1 (718) 728-0549

#403
The Second Chance Saloon
Pub
Average price: Inexpensive
District: Williamsburg - North Side
Address: 659 Grand St
Brooklyn, NY 11211
Phone: +1 (718) 387-4411

#404
Riposo 72
Wine Bar, Tapas
Average price: Moderate
District: Upper West Side
Address: 50 W 72nd St
New York, NY 10023
Phone: +1 (212) 799-4140

#405
Bell Book & Candle
American, Bar
Average price: Expensive
District: West Village
Address: 141 W 10th St
New York, NY 10014
Phone: +1 (212) 414-2355

#406
Quarter
Bar
Average price: Moderate
District: South Slope
Address: 676 5th Ave
Brooklyn, NY 11232
Phone: +1 (718) 788-0989

#407
Bar 718
Bar
Average price: Inexpensive
District: South Slope
Address: 718 5th Ave
Brooklyn, NY 11232
Phone: +1 (718) 499-2661

#408
Two Door Tavern
American, Bar, Breakfast & Brunch
Average price: Moderate
District: Williamsburg - North Side
Address: 116 N 5th St
Brooklyn, NY 11211
Phone: +1 (718) 599-0222

#409
Cubbyhole
Gay Bar
Average price: Moderate
District: West Village
Address: 281 W 12th St
New York, NY 10014
Phone: +1 (212) 243-9041

#410
Hot Bird
Pub
Average price: Inexpensive
District: Prospect Heights, Clinton Hill
Address: 546 Clinton Ave
Brooklyn, NY 11238
Phone: +1 (718) 230-5800

#411
Foley's NY
American, Pub
Average price: Moderate
District: Midtown West, Koreatown
Address: 18 W 33rd St
New York, NY 10001
Phone: +1 (212) 290-0080

#412
Mona's
Pub
Average price: Inexpensive
District: East Village, Alphabet City
Address: 224 Avenue B
New York, NY 10009
Phone: +1 (212) 353-3780

#413
Grassroots Tavern
Dive Bar
Average price: Inexpensive
District: East Village
Address: 20 St. Marks Pl
New York, NY 10003
Phone: +1 (212) 475-9443

#414
The Dove Parlour
Lounge, Wine Bar
Average price: Moderate
District: Greenwich Village
Address: 228 Thompson St
New York, NY 10012
Phone: +1 (212) 254-1435

#415
Clem's
Bar
Average price: Inexpensive
District: Williamsburg - South Side
Address: 264 Grand St
Brooklyn, NY 11211
Phone: +1 (718) 387-9617

#416
Vinus and Marc
Lounge
Average price: Moderate
District: Yorkville, Upper East Side
Address: 1825 Second Ave
New York, NY 10128
Phone: +1 (646) 692-9105

#417
Whitehall
American, Bar
Average price: Expensive
District: West Village
Address: 19 Greenwich Ave
New York, NY 10014
Phone: +1 (212) 675-7261

#418
**Charles Hanson's 169
Soul Jazz Oyster Bar**
American, Dive Bar
Average price: Inexpensive
District: Lower East Side
Address: 169 E Broadway
New York, NY 10002
Phone: +1 (212) 641-0357

#419
D.O.C. Wine Bar
Italian, Wine Bar
Average price: Expensive
District: Williamsburg - North Side
Address: 83 N 7th St
Brooklyn, NY 11211
Phone: +1 (718) 963-1925

#420
Pierre Loti Union Square
Wine Bar, Tapas Bar
Average price: Moderate
District: Union Square, Gramercy, Flatiron
Address: 53 Irving Pl
New York, NY 10003
Phone: +1 (212) 777-5684

#421
The Randolph at Broome
Coffee & Tea, Burgers, Cocktail Bar
Average price: Moderate
District: Little Italy, Nolita
Address: 349 Broome St
New York, NY 10013
Phone: +1 (212) 274-0667

#422
Toby's Public House
Pizza, Pub
Average price: Moderate
District: Little Italy, Nolita
Address: 86 Kenmare St
New York, NY 10012
Phone: +1 (212) 274-8629

#423
Entwine
Bar
Average price: Moderate
District: West Village
Address: 765 Washington St
New York, NY 10014
Phone: +1 (212) 727-8765

#424
Spritzenhaus
Bar
Average price: Moderate
District: Greenpoint
Address: 33 Nassau Ave
Brooklyn, NY 11222
Phone: +1 (347) 987-4632

#425
Camp
Bar
Average price: Moderate
District: Cobble Hill, Boerum Hill
Address: 179 Smith St
Brooklyn, NY 11201
Phone: +1 (718) 852-8086

#426
Hope Garage
American, Bar
Average price: Moderate
District: Williamsburg - North Side
Address: 163 Hope St
Brooklyn, NY 11211
Phone: +1 (718) 388-4626

#427
Pennsylvania 6 NYC
Bar, American
Average price: Expensive
District: Midtown West
Address: 132 W 31st St
New York, NY 10001
Phone: +1 (212) 727-3666

#428
Holland Bar
Dive Bar, Sport Bar
Average price: Inexpensive
District: Hell's Kitchen, Midtown West
Address: 532 Ninth Ave
New York, NY 10018
Phone: +1 (212) 502-4609

#429
High Dive
Dive Bar
Average price: Inexpensive
District: Park Slope
Address: 243 5th Ave
Brooklyn, NY 11215
Phone: +1 (718) 788-0401

#430
Tangled Vine
Mediterranean, Wine Bar
Average price: Moderate
District: Upper West Side
Address: 434 Amsterdam Ave
New York, NY 10024
Phone: +1 (646) 863-3896

#431
Von
Dance Club, Dive Bar
Average price: Moderate
District: NoHo
Address: 3 Bleecker St
New York, NY 10012
Phone: +1 (212) 473-3039

#432
Woody McHale's Bar & Grill
Bar
Average price: Moderate
District: Chelsea, West Village
Address: 234 W 14th St
New York, NY 10011
Phone: +1 (212) 206-0430

#433
Cherry Tavern
Dive Bar
Average price: Inexpensive
District: East Village, Alphabet City
Address: 441 E 6th St
New York, NY 10009
Phone: +1 (212) 777-1448

#434
Dempsey's Pub
Pub
Average price: Moderate
District: East Village
Address: 61 2nd Ave
New York, NY 10003
Phone: +1 (212) 388-0662

#435
Society Billiards + Bar
Pool Hall, Sport Bar
Average price: Moderate
District: Flatiron
Address: 10 E 21st St
New York, NY 10010
Phone: +1 (212) 420-1000

#436
The Growler Bites & Brews
Brewerie, Bar
Average price: Moderate
District: Financial District
Address: 55 Stone St
New York, NY 10004
Phone: +1 (917) 409-0251

#437
Bia
Bar, Vietnamese
Average price: Moderate
District: Williamsburg - South Side,
South Williamsburg
Address: 67 S 6th St
Brooklyn, NY 11211
Phone: +1 (718) 388-0908

#438
Richlane
Bar
Average price: Inexpensive
District: Williamsburg - North Side
Address: 595 Union Ave
Brooklyn, NY 11211
Phone: +1 (347) 422-0617

#439
Tea Lounge
Coffee & Tea, Bar
Average price: Inexpensive
District: Park Slope
Address: 837 Union St
Brooklyn, NY 11215
Phone: +1 (718) 789-2762

#440
Jeremy's Ale House
Dive Bar, Seafood
Average price: Inexpensive
District: South Street Seaport
Address: 228 Front St
New York, NY 10038
Phone: +1 (212) 964-3537

#441
Lovers of Today
Lounge
Average price: Moderate
District: East Village, Alphabet City
Address: 132 1/2 E 7th St
New York, NY 10009
Phone: +1 (212) 420-9517

#442
Fat Buddha
Bar, Asian Fusion, Korean
Average price: Moderate
District: East Village, Alphabet City
Address: 212 Ave A
New York, NY 10009
Phone: +1 (212) 598-0500

#443
Blackbird's
American, Pub
Average price: Moderate
District: Astoria
Address: 41-19 30th Ave
Astoria, NY 11103
Phone: +1 (718) 943-6899

#444
Crescent Lounge
Lounge
Average price: Moderate
District: Astoria
Address: 32-05 Crescent St
Astoria, NY 11106
Phone: +1 (718) 606-9705

#445
The Back Room
Lounge
Average price: Moderate
District: Lower East Side
Address: 102 Norfolk St
New York, NY 10002
Phone: +1 (212) 228-5098

#446
Peculier Pub
Pub, American
Average price: Inexpensive
District: Greenwich Village
Address: 145 Bleecker St
New York, NY 10012
Phone: +1 (212) 353-1327

#447
CK14 The Crooked Knife
Bar, Gastropub, American
Average price: Moderate
District: West Village
Address: 232 W 14th St
New York, NY 10011
Phone: +1 (212) 929-4534

#448
Copper Kettle Bar & Restaurant
Pub, Irish
Average price: Moderate
District: Woodside
Address: 5024 Skillman Ave
Woodside, NY 11377
Phone: +1 (718) 335-7596

#449
Buttermilk Bar
Bar
Average price: Inexpensive
District: South Slope
Address: 577 5th Ave
Brooklyn, NY 11215
Phone: +1 (718) 788-6297

#450
SOB's
Bar, Music Venue, Breakfast & Brunch
Average price: Moderate
District: South Village
Address: 204 Varick St
New York, NY 10014
Phone: +1 (212) 243-4940

#451
Sweetleaf
Lounge, Coffee & Tea
Average price: Moderate
District: Hunters Point
Address: 4615 Center Blvd
Long Island City, NY 11101
Phone: +1 (347) 527-1038

#452
South's Bar
Lounge, American
Average price: Moderate
District: TriBeCa
Address: 273 Church St
New York, NY 10013
Phone: +1 (212) 219-0640

#453
Temple Bar
Lounge, Tapas
Average price: Expensive
District: NoHo
Address: 332 Lafayette St
New York, NY 10012
Phone: +1 (212) 925-4242

#454
Rye House
Bar, American
Average price: Moderate
District: Flatiron
Address: 11 W 17th St
New York, NY 10011
Phone: +1 (212) 255-7260

#455
Evil Olive Pizza Bar
Bar, Pizza, Italian
Average price: Moderate
District: East Williamsburg
Address: 198 Union Ave
Brooklyn, NY 11211
Phone: +1 (718) 387-0707

#456
Mulholland's
Sport Bar
Average price: Moderate
District: Williamsburg - South Side
Address: 312 Grand St
Brooklyn, NY 11211
Phone: +1 (718) 486-3473

#457
Front Toward Enemy
American, Cocktail Bar
Average price: Moderate
District: Astoria
Address: 40-11 30th Avenue
Astoria, NY 11103
Phone: +1 (718) 545-2269

#458
Building On Bond
American, Pub
Average price: Moderate
District: Boerum Hill
Address: 112 Bond St
Brooklyn, NY 11217
Phone: +1 (347) 853-8687

#459
Tradesman
Bar
Average price: Moderate
District: East Williamsburg
Address: 222 Bushwick Ave
Brooklyn, NY 11206
Phone: +1 (718) 386-5300

#460
The Abbey Bar
Dive Bar, Beer, Wine & Spirits, Cocktail Bar
Average price: Inexpensive
District: Williamsburg - North Side
Address: 536 Driggs Ave
Brooklyn, NY 11211
Phone: +1 (718) 599-4400

#461
Merrion Square
Pub, Sport Bar, Dive Bar
Average price: Inexpensive
District: Yorkville, Upper East Side
Address: 1840 2nd Ave
New York, NY 10128
Phone: +1 (212) 831-7696

#462
Revision Lounge & Gallery
Lounge
Average price: Moderate
District: East Village, Alphabet City
Address: 219 Ave B
New York, NY 10009
Phone: +1 (646) 490-7271

#463
Piccolo Cafe
Italian, Cafe, Wine Bar
Average price: Moderate
District: Upper West Side
Address: 313 Amsterdam Ave
New York, NY 10023
Phone: +1 (212) 873-0962

#464
Drunken Munkey NYC
Indian, Cocktail Bar
Average price: Moderate
District: Yorkville, Upper East Side
Address: 338 E 92nd St
New York, NY 10128
Phone: +1 (646) 998-4600

#465
Snowdonia
Gastropub, Bar, American
Average price: Moderate
District: Astoria
Address: 34-55 32nd St
Astoria, NY 11106
Phone: +1 (347) 730-5783

#466
MikNic Lounge
Lounge
Average price: Inexpensive
District: Columbia Street Waterfront
Address: 200 Columbia St
Brooklyn, NY 11231
Phone: +1 (917) 770-1984

#467
Joe & MissesDoe
American, Bar
Average price: Moderate
District: East Village
Address: 45 E 1st St
New York, NY 10003
Phone: +1 (212) 780-0262

#468
The Boiler Room
Gay Bar
Average price: Inexpensive
District: East Village
Address: 86 E 4th St
New York, NY 10003
Phone: +1 (212) 254-7536

#469
Strong Place
Gastropub, Pub
Average price: Moderate
District: Cobble Hill
Address: 270 Court St
Brooklyn, NY 11231
Phone: +1 (718) 855-2105

#470
Shervins Cafe
Wine Bar, Cafe
Average price: Moderate
District: East Village, Alphabet City
Address: 131 E 7th St
New York, NY 10009
Phone: +1 (917) 596-1443

#471
12th Street Ale House
Bar
Average price: Inexpensive
District: East Village
Address: 192 2nd Ave
New York, NY 10003
Phone: +1 (212) 253-2323

#472
Venturo Osteria & Wine Bar
Italian, Wine Bar
Average price: Moderate
District: Sunnyside
Address: 44-07 Queens Blvd
Sunnyside, NY 11104
Phone: +1 (718) 406-9363

#473
Woodrow's
American, Pub
Average price: Moderate
District: TriBeCa
Address: 43 Murray St
New York, NY 10007
Phone: +1 (212) 676-0300

#474
The Globe
Pub
Average price: Moderate
District: Kips Bay, Gramercy
Address: 158 E 23rd St
New York, NY 10010
Phone: +1 (212) 477-6161

#475
Sophie's
Dive Bar
Average price: Inexpensive
District: East Village, Alphabet City
Address: 509 E 5th St
New York, NY 10003
Phone: +1 (212) 228-5680

#476
Metropolitan
Gay Bar
Average price: Inexpensive
District: Williamsburg - North Side
Address: 559 Lorimer St
Brooklyn, NY 11211
Phone: +1 (718) 599-4444

#477
The King Cole Bar And Salon
Lounge
Average price: Expensive
District: Midtown West, Midtown East
Address: 2 E 55th St
New York, NY 10022
Phone: +1 (212) 339-6857

#478
Pete's Waterfront Ale House
Pub, American
Average price: Moderate
District: Brooklyn Heights, Cobble Hill
Address: 155 Atlantic Ave
Brooklyn, NY 11201
Phone: +1 (718) 522-3794

#479
Crocodile Lounge
Lounge
Average price: Inexpensive
District: Gramercy, East Village
Address: 325 E 14th St
New York, NY 10003
Phone: +1 (212) 477-7747

#480
Inwood Local
Bar, Beer, Wine & Spirits
Average price: Moderate
District: Inwood
Address: 4957 Broadway
New York, NY 10034
Phone: +1 (212) 544-8900

#481
Banter Irish Bar and Kitchen
Pub, Irish, Breakfast & Brunch
Average price: Moderate
District: Forest Hills
Address: 108-22 Queens Blvd
Forest Hills, NY 11375
Phone: +1 (718) 268-8436

#482
5 Bar
Karaoke, Lounge, Sport Bar
Average price: Moderate
District: Midtown West, Koreatown
Address: 38 W 32 St
New York, NY 10016
Phone: +1 (212) 594-6644

#483
MASQ Restaurant & Lounge
Lounge, American
Average price: Moderate
District: Midtown East
Address: 306 E 49th St
New York, NY 10017
Phone: +1 (212) 644-8294

#484
Tracks Raw Bar & Grill
Pub, Seafood, Live/Raw Food, American
Average price: Moderate
District: Midtown West
Address: 1 Penn Plz
New York, NY 10119
Phone: +1 (212) 244-6350

#485
Glorietta Baldy
Bar
Average price: Moderate
District: Bedford Stuyvesant, Clinton Hill
Address: 502 Franklin Ave
Brooklyn, NY 11238
Phone: +1 (347) 529-1944

#486
Amity Hall
Burgers, Pub
Average price: Moderate
District: Greenwich Village
Address: 80 W 3rd St
New York, NY 10012
Phone: +1 (212) 677-2290

#487
Bonnie Vee
Cocktail Bar
Average price: Moderate
District: Lower East Side
Address: 17 Stanton St
New York, NY 10002
Phone: +1 (917) 639-3352

#488
No. 7
American, Bar
Average price: Moderate
District: Fort Greene
Address: 7 Greene Ave
Brooklyn, NY 11238
Phone: +1 (718) 522-6370

#489
Kettle of Fish
Bar
Average price: Moderate
District: West Village
Address: 59 Christopher St
New York, NY 10014
Phone: +1 (212) 414-2278

#490
Featherweight
Bar
Average price: Moderate
District: East Williamsburg
Address: 135 Graham Ave
Brooklyn, NY 11206
Phone: +1 (202) 907-3372

#491
O'Sullivan's Bar & Grill
Pub, American
Average price: Inexpensive
District: Fort Hamilton, Bay Ridge
Address: 8902 3rd Ave
Brooklyn, NY 11209
Phone: +1 (718) 745-9619

#492
Kings County
Dive Bar
Average price: Inexpensive
District: East Williamsburg
Address: 286 Seigel St
Brooklyn, NY 11206
Phone: +1 (718) 418-8823

#493
Triona's
Sport Bar, Irish Pub
Average price: Inexpensive
District: Greenwich Village
Address: 237 Sullivan St
New York, NY 10012
Phone: +1 (212) 982-5222

#494
Ryan Maguire's Ale House
Pub, American, Irish
Average price: Moderate
District: Financial District
Address: 28 Cliff St
New York, NY 10038
Phone: +1 (212) 566-6906

#495
The Patriot Saloon
Dive Bar
Average price: Inexpensive
District: TriBeCa
Address: 110 Chambers St
New York, NY 10007
Phone: +1 (212) 748-1162

#496
Barfly NY
Sport Bar, American
Average price: Moderate
District: Gramercy
Address: 244 3rd Ave
New York, NY 10010
Phone: +1 (212) 473-9660

#497
Cooper's Craft & Kitchen
Bar, American
Average price: Moderate
District: East Village
Address: 87 2nd Ave
New York, NY 10003
Phone: +1 (646) 606-2384

#498
Fish Bar
Restaurant, Bar
Average price: Inexpensive
District: East Village
Address: 237 E 5th St
New York, NY 10003
Phone: +1 (212) 475-4949

#499
Jacques 1534
Gastropub, Lounge, French
Average price: Moderate
District: Nolita
Address: 20 Prince St
New York, NY 10012
Phone: +1 (212) 966-8886

#500
Croxley's Abbey
Sport Bar, Chicken Wings,
Breakfast & Brunch
Average price: Moderate
District: Williamsburg - North Side
Address: 63 Grand St
Brooklyn, NY 11211
Phone: +1 (718) 387-4290

TOP 500 BARS & PUBS

Most Recommended by Locals & Trevelers
Ranking (from #1 to #500)

#1
Sunny's Bar
Bar
Average price: Inexpensive
District: Red Hook
Address: 253 Conover St
Brooklyn, NY 11231
Phone: +1 (718) 625-8211

#2
Bed-Vyne Wine
Beer, Wine & Spirits, Wine Bar,
Food Delivery Services
Average price: Moderate
District: Bedford Stuyvesant
Address: 370 Tompkins Ave
Brooklyn, NY 11216
Phone: +1 (347) 915-1080

#3
South
Bar
Average price: Inexpensive
District: South Slope
Address: 629 5th Ave
Brooklyn, NY 11215
Phone: +1 (718) 832-4720

#4
Angel's Share
Lounge, Cocktail Bar
Average price: Expensive
District: East Village
Address: 8 Stuyvesant St
New York, NY 10003
Phone: +1 (212) 777-5415

#5
Amor y Amargo
Cocktail Bar
Average price: Moderate
District: East Villagea, Alphabet City
Address: 443 E 6th St
New York, NY 10009
Phone: +1 (212) 614-6818

#6
Mosaic Cafe & Lounge
Wine Bar, Lounge,
Venue &Event Space
Average price: Moderate
District: Astoria
Address: 25-19 24th Ave
Astoria, NY 11102
Phone: +1 (718) 728-0708

#7
The Pony Bar
Bar
Average price: Moderate
District: Hell's Kitchen, Midtown West
Address: 637 10th Ave
New York, NY 10036
Phone: +1 (212) 586-2707

#8
Brooklyn Ice House
Barbeque, Pub
Average price: Inexpensive
District: Red Hook
Address: 318 Van Brunt St
Brooklyn, NY 11231
Phone: +1 (718) 222-1865

#9
Amélie
French, Wine Bar
Average price: Moderate
District: Greenwich Village
Address: 22 W 8th St
New York, NY 10011
Phone: +1 (212) 533-2962

#10
Whiskey Tavern
Pub
Average price: Moderate
District: Chinatown
Address: 79 Baxter St
New York, NY 10013
Phone: +1 (212) 374-9119

#11
Blue Ribbon Downing Street Bar
Lounge
Average price: Expensive
District: West Village
Address: 34 Downing St
New York, NY 10014
Phone: +1 (212) 691-0404

#12
Flatiron Room
Lounge, Jazz & Blues
Average price: Expensive
District: Flatiron
Address: 37 W 26th St
New York, NY 10010
Phone: +1 (212) 725-3860

#13
Caledonia Scottish Pub
Pub, Scottish
Average price: Moderate
District: Yorkville, Upper East Side
Address: 1609 2nd Ave
New York, NY 10028
Phone: +1 (212) 879-0402

#14
The Dead Rabbit
Grocery, Bar, American
Average price: Expensive
District: Financial District
Address: 30 Water St
New York, NY 10004
Phone: +1 (646) 422-7906

#15
Bergen Hill
Cocktail Bar, Seafood
Average price: Expensive
District: Carroll Gardens
Address: 387 Court St
Brooklyn, NY 11231
Phone: +1 (718) 858-5483

#16
Post Office
Bar, American
Average price: Moderate
District: Williamsburg - South Side
Address: 188 Havemeyer St
Brooklyn, NY 11211
Phone: +1 (718) 963-2574

#17
The Wayland
Bar
Average price: Moderate
District: East Villagea, Alphabet City
Address: 700 E 9th St
New York, NY 10009
Phone: +1 (212) 777-7022

#18
Little Branch
Lounge, Cocktail Bar
Average price: Expensive
District: West Village
Address: 22 7th Ave S
New York, NY 10014
Phone: +1 (212) 929-4360

#19
Burning Waters Cantina
Cocktail Bar
Average price: Moderate
District: Greenwich Village
Address: 116 MacDougal St
New York, NY 10012
Phone: +1 (646) 707-0078

#20
Dizzy's Club Coca Cola
Jazz & Blues
Average price: Expensive
District: Upper West Side
Address: 10 Columbus Cir
New York, NY 10019
Phone: +1 (212) 258-9595

#21
Distilled
American, Cocktail Bar
Average price: Expensive
District: TriBeCa
Address: 211 W Broadway
New York, NY 10013
Phone: +1 (212) 601-9514

#22
Spuyten Duyvil
Pub
Average price: Moderate
District: Williamsburg - North Side
Address: 359 Metropolitan Ave
Brooklyn, NY 11211
Phone: +1 (718) 963-4140

#23
The Jeffrey Craft Beer & Bites
Bar, Cafe
Average price: Moderate
District: Upper East Side
Address: 311 East 60th St
New York, NY 10022
Phone: +1 (212) 355-2337

#24
Vin Sur Vingt
Wine Bar, French
Average price: Expensive
District: West Village
Address: 201 W 11th St
New York, NY 10014
Phone: +1 (212) 924-4442

#25
The Pickle Shack
Bar, Vegetarian
Average price: Moderate
District: Park Slope, Gowanus
Address: 256 4th Ave
Brooklyn, NY 11215
Phone: +1 (347) 763-2127

#26
Blueprint
Cocktail Bar
Average price: Moderate
District: Park Slope
Address: 196 5th Ave
Brooklyn, NY 11217
Phone: +1 (718) 622-6644

#27
The Quays Pub
Pub
Average price: Inexpensive
District: Astoria
Address: 45-02 30th Ave
Astoria, NY 11103
Phone: +1 (718) 204-8435

#28
Blind Tiger Ale House
American, Pub
Average price: Moderate
District: West Village
Address: 281 Bleecker St
New York, NY 10014
Phone: +1 (212) 462-4682

#29
The Wayland
Bar
Average price: Moderate
District: East Villagea, Alphabet City
Address: 700 E 9th St
New York, NY 10009
Phone: +1 (212) 777-7022

#30
Barboncino
Pizza, Bar
Average price: Moderate
District: Crown Heights
Address: 781 Franklin Ave
Brooklyn, NY 11238
Phone: +1 (718) 483-8834

#31
Harlem Public
American, Pub
Average price: Moderate
District: Harlem
Address: 3612 Broadway
New York, NY 10031
Phone: +1 (212) 939-9404

#32
Village Vanguard
Music Venue, Jazz & Blues
Average price: Moderate
District: West Village
Address: 178 7th Ave S
New York, NY 10014
Phone: +1 (212) 255-4037

#33
Earl's Beer & Cheese
Bar, Comfort Food, Beer,
Wine & Spirits
Average price: Moderate
District: East Harlem
Address: 1259 Park Ave
New York, NY 10029
Phone: +1 (212) 289-1581

#34
Tip Top Bar & Grill
Dive Bar
Average price: Inexpensive
District: Bedford Stuyvesant, Clinton Hill
Address: 432 Franklin Ave
Brooklyn, NY 11238
Phone: +1 (718) 857-9744

#35
The Jeffrey Craft Beer & Bites
Bar, Cafe
Average price: Moderate
District: Upper East Side
Address: 311 East 60th St
New York, NY 10022
Phone: +1 (212) 355-2337

#36
Little Branch
Lounge, Cocktail Bar
Average price: Expensive
District: West Village
Address: 22 7th Ave S
New York, NY 10014
Phone: +1 (212) 929-4360

#37
Rudy's Bar & Grill
Dive Bar, Hot Dogs
Average price: Inexpensive
District: Hell's Kitchen,
Midtown West, Theater District
Address: 627 9th Ave
New York, NY 10036
Phone: +1 (646) 707-0890

#38
Burning Waters Cantina
Cocktail Bar
Average price: Moderate
District: Greenwich Village
Address: 116 MacDougal St
New York, NY 10012
Phone: +1 (646) 707-0078

#39
Spuyten Duyvil
Pub
Average price: Moderate
District: Williamsburg - North Side
Address: 359 Metropolitan Ave
Brooklyn, NY 11211
Phone: +1 (718) 963-4140

#40
Bemelmans Bar
Lounge
Average price: Exclusive
District: Upper East Side
Address: 35 E 76th St
New York, NY 10021
Phone: +1 (212) 744-1600

#41
The Pickle Shack
Bar, Vegetarian
Average price: Moderate
District: Park Slope, Gowanus
Address: 256 4th Ave
Brooklyn, NY 11215
Phone: +1 (347) 763-2127

#42
Distilled
American, Cocktail Bar
Average price: Expensive
District: TriBeCa
Address: 211 W Broadway
New York, NY 10013
Phone: +1 (212) 601-9514

#43
Blueprint
Cocktail Bar
Average price: Moderate
District: Park Slope
Address: 196 5th Ave
Brooklyn, NY 11217
Phone: +1 (718) 622-6644

#44
Vin Sur Vingt
Wine Bar, French
Average price: Expensive
District: West Village
Address: 201 W 11th St
New York, NY 10014
Phone: +1 (212) 924-4442

#45
ChikaLicious Dessert Bar
Desserts, Coffee & Tea, Wine Bar
Average price: Moderate
District: East Village
Address: 203 E 10th St
New York, NY 10003
Phone: +1 (212) 995-9511

#46
Graffiti Food & Wine Bar
American, Wine Bar
Average price: Expensive
District: East Village
Address: 224 E 10th St
New York, NY 10003
Phone: +1 (212) 677-0695

#47
Lulu's
Pizza, Dive Bar
Average price: Inexpensive
District: Greenpoint
Address: 113 Franklin St
Brooklyn, NY 11222
Phone: +1 (718) 383-6000

#48
Der Kommissar
Bar, Austrian
Average price: Moderate
District: South Slope, Park Slope
Address: 559 5th Ave
Brooklyn, NY 11215
Phone: +1 (718) 788-0789

#49
Dutch Kills
Lounge, Cocktail Bar
Average price: Moderate
District: Long Island City
Address: 27-24 Jackson Ave
Long Island City, NY 11101
Phone: +1 (718) 383-2724

#50
Duff's Brooklyn
Dive Bar
Average price: Inexpensive
District: Williamsburg - South Side
Address: 168 Marcy Ave
Brooklyn, NY 11211
Phone: +1 (718) 599-2092

#51
Black Mountain Wine House
Wine Bar
Average price: Moderate
District: Gowanus
Address: 415 Union St
Brooklyn, NY 11231
Phone: +1 (718) 522-4340

#52
Freddy's Bar
Bar
Average price: Inexpensive
District: South Slope
Address: 627 5th Ave
Brooklyn, NY 11215
Phone: +1 (718) 768-0131

#53
Blind Tiger Ale House
American, Pub
Average price: Moderate
District: West Village
Address: 281 Bleecker St
New York, NY 10014
Phone: +1 (212) 462-4682

#54
Hummus Place
Bar, American
Average price: Inexpensive
District: East Villagea, Alphabet City
Address: 109 St Marks Pl
New York, NY 10009
Phone: +1 (212) 529-9198

#55
2nd Floor on Clinton
Lounge
Average price: Expensive
District: Lower East Side
Address: 67 Clinton St
New York, NY 10002
Phone: +1 (212) 529-6900

#56
The Richardson
Bar
Average price: Moderate
District: Williamsburg - North Side
Address: 451 Graham Ave
Brooklyn, NY 11222
Phone: +1 (718) 389-0839

#57
South 4th Bar & Café
Coffee & Tea, Bar
Average price: Inexpensive
District: Williamsburg - South Side
Address: 90 S 4th St
Brooklyn, NY 11249
Phone: +1 (718) 218-7478

#58
Noorman's Kil
Bar, Sandwiches
Average price: Moderate
District: Williamsburg - North Side
Address: 609 Grand St
Brooklyn, NY 11211
Phone: +1 (347) 384-2526

#59
Ost Café
Coffee & Tea, Wine Bar
Average price: Inexpensive
District: East Villagea, Alphabet City
Address: 441 E 12th St
New York, NY 10009
Phone: +1 (212) 477-5600

#60
Desnuda
Seafood, Peruvian, Cocktail Bar
Average price: Expensive
District: Williamsburg - South Side
Address: 221 S 1st St
Brooklyn, NY 11211
Phone: +1 (718) 387-0563

#61
The Winslow
Bar
Average price: Moderate
District: Gramercy
Address: 243 E 14th St
New York, NY 10003
Phone: +1 (212) 777-7717

#62
Whynot Coffee & Wine
Cafe, Wine Bar
Average price: Moderate
District: West Village
Address: 14 Christopher St
New York, NY 10014
Phone: +1 (646) 756-4145

#63
Murray's Cheese Bar
Bar, American
Average price: Moderate
District: West Village
Address: 264 Bleecker St
New York, NY 10014
Phone: +1 (646) 476-8882

#64
Taqueria Lower East Side
Mexican, Bar
Average price: Inexpensive
District: Lower East Side
Address: 198 Orchard St
New York, NY 10002
Phone: +1 (212) 677-3910

#65
HunkOMania
Adult Entertainment
Average price: Expensive
District: Hell's Kitchen, Midtown West
Address: 301 W 39th St
New York, NY 10018
Phone: +1 (866) 872-4865

#66
In Vino
Wine Bar, Italian
Average price: Expensive
District: East Villagea, Alphabet City
Address: 215 E 4th St
New York, NY 10009
Phone: +1 (212) 539-1011

#67
Jadis
French, Wine Bar
Average price: Moderate
District: Lower East Side
Address: 42 Rivington St
New York, NY 10002
Phone: +1 (212) 254-1675

#68
Clover Club
Lounge, American
Average price: Expensive
District: Cobble Hill, Gowanus
Address: 210 Smith St
Brooklyn, NY 11201
Phone: +1 (718) 855-7939

#69
Brookvin
Wine Bar, Tapas Bar
Average price: Moderate
District: South Slope, Park Slope
Address: 381 7th Ave
Brooklyn, NY 11215
Phone: +1 (718) 768-9463

#70
Sake Bar Decibel
Bar, Japanese
Average price: Moderate
District: East Village
Address: 240 E 9th St
New York, NY 10003
Phone: +1 (212) 979-2733

#71
Beacon Theatre
Music Venue, Performing Arts
Average price: Expensive
District: Upper West Side
Address: 2124 Broadway
New York, NY 10023
Phone: +1 (212) 465-6500

#72
Elsa
Bar
Average price: Moderate
District: East Villagea, Alphabet City
Address: 217 E 3rd St
New York, NY 10009
Phone: +1 (917) 882-7395

#73
Sunita Bar
Lounge
Average price: Moderate
District: Lower East Side
Address: 106 Norfolk St
New York, NY 10002
Phone: +1 (212) 253-8860

#74
Domaine Wine Bar
Wine Bar, Jazz & Blues
Average price: Moderate
District: Hunters Point, Long Island City
Address: 50-04 Vernon Blvd
Long Island City, NY 11101
Phone: +1 (718) 784-2350

#75
Vintry Wine and Whiskey
Bar
Average price: Expensive
District: Financial District
Address: 57 Stone St
New York, NY 10004
Phone: +1 (212) 480-9800

#76
Hotel Delmano
Lounge
Average price: Expensive
District: Williamsburg - North Side
Address: 82 Berry St
Brooklyn, NY 11211
Phone: +1 (718) 387-1945

#77
The Bourgeois Pig
Lounge, Wine Bar
Average price: Moderate
District: East Villagea, Alphabet City
Address: 111 E 7th St
New York, NY 10009
Phone: +1 (212) 475-2246

#78
Proletariat
Bar
Average price: Moderate
District: East Villagea, Alphabet City
Address: 102 St Marks Pl
New York, NY 10009
Phone: +1 (212) 777-6707

#79
The Shakespeare
Pub, British
Average price: Expensive
District: Midtown East, Murray Hill
Address: 24 E 39th St
New York, NY 10016
Phone: +1 (646) 837-6779

#80
Sweet Afton
Bar, American
Average price: Moderate
District: Astoria
Address: 30-09 34th St
Astoria, NY 11103
Phone: +1 (718) 777-2570

#81
The Owl's Head
Wine Bar
Average price: Moderate
District: Bay Ridge
Address: 479 74th St
Brooklyn, NY 11209
Phone: +1 (718) 680-2436

#82
SriPraPhai Thai Restaurant
Thai, Bar
Average price: Moderate
District: Woodside
Address: 6413 39th Ave
Woodside, NY 11377
Phone: +1 (718) 899-9599

#83
Keuka Kafe a Wine Bar
American, Wine Bar
Average price: Moderate
District: Forest Hills
Address: 112-04 Queens Blvd
Forest Hills, NY 11375
Phone: +1 (718) 880-1478

#84
Crescent & Vine
Wine Bar
Average price: Moderate
District: Astoria
Address: 25-01 Ditmars Blvd
Astoria, NY 11105
Phone: +1 (718) 204-4774

#85
Magnet Theater
Comedy Club, Performing Arts,
Average price: Inexpensive
District: Chelsea, Midtown West
Address: 254 W 29th St
New York City, NY 10001
Phone: +1 (212) 244-8824

#86
Employees Only
American, Lounge
Average price: Expensive
District: West Village
Address: 510 Hudson St
New York, NY 10014
Phone: +1 (212) 242-3021

#87
The Immigrant
Wine Bar
Average price: Moderate
District: East Village
Address: 341 E 9th St
New York, NY 10003
Phone: +1 (646) 308-1724

#88
Brandy Library
American, Lounge, Wine Bar
Average price: Expensive
District: TriBeCa
Address: 25 N Moore St
New York, NY 10013
Phone: +1 (212) 226-5545

#89
Café Moto
Cafe, Bar
Average price: Moderate
District: Williamsburg - South Side,
South Williamsburg
Address: 394 Broadway
Brooklyn, NY 11211
Phone: +1 (718) 599-6895

#90
Wine Escape
Wine Bar
Average price: Moderate
District: Hell's Kitchen, Midtown West
Address: 405 W 44th St
New York, NY 10036
Phone: +1 (212) 262-7000

#91
Pouring Ribbons
Lounge, Cocktail Bar
Average price: Expensive
District: East Villagea, Alphabet City
Address: 225 Ave B
New York, NY 10009
Phone: +1 (917) 656-6788

#92
Black Crescent
Cocktail Bar
Average price: Moderate
District: Lower East Side
Address: 76 Clinton St
New York, NY 10002
Phone: +1 (212) 477-1771

#93
Atera
American, Lounge
Average price: Exclusive
District: Civic Center, TriBeCa
Address: 77 Worth St
New York, NY 10013
Phone: +1 (212) 226-1444

#94
Manitoba's
Bar
Average price: Inexpensive
District: East Villagea, Alphabet City
Address: 99 Ave B
New York, NY 10009
Phone: +1 (212) 982-2511

#95
Bill's Place
Jazz & Blues
Average price: Inexpensive
District: Harlem
Address: 148 W 133rd St
New York, NY 10030
Phone: +1 (212) 281-0777

#96
Sycamore
Bar, Florist, Music Venue
Average price: Moderate
District: Flatbush
Address: 1118 Cortelyou Rd
Brooklyn, NY 11218
Phone: +1 (347) 240-5850

#97
Watawa Sushi
Sushi Bar, Japanese, Wine Bar
Average price: Moderate
District: Astoria
Address: 33-10 Ditmars Blvd
Astoria, NY 11105
Phone: +1 (718) 545-9596

#98
The Diamond
Bar, Beer, Wine & Spirits
Average price: Moderate
District: Greenpoint
Address: 43 Franklin St
Brooklyn, NY 11222
Phone: +1 (718) 383-5030

#99
Death & Co
Lounge, Music Venue
Average price: Expensive
District: East Villagea, Alphabet City
Address: 433 E 6th St
New York, NY 10009
Phone: +1 (212) 388-0882

#100
Lock Yard
American, Hot Dogs, Pub
Average price: Moderate
District: Fort Hamilton, Bay Ridge
Address: 9221 5th Ave
Brooklyn, NY 11209
Phone: +1 (718) 333-5282

#101
Pegu Club
Lounge
Average price: Expensive
District: SoHo
Address: 77 W Houston St
New York, NY 10012
Phone: +1 (212) 473-7348

#102
124 Old Rabbit Club
Bar
Average price: Moderate
District: Greenwich Village
Address: 124 MacDougal St
New York, NY 10012
Phone: +1 (212) 254-0575

#103
Corkbuzz Wine Studio
Wine Bar, American
Average price: Expensive
District: Greenwich Village, Union Square
Address: 13 E 13 St
New York, NY 10003
Phone: +1 (646) 873-6071

#104
Los Perros Locos
Hot Dogs, Colombian
Average price: Inexpensive
District: Lower East Side
Address: 201 Allen St
New York, NY 10002
Phone: +1 (212) 473-1200

#105
Jacob's Pickles
American, Bar
Average price: Moderate
District: Upper West Side
Address: 509 Amsterdam Ave
New York, NY 10024
Phone: +1 (212) 470-5566

#106
Baby Grand
Karaoke, Lounge
Average price: Moderate
District: SoHo
Address: 161 Lafayette St
New York, NY 10013
Phone: +1 (212) 219-8110

#107
Brooklyn Star
Southern, Bar
Average price: Moderate
District: Williamsburg - North Side
Address: 593 Lorimer St
Brooklyn, NY 11211
Phone: +1 (718) 599-9899

#108
La Pulperia
Latin American, Seafood, Bar
Average price: Expensive
District: Hell's Kitchen,
Midtown West, Theater District
Address: 371 W 46 St
New York, NY 10036
Phone: +1 (212) 956-3055

#109
BAM Café
Lounge, Music Venue
Average price: Moderate
District: Fort Greene
Address: 30 Lafayette Ave
Brooklyn, NY 11217
Phone: +1 (718) 623-7811

#110
8th Street Wine Cellar
Wine Bar
Average price: Moderate
District: Greenwich Village
Address: 28 W 8th St
New York, NY 10011
Phone: +1 (212) 260-9463

#111
Barcade
Bar, Arcade, Do-It-Yourself Food
Average price: Moderate
District: Williamsburg - North Side
Address: 388 Union Ave
Brooklyn, NY 11224
Phone: +1 (718) 302-6464

#112
Diamante's Brooklyn Cigar Lounge
Tobacco Shop, Lounge
Average price: Moderate
District: Fort Greene
Address: 108 S Oxford St
Brooklyn, NY 11217
Phone: +1 (646) 462-3876

#113
The Levee
American, Bar
Average price: Inexpensive
District: Williamsburg - North Side
Address: 212 Berry St
Brooklyn, NY 11211
Phone: +1 (718) 218-8787

#114
The Bar Room at The Modern
Lounge, French
Average price: Expensive
District: Midtown West
Address: 9 W 53rd St
New York, NY 10019
Phone: +1 (212) 333-1220

#115
Lobster Joint
Sport Bar, Seafood
Average price: Moderate
District: Lower East Side
Address: 201 E Houston St
New York, NY 10002
Phone: +1 (646) 896-1110

#116
Prima
Seafood, Bar
Average price: Expensive
District: East Village
Address: 58 East 1 St
New York, NY 10003
Phone: +1 (646) 559-4823

#117
Ryan's Daughter
Pub, American
Average price: Moderate
District: Yorkville, Upper East Side
Address: 350 E 85th St
New York, NY 10028
Phone: +1 (212) 628-2613

#118
Sofia Wine Bar & Cafe
Italian, Wine Bar
Average price: Moderate
District: Midtown East
Address: 242 E 50th St
New York, NY 10022
Phone: +1 (212) 888-8660

#119
Zum Schneider
Pub, German
Average price: Moderate
District: East Villagea, Alphabet City
Address: 107 Ave C
New York, NY 10009
Phone: +1 (212) 598-1098

#120
Terroir Wine Bar
Wine Bar, American
Average price: Moderate
District: East Village
Address: 413 E 12th St
New York, NY 10009
Phone: +1 (646) 602-1300

#121
The Habitat
Pub
Average price: Moderate
District: Greenpoint
Address: 988 Manhattan Ave
Brooklyn, NY 11222
Phone: +1 (718) 383-5615

#122
Pata Negra
Tapas Bar, Wine Bar, Spanish
Average price: Moderate
District: East Village
Address: 345 E 12th St
New York, NY 10003
Phone: +1 (212) 228-1696

#123
Royale
Burgers, Bar
Average price: Inexpensive
District: East Villagea, Alphabet City
Address: 157 Ave C
New York, NY 10009
Phone: +1 (212) 254-6600

#124
Maraya
Tobacco Shop, Lounge
Average price: Moderate
District: Lower East Side
Address: 87 Orchard St
New York, NY 10002
Phone: +1 (212) 334-3499

#125
Verlaine
Tapas, Small Plates, Lounge
Average price: Moderate
District: Lower East Side
Address: 110 Rivington St
New York, NY 10002
Phone: +1 (212) 614-2494

#126
Beer Culture
Beer, Wine & Spirits, Bar
Average price: Moderate
District: Hell's Kitchen,
Midtown West, Theater District
Address: 328 W 45th St
New York, NY 10036
Phone: +1 (646) 590-2139

#127
The Shanty
Bar
Average price: Moderate
District: Williamsburg - North Side
Address: 79 Richardson St
Brooklyn, NY 11211
Phone: +1 (718) 412-0874

#128
Radegast Hall and Biergarten
Pub, German
Average price: Moderate
District: Williamsburg - North Side
Address: 113 N 3rd St
Brooklyn, NY 11249
Phone: +1 (718) 963-3973

#129
B Flat
Lounge, Jazz & Blues
Average price: Moderate
District: TriBeCa
Address: 277 Church St
New York, NY 10013
Phone: +1 (212) 219-2970

#130
Culturefix
Art Gallery, Bar
Average price: Moderate
District: Lower East Side
Address: 9 Clinton St
New York, NY 10002
Phone: +1 (646) 863-7171

#131
Cask Bar + Kitchen
Bar, American, Seafood
Average price: Moderate
District: Midtown East, Murray Hill
Address: 167 E 33rd St
New York, NY 10016
Phone: +1 (212) 300-4924

#132
TØRST
Pub
Average price: Expensive
District: Greenpoint
Address: 615 Manhattan Ave
Brooklyn, NY 11222
Phone: +1 (718) 389-6034

#133
Khe-Yo
Laotian, Wine Bar
Average price: Expensive
District: TriBeCa
Address: 157 Duane St
New York, NY 10013
Phone: +1 (212) 587-1089

#134
Freemans Restaurant
Breakfast & Brunch, American, Lounge
Average price: Expensive
District: Lower East Side
Address: 8 Rivington St
New York, NY 10002
Phone: +1 (212) 420-0012

#135
The Anchored Inn
Bar, American
Average price: Moderate
District: East Williamsburg
Address: 57 Waterbury St
Brooklyn, NY 11206
Phone: +1 (718) 576-3297

#136
Windy City Ale House
Sport Bar, American
Average price: Moderate
District: Bay Ridge
Address: 7915 3rd Ave
Brooklyn, NY 11209
Phone: +1 (718) 630-5700

#137
Greenpoint Heights
Bar, American
Average price: Moderate
District: Greenpoint
Address: 278 Nassau Ave
Brooklyn, NY 11222
Phone: +1 (718) 389-0110

#138
The Stanton Social
Tapas, Small Plates, Bar
Average price: Expensive
District: Lower East Side
Address: 99 Stanton St
New York, NY 10002
Phone: +1 (212) 995-0099

#139
Jazz Standard
Jazz & Blues, Barbeque
Average price: Expensive
District: Flatiron
Address: 116 E 27th St
New York, NY 10016
Phone: +1 (212) 576-2232

#140
The Castello Plan
Bar, American
Average price: Moderate
District: Flatbush
Address: 1213 Cortelyou Rd
Brooklyn, NY 11218
Phone: +1 (718) 856-8888

#141
Cronin & Phelan's
Pub, American
Average price: Moderate
District: Astoria
Address: 38-14 Broadway
Astoria, NY 11102
Phone: +1 (718) 545-8999

#142
Station House
Pub, American, Gastropub
Average price: Moderate
District: Forest Hills
Address: 106-11 71st Ave
Forest Hills, NY 11375
Phone: +1 (718) 544-5000

#143
Barrio Chino
Mexican, Bar
Average price: Moderate
District: Lower East Side
Address: 253 Broome St
New York, NY 10002
Phone: +1 (212) 228-6710

#144
Print
American, Lounge
Average price: Expensive
District: Hell's Kitchen, Midtown West
Address: 653 11th Ave
New York, NY 10036
Phone: +1 (212) 757-2224

#145
Karaoke Duet 35
Karaoke, Music Venue
Average price: Moderate
District: Midtown West
Address: 53 W 35th St
New York, NY 10001
Phone: +1 (646) 473-0826

#146
SakaMai
Japanese, Lounge
Average price: Expensive
District: Lower East Side
Address: 157 Ludlow St
New York, NY 10002
Phone: +1 (646) 590-0684

#147
Keybar
Lounge, Pub
Average price: Inexpensive
District: East Villagea, Alphabet City
Address: 432 E 13th St
New York, NY 10009
Phone: +1 (212) 478-3021

#148
Lelabar
Wine Bar, Lounge
Average price: Moderate
District: West Village
Address: 422 Hudson St
New York, NY 10014
Phone: +1 (212) 206-0594

#149
Pete's Candy Store
Music Venue, Dive Bar, Pub
Average price: Inexpensive
District: Williamsburg - North Side
Address: 709 Lorimer St
Brooklyn, NY 11211
Phone: +1 (718) 302-3770

#150
Fat Cat
Pool Hall, Jazz & Blues,
Music Venue
Average price: Inexpensive
District: West Village
Address: 75 Christopher St
New York, NY 10014
Phone: +1 (212) 675-6056

#151
Kaia Wine Bar
Wine Bar
Average price: Moderate
District: Yorkville, Upper East Side
Address: 1614 3rd Ave
New York, NY 10128
Phone: +1 (212) 722-0490

#152
Birdland
Jazz & Blues, Cajun/Creole, Southern
Average price: Expensive
District: Hell's Kitchen,
Midtown West, Theater District
Address: 315 W 44th St
New York, NY 10036
Phone: +1 (212) 581-3080

#153
Circa Tabac
Lounge, Cocktail Bar,
Tobacco Shop
Average price: Moderate
District: South Village
Address: 32 Watts St
New York, NY 10013
Phone: +1 (212) 941-1781

#154
Two 8 Two
Burgers, Bar
Average price: Moderate
District: Cobble Hill, Boerum Hill
Address: 282 Atlantic Ave
Brooklyn, NY 11201
Phone: +1 (718) 596-2282

#155
Turntable Mad for Chicken
Chicken Wings, Lounge
Average price: Moderate
District: Midtown West, Koreatown
Address: 314 5th Ave
New York, NY 10001
Phone: +1 (212) 714-9700

#156
Huckleberry Bar
Bar, American
Average price: Moderate
District: East Williamsburg
Address: 588 Grand St
Brooklyn, NY 11211
Phone: +1 (718) 218-8555

#157
Marshall Stack
Bar
Average price: Moderate
District: Lower East Side
Address: 66 Rivington St
New York, NY 10002
Phone: +1 (212) 228-4667

#158
Ear Inn
Bar, American
Average price: Moderate
District: South Village
Address: 326 Spring St
New York, NY 10013
Phone: +1 (212) 226-9060

#159
The Room
Lounge, Wine Bar
Average price: Moderate
District: South Village
Address: 144 Sullivan St
New York, NY 10012
Phone: +1 (212) 477-2102

#160
Aroma Kitchen & Winebar
Italian, Wine Bar
Average price: Expensive
District: NoHo
Address: 36 E 4th St
New York, NY 10003
Phone: +1 (212) 375-0100

#161
Flatiron Lounge
Lounge
Average price: Expensive
District: Flatiron
Address: 37 W 19th St
New York, NY 10011
Phone: +1 (212) 727-7741

#162
Lucky 13 Saloon
Bar
Average price: Inexpensive
District: South Slope, Park Slope
Address: 273 13th St
Brooklyn, NY 11215
Phone: +1 (718) 499-7553

#163
The Sackett
Bar
Average price: Moderate
District: Park Slope, Gowanus
Address: 661 Sackett St
Brooklyn, NY 11217
Phone: +1 (718) 622-0437

#164
Do or Dine
Bar, American, Breakfast & Brunch
Average price: Moderate
District: Bedford Stuyvesant
Address: 1108 Bedford Ave
Brooklyn, NY 11216
Phone: +1 (718) 684-2290

#165
Karaoke DUET 48
Karaoke
Average price: Moderate
District: Midtown East
Address: 304 E 48th St
New York, NY 10017
Phone: +1 (212) 753-0030

#166
Inwood Local
Bar, Beer, Wine & Spirits
Average price: Moderate
District: Inwood
Address: 4957 Broadway
New York, NY 10034
Phone: +1 (212) 544-8900

#167
Kristophe
Comfort Food, Bar, American
Average price: Moderate
District: Williamsburg - North Side
Address: 221 N 4th St
Brooklyn, NY 11211
Phone: +1 (718) 302-5100

#168
Matt Torrey's
Bar
Average price: Moderate
District: East Williamsburg
Address: 46 Bushwick Ave
Brooklyn, NY 11211
Phone: +1 (718) 218-7646

#169
Cull & Pistol Oyster Bar
Seafood, Wine Bar
Average price: Expensive
District: Chelsea, Meatpacking District
Address: 75 Ninth Ave
New York, NY 10011
Phone: +1 (646) 568-1223

#170
Russian Vodka Room
Lounge, Russian, Jazz & Blues
Average price: Moderate
District: Midtown West, Theater District
Address: 265 W 52nd St
New York, NY 10019
Phone: +1 (212) 307-5835

#171
Ward III
American, Lounge
Average price: Moderate
District: TriBeCa
Address: 111 Reade St
New York, NY 10013
Phone: +1 (212) 240-9194

#172
Bua
Bar
Average price: Moderate
District: East Villagea, Alphabet City
Address: 122 St Marks Pl
New York, NY 10009
Phone: +1 (212) 979-6276

#173
The Bell House
Music Venue, Lounge
Average price: Moderate
District: Gowanus
Address: 149 7th St
Brooklyn, NY 11215
Phone: +1 (718) 643-6510

#174
The Pony Bar
Bar
Average price: Moderate
District: Yorkville, Upper East Side
Address: 1444 1st Ave
New York, NY 10021
Phone: +1 (212) 288-0090

#175
Brooklyn Winery
Wineries, Wine Bar,
Venue &Event Space
Average price: Moderate
District: Williamsburg - North Side
Address: 213 N 8th St
Brooklyn, NY 11211
Phone: +1 (347) 763-1506

#176
Pravda
Lounge, Cocktail Bar
Average price: Expensive
District: Nolita
Address: 281 Lafayette St
New York, NY 10012
Phone: +1 (212) 226-4944

#177
The Bodega
Pub, Breakfast & Brunch
Average price: Moderate
District: Bushwick
Address: 24 St. Nicholas Ave
Brooklyn, NY 11237
Phone: +1 (347) 305-3344

#178
**The Cellar at Beecher's
Handmade Cheese**
Wine Bar, American, American
Average price: Moderate
District: Flatiron
Address: 900 Broadway
New York, NY 10003
Phone: +1 (212) 466-3340

#179
Dram
Cocktail Bar
Average price: Moderate
District: Williamsburg - South Side
Address: 177 S 4th St
Brooklyn, NY 11211
Phone: +1 (718) 486-3726

#180
George Keeley's
Pub, American, Sport Bar
Average price: Moderate
District: Upper West Side
Address: 485 Amsterdam Ave
New York, NY 10024
Phone: +1 (212) 873-0251

#181
Full Circle Bar
Bar
Average price: Inexpensive
District: Williamsburg - South Side
Address: 318 Grand St
Brooklyn, NY 11211
Phone: +1 (347) 725-4588

#182
Ten Degrees Bar
Wine Bar, Gastropub
Average price: Moderate
District: East Villagea, Alphabet City
Address: 121 St. Marks Pl
New York, NY 10009
Phone: +1 (212) 358-8600

#183
Apothéke
Lounge, Cocktail Bar
Average price: Expensive
District: Chinatown, Civic Center
Address: 9 Doyers St
New York, NY 10013
Phone: +1 (212) 406-0400

#184
DTUT
Bar, Cafe
Average price: Inexpensive
District: Yorkville, Upper East Side
Address: 1744 2nd Ave
New York, NY 10128
Phone: +1 (212) 410-6449

#185
Toby's Public House
Pizza, Bar
Average price: Moderate
District: South Slope
Address: 686 6th Ave
Brooklyn, NY 11215
Phone: +1 (718) 788-1186

#186
Dirty Pierre's
Pub, Burgers
Average price: Moderate
District: Forest Hills
Address: 13 Station Sq
Forest Hills, NY 11375
Phone: +1 (718) 830-9698

#187
Middle Branch
Bar
Average price: Moderate
District: Midtown East, Murray Hill
Address: 154 E 33rd St
New York, NY 10016
Phone: +1 (212) 213-1350

#188
The Owl Farm
Pub
Average price: Moderate
District: Park Slope, Gowanus
Address: 297 9th St
Brooklyn, NY 11215
Phone: +1 (718) 499-4988

#189
Vetro by Russo's on the Bay
Italian, Lounge
Average price: Expensive
District: Howard Beach
Address: 164-49 Crossbay Blvd
Howard Beach, NY 11414
Phone: +1 (718) 843-8387

#190
Le Bateau Ivre
French, Wine Bar
Average price: Expensive
District: Midtown East
Address: 230 E 51st St
New York, NY 10022
Phone: +1 (212) 583-0579

#191
Ed's Lobster Bar
Bar
Average price: Expensive
District: SoHo
Address: 222 Lafayette St
New York, NY 10012
Phone: +1 (212) 343-3236

#192
Miriam
Wine Bar, Mediterranean,
Breakfast & Brunch
Average price: Moderate
District: Park Slope
Address: 79 5th Ave
Brooklyn, NY 11215
Phone: +1 (718) 622-2250

#193
Sweet Revenge
Desserts, Wine Bar
Average price: Moderate
District: West Village
Address: 62 Carmine St
New York, NY 10014
Phone: +1 (212) 242-2240

#194
Pacific Standard Brooklyn
Bar
Average price: Inexpensive
District: Park Slope, Gowanus
Address: 82 4th Ave
Brooklyn, NY 11217
Phone: +1 (718) 858-1951

#195
The Ginger Man
Bar, Brewerie
Average price: Moderate
District: Midtown East
Address: 11 E 36th St
New York, NY 10016
Phone: +1 (212) 532-3740

#196
The Otheroom
Lounge, Wine Bar, American
Average price: Moderate
District: West Village
Address: 143 Perry St
New York, NY 10014
Phone: +1 (212) 645-9758

#197
Ardesia
Wine Bar, Tapas, Small Plates
Average price: Moderate
District: Hell's Kitchen, Midtown West
Address: 510 W 52nd St
New York, NY 10019
Phone: +1 (212) 247-9191

#198
Please Don't Tell
Lounge
Average price: Expensive
District: East Villagea, Alphabet City
Address: 113 St. Marks Pl
New York, NY 10009
Phone: +1 (212) 614-0386

#199
The Campbell Apartment
Lounge
Average price: Expensive
District: Midtown East
Address: 15 Vanderbilt Ave
New York, NY 10017
Phone: +1 (212) 953-0409

#200
Minibar
Wine Bar, Lounge
Average price: Moderate
District: Carroll Gardens
Address: 482 Court St
Brooklyn, NY 11231
Phone: +1 (718) 569-2321

#201
Bowery Poetry Club
Performing Arts, Music Venue
Average price: Inexpensive
District: NoHo
Address: 308 Bowery
New York, NY 10012
Phone: +1 (212) 614-0505

#202
Weather Up
Bar
Average price: Moderate
District: Prospect Heights
Address: 589 Vanderbilt Ave
Brooklyn, NY 11226
Phone: +1 (212) 766-3202

#203
Don's Bogam
Korean, Barbeque, Wine Bar
Average price: Expensive
District: Midtown East
Address: 17 E 32nd St
New York, NY 10016
Phone: +1 (212) 683-2200

#204
Shoolbred's
Lounge
Average price: Moderate
District: East Village
Address: 197 2nd Ave
New York, NY 10003
Phone: +1 (212) 529-0340

#205
Gottino
Wine Bar, Italian
Average price: Moderate
District: West Village
Address: 52 Greenwich Ave
New York, NY 10011
Phone: +1 (212) 633-2590

#206
Beloved
Cocktail Bar
Average price: Moderate
District: Greenpoint
Address: 674 Manhattan Ave
Brooklyn, NY 11222
Phone: +1 (347) 457-5448

#207
Karaoke Duet 53
Karaoke
Average price: Moderate
District: Midtown West, Theater District
Address: 900 8th Ave
New York, NY 10019
Phone: +1 (212) 757-4676

#208
Laughing Devil Comedy Club
Comedy Club
Average price: Moderate
District: Hunters Point, Long Island City
Address: 4738 Vernon Blvd
Long Island City, NY 11101
Phone: +1 (347) 913-3845

#209
Wheated
Pizza, Vegan, Cocktail Bar
Average price: Moderate
District: Flatbush
Address: 905 Church Ave
Brooklyn, NY 11218
Phone: +1 (347) 240-2813

#210
Milk And Roses
Coffee & Tea, Wine Bar, Italian
Average price: Moderate
District: Greenpoint
Address: 1110 Manhattan Ave
Brooklyn, NY 11222
Phone: +1 (718) 389-0160

#211
Via Trenta Osteria & Wine Bar
Italian, Wine Bar, Pizza
Average price: Moderate
District: Astoria
Address: 36-19 30th Ave
Astoria, NY 11103
Phone: +1 (718) 545-2090

#212
Harefield Road
Bar, Breakfast & Brunch
Average price: Moderate
District: East Williamsburg
Address: 769 Metropolitan Ave
Brooklyn, NY 11211
Phone: +1 (718) 388-6870

#213
Idle Hands Bar
Bar, American
Average price: Moderate
District: East Villagea, Alphabet City
Address: 25 Ave B
New York, NY 10009
Phone: +1 (917) 338-7090

#214
The Way Station
Bar, Music Venue
Average price: Moderate
District: Crown Heights, Prospect Heights
Address: 683 Washington Ave
Brooklyn, NY 11238
Phone: +1 (347) 627-4949

#215
Bondurants
Cocktail Bar, American, Gastropub
Average price: Moderate
District: Yorkville, Upper East Side
Address: 303 E 85th St
New York, NY 10028
Phone: +1 (212) 249-1509

#216
Sorella
Italian, Wine Bar
Average price: Expensive
District: Lower East Side
Address: 95 Allen St
New York, NY 10002
Phone: +1 (212) 274-9595

#217
The Jakewalk
Wine Bar, Fondue
Average price: Moderate
District: Carroll Gardens, Gowanus
Address: 282 Smith St
Brooklyn, NY 11231
Phone: +1 (347) 599-0294

#218
Bijan's
Bar, American
Average price: Moderate
District: Downtown
Brooklyn, Boerum Hill
Address: 81 Hoyt St
Brooklyn, NY 11201
Phone: +1 (718) 855-5574

#219
Sunswick
Bar, American
Average price: Moderate
District: Astoria
Address: 3502 35th St
Astoria, NY 11106
Phone: +1 (718) 752-0620

#220
Maracuja Bar & Grill
Lounge
Average price: Inexpensive
District: Williamsburg - North Side
Address: 279 Grand St
Brooklyn, NY 11211
Phone: +1 (718) 302-9023

#221
Brooklyn Bowl
Bowling, Music Venue, American
Average price: Moderate
District: Williamsburg - North Side
Address: 61 Wythe Ave
Brooklyn, NY 11211
Phone: +1 (718) 963-3369

#222
Zampa
Italian, Wine Bar, Tapas Bar
Average price: Expensive
District: West Village
Address: 306 W 13th St
New York, NY 10014
Phone: +1 (212) 206-0601

#223
Finnerty's
Pub, Sport Bar
Average price: Inexpensive
District: East Village
Address: 221 2nd Ave
New York, NY 10003
Phone: +1 (212) 677-2655

#224
Mission Dolores Bar
Bar
Average price: Moderate
District: Park Slope, Gowanus
Address: 249 4th Ave
Brooklyn, NY 11215
Phone: +1 (347) 457-5606

#225
Uncle Barry's
Pub
Average price: Inexpensive
District: Park Slope
Address: 58 5th Ave
Brooklyn, NY 11217
Phone: +1 (718) 622-4980

#226
Petite Abeille .
Breakfast & Brunch, Belgian, Bar
Average price: Moderate
District: Flatiron
Address: 44 W 17th St
New York, NY 10011
Phone: +1 (212) 727-2989

#227
Little Zelda
Coffee & Tea, Wine Bar
Average price: Moderate
District: Crown Heights
Address: 728 Franklin Ave
New York, NY 11238
Phone: +1 (917) 499-3244

#228
The Village Underground
Dance Club, Lounge
Average price: Moderate
District: Greenwich Village
Address: 130 W 3rd St
New York, NY 10012
Phone: +1 (212) 777-7745

#229
Vbar
Wine Bar, American
Average price: Moderate
District: Greenwich Village
Address: 225 Sullivan St
New York, NY 10012
Phone: +1 (212) 253-5740

#230
Shalel Lounge
Lounge, Moroccan
Average price: Moderate
District: Upper West Side
Address: 65 W 70th St
New York, NY 10023
Phone: +1 (212) 873-2300

#231
Trinity Pub
Pub
Average price: Moderate
District: Yorkville, Upper East Side
Address: 229 E 84th St
New York, NY 10028
Phone: +1 (212) 327-4450

#232
Jack & Nellie's
American, Wine Bar,
Breakfast & Brunch
Average price: Moderate
District: Forest Hills
Address: 108-25 Ascan Ave
Forest Hills, NY 11375
Phone: +1 (718) 268-2696

#233
The Auction House
Lounge
Average price: Moderate
District: Yorkville, Upper East Side
Address: 300 E 89th St
New York, NY 10128
Phone: +1 (212) 427-4458

#234
Boulevard Tavern
Pub
Average price: Inexpensive
District: Greenpoint
Address: 579 Meeker Ave
Brooklyn, NY 11222
Phone: +1 (718) 389-3252

#235
Grape and Grain
Wine Bar, American
Average price: Moderate
District: East Villagea, Alphabet City
Address: 620 E 6th St
New York, NY 10009
Phone: +1 (212) 420-0002

#236
Subject
Cocktail Bar
Average price: Moderate
District: Lower East Side
Address: 188 Suffolk St
New York, NY 10002
Phone: +1 (646) 422-7898

#237
Vol de Nuit
Lounge, American
Average price: Moderate
District: Greenwich Village
Address: 148 W 4th St
New York, NY 10012
Phone: +1 (212) 982-3388

#238
Red Hook Bait & Tackle
Dive Bar
Average price: Inexpensive
District: Red Hook
Address: 320 Van Brunt St
Brooklyn, NY 11231
Phone: +1 (718) 797-4892

#239
The Redhead
American, Bar
Average price: Moderate
District: East Village
Address: 349 E 13th St
New York, NY 10003
Phone: +1 (212) 533-6212

#240
Shade
Bar, American, Crêperie
Average price: Moderate
District: Greenwich Village
Address: 241 Sullivan St
New York, NY 10012
Phone: +1 (212) 982-6275

#241
Sanford's Restaurant
American, Breakfast & Brunch, Bar
Average price: Moderate
District: Astoria
Address: 30-13 Broadway
Astoria, NY 11106
Phone: +1 (718) 932-9569

#242
Jimmy's Corner
Pub, Sport Bar, Dive Bar
Average price: Inexpensive
District: Midtown West, Theater District
Address: 140 W 44th St
New York, NY 10036
Phone: +1 (212) 221-9510

#243
Char No. 4
Bar, Southern
Average price: Expensive
District: Cobble Hill, Gowanus
Address: 196 Smith St
Brooklyn, NY 11201
Phone: +1 (718) 643-2106

#244
The Narrows
Bar, American
Average price: Moderate
District: East Williamsburg, Bushwick
Address: 1037 Flushing Ave
Brooklyn, NY 11237
Phone: +1 (281) 827-1800

#245
Molly Blooms
Irish, Pub
Average price: Moderate
District: Sunnyside
Address: 43-13 Queens Blvd
Sunnyside, NY 11104
Phone: +1 (718) 433-1916

#246
Wine:30
Wine Bar, American
Average price: Moderate
District: Midtown East
Address: 41 E 30th St
New York, NY 10016
Phone: +1 (212) 481-0197

#247
Bohemian Hall & Beer Garden
Pub, Music Venue, Czech
Average price: Moderate
District: Astoria
Address: 2919 24th Ave
Astoria, NY 11102
Phone: +1 (718) 274-4925

#248
Alphabet City Beer Company
Bar, Beer, Wine & Spirits
Average price: Moderate
District: East Villagea, Alphabet City
Address: 96 Ave C
New York, NY 10009
Phone: +1 (646) 422-7103

#249
Clandestino
Wine Bar
Average price: Moderate
District: Chinatown, Lower East Side
Address: 35 Canal St
New York, NY 10002
Phone: +1 (212) 475-5505

#250
The Double Windsor
Pub, Gastropub
Average price: Moderate
District: South Slope, Windsor Terrace
Address: 210 Prospect Park W
Brooklyn, NY 11215
Phone: +1 (347) 725-3479

#251
Jones Wood Foundry
British, Pub, Gastropub
Average price: Moderate
District: Yorkville, Upper East Side
Address: 401 E 76th St
New York, NY 10021
Phone: +1 (212) 249-2700

#252
The Bar Downstairs
Lounge
Average price: Expensive
District: Midtown East
Address: 485 5th Ave
New York, NY 10017
Phone: +1 (212) 601-1234

#253
Woodwork
Sport Bar, Gastropub, Beer,
Wine & Spirits
Average price: Moderate
District: Prospect Heights
Address: 583 Vanderbilt Ave
Brooklyn, NY 11238
Phone: +1 (718) 857-5777

#254
Uvarara
Italian, Wine Bar
Average price: Expensive
District: Middle Village
Address: 79-28 Metropolitan Ave
Middle Village, NY 11379
Phone: +1 (718) 894-0052

#255
The Whiskey Ward
Bar
Average price: Moderate
District: Lower East Side
Address: 121 Essex St
New York, NY 10002
Phone: +1 (212) 477-2998

#256
Lighthouse
Bar, Modern European, American
Average price: Moderate
District: Williamsburg - South Side
Address: 145 Borinquen Pl
Brooklyn, NY 11211
Phone: +1 (347) 789-7742

#257
Beauty & Essex
Bar, American, Tapas, Small Plates
Average price: Expensive
District: Lower East Side
Address: 146 Essex St
New York, NY 10002
Phone: +1 (212) 614-0146

#258
Valhalla
Pub
Average price: Moderate
District: Hell's Kitchen,
Midtown West, Theater District
Address: 815 9th Ave
New York, NY 10019
Phone: +1 (212) 757-2747

#259
Bushwick Country Club
Bar, Mini Golf
Average price: Inexpensive
District: East Williamsburg
Address: 618 Grand St
Brooklyn, NY 11211
Phone: +1 (718) 388-2114

#260
Bar Great Harry
Pub
Average price: Moderate
District: Carroll Gardens, Gowanus
Address: 280 Smith St
Brooklyn, NY 11231
Phone: +1 (718) 222-1103

#261
Banter
Bar
Average price: Moderate
District: Williamsburg - South Side
Address: 132 Havemeyer St
Brooklyn, NY 11211
Phone: +1 (718) 599-5200

#262
Doris
Bar
Average price: Moderate
District: Bedford Stuyvesant, Clinton Hill
Address: 1088 Fulton St
Brooklyn, NY 11238
Phone: +1 (347) 240-3350

#263
Skinny Dennis
Bar
Average price: Inexpensive
District: Williamsburg - North Side
Address: 152 Metropolitan Ave
Brooklyn, NY 11249
Phone: +1 (212) 555-1212

#264
Louis 649
Jazz & Blues, Cocktail Bar
Average price: Moderate
District: East Villagea, Alphabet City
Address: 649 East 9th Street
New York, NY 10009
Phone: +1 (212) 673-1190

#265
Cork 'n Fork
Tapas, Small Plates, Wine Bar
Average price: Moderate
District: East Villagea, Alphabet City
Address: 186 Ave A
New York, NY 10009
Phone: +1 (646) 707-0707

#266
The Royal Palms Shuffleboard Club
Social Club, Bar, Recreation Center
Average price: Moderate
District: Gowanus
Address: 514 Union St
Brooklyn, NY 11215
Phone: +1 (347) 223-4410

#267
Smoke Jazz Club
Jazz & Blues, Music Venue,
Soul Food
Average price: Moderate
District: Manhattan Valley
Address: 2751 Broadway
New York, NY 10025
Phone: +1 (212) 864-6662

#268
Sweet Science
Bar, Burgers, American
Average price: Moderate
District: East Williamsburg
Address: 135 Graham Ave
Brooklyn, NY 11206
Phone: +1 (347) 763-0872

#269
Corner Bistro
Burgers, Bar
Average price: Inexpensive
District: West Village
Address: 331 W 4th St
New York, NY 10014
Phone: +1 (212) 242-9502

#270
New York Philharmonic
Performing Arts, Music Venue
Average price: Expensive
District: Upper West Side
Address: 10 Lincoln Center Plz
New York, NY 10023
Phone: +1 (212) 875-5656

#271
Rosamunde Sausage Grill
Hot Dogs, German, Bar
Average price: Moderate
District: Williamsburg - South Side
Address: 285 Bedford Ave
Brooklyn, NY 11211
Phone: +1 (718) 388-2170

#272
Old Man Hustle
Wine Bar, Dive Bar, Music Venue
Average price: Inexpensive
District: Lower East Side
Address: 39 Essex St
New York, NY 10002
Phone: +1 (212) 253-7747

#273
V-Note
Vegan, Vegetarian, Wine Bar
Average price: Moderate
District: Yorkville, Upper East Side
Address: 1522 1st Ave
New York, NY 10075
Phone: +1 (212) 249-5009

#274
Michaelangelo's Little Italy
Lounge, Italian, Pizza
Average price: Moderate
District: Belmont
Address: 2477 Arthur Ave
Bronx, NY 10458
Phone: +1 (718) 220-8355

#275
Onieal's Grand St. Bar
& Restaurant
Bar, American
Average price: Moderate
District: Little Italy
Address: 174 Grand St
New York, NY 10013
Phone: +1 (212) 941-9119

#276
The Path Cafe
Music Venue, Salad,
Breakfast & Brunch
Average price: Inexpensive
District: West Village
Address: 131 Christopher St
New York, NY 10014
Phone: +1 (212) 243-1311

#277
Pierre Loti Midtown
Wine Bar, Tapas, Turkish
Average price: Moderate
District: Midtown East
Address: 300 E 52nd St
New York, NY 10022
Phone: +1 (212) 755-5684

#278
B Side
Dive Bar
Average price: Inexpensive
District: East Villagea, Alphabet City
Address: 204 Ave B
New York, NY 10009
Phone: +1 (212) 475-4600

#279
Five Points
American, Mediterranean, Bar
Average price: Moderate
Address: 31 Great Jones St
New York, NY 10012
Phone: +1 (212) 253-5700

#280
Bembe
Dance Club
Average price: Moderate
District: Williamsburg - South Side,
South Williamsburg
Address: 81 S 6th St
Brooklyn, NY 11211
Phone: +1 (718) 387-5389

#281
The Whiskey Brooklyn
Bar, American
Average price: Moderate
District: Williamsburg - North Side
Address: 44 Berry St
Brooklyn, NY 11211
Phone: +1 (718) 387-8444

#282
Canal Bar
Dive Bar, Cocktail Bar
Average price: Inexpensive
District: Gowanus
Address: 270 3rd Ave
Brooklyn, NY 11215
Phone: +1 (718) 246-0011

#283
Session House
Irish, Pub
Average price: Moderate
District: Midtown East
Address: 1009 2nd Ave
New York, NY 10022
Phone: +1 (646) 559-4404

#284
Saxon + Parole
American, Bar
Average price: Expensive
District: NoHo
Address: 316 Bowery
New York, NY 10012
Phone: +1 (212) 254-0350

#285
The Rum House
Lounge, Cocktail Bar
Average price: Expensive
District: Midtown West, Theater District
Address: 228 W 47th St
New York, NY 10036
Phone: +1 (646) 490-6924

#286
Maysville
American, Wine Bar
Average price: Expensive
District: Flatiron
Address: 17 W 26th St
New York, NY 10010
Phone: +1 (646) 490-8240

#287
International Bar
Dive Bar, Lounge
Average price: Inexpensive
District: East Village
Address: 120 1/2 1st Ave
New York, NY 10009
Phone: +1 (212) 777-1643

#288
Floyd, NY
Bar
Average price: Inexpensive
District: Brooklyn Heights
Address: 131 Atlantic Ave
Brooklyn, NY 11201
Phone: +1 (718) 858-5810

#289
Mar's
Seafood, Bar
Average price: Expensive
District: Astoria
Address: 34-21 34th Ave
Astoria, NY 11106
Phone: +1 (718) 685-2480

#290
Puck Fair
Pub, Irish
Average price: Moderate
District: SoHo, Nolita
Address: 298 Lafayette St
New York, NY 10012
Phone: +1 (212) 431-1200

#291
The Tippler
Bar
Average price: Moderate
District: Chelsea, Meatpacking
Address: 425 W 15th St
New York, NY 10011
Phone: +1 (212) 206-0000

#292
Pinkerton Wine Bar
Wine Bar
Average price: Moderate
District: Williamsburg - North Side
Address: 263 N 6th St
Brooklyn, NY 11211
Phone: +1 (718) 782-7171

#293
Sharlene's
Bar
Average price: Inexpensive
District: Prospect Heights
Address: 353 Flatbush Ave
Brooklyn, NY 11238
Phone: +1 (347) 350-8225

#294
Zombie Hut
Bar
Average price: Moderate
District: Gowanus
Address: 273 Smith St
Brooklyn, NY 11231
Phone: +1 (718) 875-3433

#295
Botanica Bar
Bar
Average price: Inexpensive
District: Nolita
Address: 47 E Houston St
New York, NY 10012
Phone: +1 (212) 343-7251

#296
Iron Horse NYC
Dive Bar, Pub
Average price: Inexpensive
District: Financial District
Address: 32 Cliff St
New York, NY 10038
Phone: +1 (646) 546-5426

#297
Gottscheer Hall
Caterers, German, Pub
Average price: Inexpensive
District: Ridgewood
Address: 657 Fairview Ave
Ridgewood, NY 11385
Phone: +1 (718) 366-3030

#298
Dram Shop
Burgers, Bar
Average price: Moderate
District: South Slope, Park Slope
Address: 339 9th St
Brooklyn, NY 11215
Phone: +1 (718) 788-1444

#299
Swift
Restaurant, Bar
Average price: Moderate
District: NoHo
Address: 34 E 4th St
New York, NY 10003
Phone: +1 (212) 227-9438

#300
Terra Blues
Jazz & Blues
Average price: Moderate
District: Greenwich Village
Address: 149 Bleecker St
New York, NY 10012
Phone: +1 (212) 777-7776

#301
Ba'sik
Cocktail Bar, Salad, Sandwiches
Average price: Moderate
District: Williamsburg - North Side
Address: 323 Graham Ave
Brooklyn, NY 11211
Phone: +1 (347) 889-7597

#302
Klimat Lounge
Polish, Lounge, Wine Bar
Average price: Moderate
District: East Village
Address: 77 E 7th St
New York, NY 10003
Phone: +1 (917) 214-0589

#303
Miller's Tavern
American, Cocktail Bar,
Breakfast & Brunch
Average price: Moderate
District: Williamsburg - North Side
Address: 2 Hope St
Brooklyn, NY 11211
Phone: +1 (347) 335-0330

#304
Colonie
American, Bar
Average price: Expensive
District: Brooklyn Heights
Address: 127 Atlantic Ave
Brooklyn, NY 11201
Phone: +1 (718) 855-7500

#305
The Fulton Grand
Bar
Average price: Moderate
District: Clinton Hill
Address: 1011 Fulton St
Brooklyn, NY 11238
Phone: +1 (718) 399-2240

#306
Palace Cafe
Bar
Average price: Inexpensive
District: Greenpoint
Address: 206 Nassau Ave
Brooklyn, NY 11222
Phone: +1 (718) 383-9848

#307
Analogue
Cocktail Bar, Jazz & Blues, Lounge
Average price: Expensive
District: Greenwich Village
Address: 19 W 8th St
New York, NY 10011
Phone: +1 (212) 432-0200

#308
Burp Castle
Pub, Lounge
Average price: Moderate
District: East Village
Address: 41 E 7th St
New York, NY 10003
Phone: +1 (212) 982-4576

#309
The Monro Pub
Pub
Average price: Inexpensive
District: South Slope, Park Slope
Address: 481 5th Ave
Brooklyn, NY 11215
Phone: +1 (718) 499-2005

#310
Iona
Bar
Average price: Moderate
District: Williamsburg - South Side,
Williamsburg - North Side
Address: 180 Grand St
Brooklyn, NY 11211
Phone: +1 (718) 384-5008

#311
Briciola
Italian, Wine Bar
Average price: Moderate
District: Hell's Kitchen,
Midtown West, Theater District
Address: 370 W 51 St
New York, NY 10019
Phone: +1 (646) 678-5763

#312
Larry Lawrence
Lounge
Average price: Moderate
District: Williamsburg - North Side
Address: 295 Grand St
Brooklyn, NY 11211
Phone: +1 (718) 218-7866

#313
Johnny's Bar
Dive Bar
Average price: Inexpensive
District: West Village
Address: 90 Greenwich Ave
New York, NY 10011
Phone: +1 (212) 741-5279

#314
Sake Bar Satsko
Japanese, Bar
Average price: Moderate
District: East Villagea, Alphabet City
Address: 202 E 7th St
New York, NY 10009
Phone: +1 (212) 614-0933

#315
Fresh Salt
Bar, American
Average price: Moderate
District: South Street Seaport
Address: 146 Beekman St
New York, NY 10038
Phone: +1 (212) 962-0053

#316
Upright Brew House
American, Bar
Average price: Moderate
District: West Village
Address: 547 Hudson St
New York, NY 10014
Phone: +1 (212) 810-9944

#317
Black Rabbit
Pub
Average price: Moderate
District: Greenpoint
Address: 91 Greenpoint Ave
Brooklyn, NY 11222
Phone: +1 (718) 349-1595

#318
Alligator Lounge
Lounge, Dive Bar, Karaoke
Average price: Inexpensive
District: Williamsburg - North Side
Address: 600 Metropolitan Ave
Brooklyn, NY 11211
Phone: +1 (718) 599-4440

#319
The Stag's Head
Pub
Average price: Moderate
District: Midtown East
Address: 252 E 51st St
New York, NY 10022
Phone: +1 (212) 888-2453

#320
Two Bit's Retro Arcade
Arcade, Dive Bar
Average price: Inexpensive
District: Lower East Side
Address: 153 Essex St
New York, NY 10002
Phone: +1 (212) 477-8161

#321
Commonwealth
Bar
Average price: Moderate
District: South Slope, Park Slope
Address: 497 5th Ave
Brooklyn, NY 11215
Phone: +1 (718) 768-2040

#322
Locksmith Wine & Burger Bar
Wine Bar, Burgers
Average price: Moderate
District: Washington Heights
Address: 4463 Broadway
New York, NY 10040
Phone: +1 (212) 304-9463

#323
Hibernia
Bar, American
Average price: Moderate
District: Hell's Kitchen, Midtown West
Address: 401 W 50th St
New York, NY 10019
Phone: +1 (212) 969-9703

#324
Double Wide
Southern, Bar, Breakfast & Brunch
Average price: Moderate
District: East Villagea, Alphabet City
Address: 505 E 12th St
New York, NY 10009
Phone: +1 (917) 261-6461

#325
Destination Bar & Grill
American, Cocktail Bar
Average price: Inexpensive
District: East Villagea, Alphabet City
Address: 211 Ave A
New York, NY 10009
Phone: +1 (212) 388-9844

#326
Réunion
Cocktail Bar
Average price: Moderate
District: Hell's Kitchen,
Midtown West, Theater District
Address: 357 W 44th St
New York, NY 10036
Phone: +1 (212) 582-3200

#327
Shrine
Bar, Music Venue
Average price: Moderate
District: Harlem
Address: 2271 Adam Clayton Powell Blvd
New York, NY 10030
Phone: +1 (212) 690-7807

#328
On The Rocks
Lounge
Average price: Moderate
District: Hell's Kitchen, Midtown West
Address: 696 10th Ave
New York, NY 10019
Phone: +1 (212) 247-2055

#329
Stonehome Wine Bar
Wine Bar, American
Average price: Expensive
District: Fort Greene
Address: 87 Lafayette Ave
Brooklyn, NY 11217
Phone: +1 (718) 624-9443

#330
reBar
Bar, Venue & Event Space
Average price: Moderate
District: DUMBO
Address: 147 Front St.
Brooklyn, NY 11201
Phone: +1 (718) 766-9110

#331
P J Horgan Tavern
Pub, Irish
Average price: Moderate
District: Sunnyside
Address: 4217 Queens Blvd
Sunnyside, NY 11104
Phone: +1 (718) 361-9680

#332
Anotheroom
Lounge
Average price: Moderate
District: TriBeCa
Address: 249 W Broadway
New York, NY 10013
Phone: +1 (212) 226-1418

#333
Barbes
Bar, Jazz & Blues
Average price: Moderate
District: South Slope, Park Slope
Address: 376 9th St
Brooklyn, NY 11215
Phone: +1 (347) 422-0248

#334
Ugly Kitchen
Bar, Asian Fusion, Filipino
Average price: Moderate
District: East Village
Address: 103 1st Ave
New York, NY 10003
Phone: +1 (212) 777-6677

#335
Hourglass Tavern
American, Lounge, American
Average price: Moderate
District: Hell's Kitchen,
Midtown West, Theater District
Address: 373 W 46th St
New York, NY 10036
Phone: +1 (212) 265-2060

#336
Standings
Sport Bar, Pub
Average price: Moderate
District: East Village
Address: 43 E 7th St
New York, NY 10003
Phone: +1 (212) 420-0671

#337
Club Macanudo
Tobacco Shop, Dance Club
Average price: Expensive
District: Upper East Side
Address: 26 E 63rd St
New York, NY 10021
Phone: +1 (212) 752-8200

#338
Hell Gate Social
Lounge, Pub
Average price: Inexpensive
District: Astoria
Address: 1221 Astoria Blvd
Astoria, NY 11102
Phone: +1 (718) 204-8313

#339
Black Swan
Pub, Gastropub
Average price: Moderate
District: Bedford Stuyvesant
Address: 1048 Bedford Ave
Brooklyn, NY 11205
Phone: +1 (718) 783-4744

#340
Greenpoint Tavern
Dive Bar
Average price: Inexpensive
District: Williamsburg - North Side
Address: 188 Bedford Ave
Brooklyn, NY 11211
Phone: +1 (718) 384-9539

#341
Molly's
American, Irish, Pub
Average price: Moderate
District: Gramercy
Address: 287 3rd Ave
New York, NY 10010
Phone: +1 (212) 889-3361

#342
Barcelona Bar
Dive Bar
Average price: Moderate
District: Hell's Kitchen, Midtown West
Address: 923 8th Ave
New York, NY 10019
Phone: +1 (212) 245-3212

#343
Lantern's Keep
Cocktail Bar
Average price: Expensive
District: Midtown West
Address: 49 W 44th St
New York, NY 10036
Phone: +1 (212) 453-4287

#344
Barramundi
Venue &Event Space, Lounge
Average price: Inexpensive
District: Lower East Side
Address: 67 Clinton St
New York, NY 10002
Phone: +1 (212) 529-6999

#345
61 Local
Pub, Venue &Event Space, Coffee & Tea
Average price: Moderate
District: Cobble Hill
Address: 61 Bergen St
Brooklyn, NY 11201
Phone: +1 (718) 875-1150

#346
Lillie's Victorian Bar & Restaurant
Irish, Pub
Average price: Moderate
District: Union Square, Flatiron
Address: 13 E 17th St
New York, NY 10003
Phone: +1 (212) 337-1970

#347
The Horse Box
Sport Bar
Average price: Inexpensive
District: East Villagea, Alphabet City
Address: 218 Ave A
New York, NY 10009
Phone: +1 (646) 370-1791

#348
Brandy's Piano Bar
Bar, Music Venue
Average price: Moderate
District: Yorkville, Upper East Side
Address: 235 E 84th St
New York, NY 10028
Phone: +1 (212) 744-4949

#349
Heidelberg Restaurant
German, Bar
Average price: Moderate
District: Yorkville, Upper East Side
Address: 1648 2nd Ave
New York, NY 10028
Phone: +1 (212) 628-2332

#350
11th Street Bar
Pub
Average price: Inexpensive
District: East Villagea, Alphabet City
Address: 510 E 11th St
New York, NY 10009
Phone: +1 (212) 982-3929

#351
Lion's Head Tavern
Bar
Average price: Inexpensive
District: Manhattan Valley
Address: 995 Amsterdam Ave
New York, NY 10025
Phone: +1 (212) 866-1030

#352
Mother's Ruin
Bar, American, Breakfast & Brunch
Average price: Moderate
District: Nolita
Address: 18 Spring St
New York, NY 10012
Phone: +1 (212) 219-0942

#353
Jules Bistro
French, Bar
Average price: Moderate
District: East Village
Address: 65 Saint Marks Pl
New York, NY 10003
Phone: +1 (212) 477-5560

#354
Otto's Shrunken Head
Dive Bar
Average price: Moderate
District: East Villagea, Alphabet City
Address: 538 E 14th St
New York, NY 10009
Phone: +1 (212) 228-2240

#355
The Library
Dive Bar, Jazz & Blues
Average price: Inexpensive
District: East Villagea, Alphabet City
Address: 7 Ave A
New York, NY 10009
Phone: +1 (212) 375-1352

#356
The Sparrow Tavern
Bar, Breakfast & Brunch, American
Average price: Moderate
District: Astoria
Address: 24-01 29th St
Astoria, NY 11102
Phone: +1 (718) 606-2260

#357
Darbar Grill
Indian, Buffets, Bar
Average price: Moderate
District: Midtown East
Address: 157 E 55th St
New York, NY 10022
Phone: +1 (212) 751-4600

#358
Tom & Jerry's
Bar
Average price: Moderate
District: NoHo
Address: 288 Elizabeth St
New York, NY 10012
Phone: +1 (212) 260-5045

#359
Washington Commons
Pub
Average price: Inexpensive
District: Crown Heights, Prospect Heights
Address: 748 Washington Ave
Brooklyn, NY 11238
Phone: +1 (718) 230-3666

#360
Union Hall
Pub, Music Venue
Average price: Moderate
District: Park Slope
Address: 702 Union St
Brooklyn, NY 11215
Phone: +1 (718) 638-4400

#361
Oro Bakery and Bar
Wine Bar, Bakery
Average price: Moderate
District: Little Italy, Nolita
Address: 375 Broome St
New York, NY 10013
Phone: +1 (212) 941-6368

#362
Corcho Wine Room
Wine Bar, Tapas Bar
Average price: Moderate
District: Washington Heights, Inwood
Address: 231 Dykman St
New York, NY 10034
Phone: +1 (212) 203-3371

#363
Rattle 'N' Hum
Pub, American
Average price: Moderate
District: Midtown East
Address: 14 E 33rd St
New York, NY 10016
Phone: +1 (212) 481-1586

#364
Wolf and Deer
Wine Bar, American
Average price: Moderate
District: Park Slope
Address: 74 5th Ave
Brooklyn, NY 11217
Phone: +1 (718) 398-3181

#365
Good Co.
Bar
Average price: Inexpensive
District: Williamsburg - North Side
Address: 10 Hope St
Brooklyn, NY 11211
Phone: +1 (718) 218-7191

#366
Egyptian Coffee Shop
Coffee & Tea, Hookah Bar, Egyptian
Average price: Inexpensive
District: Astoria
Address: 25-09 Steinway St
Astoria, NY 11103
Phone: +1 (718) 777-5517

#367
Drop Off Service
Bar
Average price: Inexpensive
District: East Villagea, Alphabet City
Address: 211 Ave A
New York, NY 10009
Phone: +1 (212) 260-2914

#368
Catfish
Cajun/Creole, Cocktail Bar,
Breakfast & Brunch
Average price: Moderate
District: Crown Heights
Address: 1433 Bedford Ave
Brooklyn, NY 11216
Phone: +1 (347) 305-3233

#369
Antibes Bistro
French, Jazz & Blues
Average price: Moderate
District: Lower East Side
Address: 112 Suffolk St
New York, NY 10002
Phone: +1 (212) 533-6088

#370
Kilo
Tapas Bar, Wine Bar
Average price: Moderate
District: Hell's Kitchen, Midtown West
Address: 857 9th Ave
New York, NY 10019
Phone: +1 (212) 707-8770

#371
The Peoples Improv Theater
Performing Arts, Comedy Club
Average price: Inexpensive
District: Flatiron
Address: 123 E 24th St
New York, NY 10010
Phone: +1 (212) 563-7488

#372
Uncorked Wine & Tapas
Wine Bar, Lounge,
Tapas, Small Plates
Average price: Moderate
District: Midtown East
Address: 344 E 59th St
New York, NY 10022
Phone: +1 (646) 429-8365

#373
Bathtub Gin
Bar
Average price: Expensive
District: Chelsea
Address: 132 9th Ave
New York, NY 10011
Phone: +1 (646) 559-1671

#374
Amsterdam Tavern
Bar
Average price: Moderate
District: Manhattan Valley
Address: 938 Amsterdam Ave
New York, NY 10025
Phone: +1 (212) 280-8070

#375
At Nine Restaurant & Bar
Thai, Cocktail Bar
Average price: Moderate
District: Hell's Kitchen,
Midtown West, Theater District
Address: 592 9th Ave
New York, NY 10036
Phone: +1 (212) 265-4499

#376
Zablozki's
Pub
Average price: Inexpensive
District: Williamsburg - North Side
Address: 107 N 6th St
Brooklyn, NY 11211
Phone: +1 (718) 384-1903

#377
Lansdowne Road
Pub, Sport Bar
Average price: Moderate
District: Hell's Kitchen, Midtown West
Address: 599 10th Ave
New York, NY 10036
Phone: +1 (212) 239-8020

#378
Riposo 46
Wine Bar, Italian
Average price: Moderate
District: Hell's Kitchen,
Midtown West, Theater District
Address: 667 9th Ave
New York, NY 10036
Phone: +1 (212) 247-8018

#379
Lamoza
Middle Eastern, Hookah Bar
Average price: Moderate
District: Bay Ridge
Address: 7704 3rd Ave
Brooklyn, NY 11209
Phone: +1 (718) 238-3625

#380
Boat Bar
Dive Bar
Average price: Inexpensive
District: Cobble Hill, Boerum Hill
Address: 175 Smith St
Brooklyn, NY 11201
Phone: +1 (718) 254-0607

#381
Prime Meats
Bar, American
Average price: Expensive
District: Carroll Gardens
Address: 465 Court St
Brooklyn, NY 11231
Phone: +1 (718) 254-0327

#382
Common Ground
Bar, American
Average price: Moderate
District: East Villagea, Alphabet City
Address: 206 Ave A
New York, NY 10009
Phone: +1 (212) 228-6231

#383
Fedora
American, French, Bar
Average price: Expensive
District: West Village
Address: 239 W 4th St
New York, NY 10014
Phone: +1 (646) 449-9336

#384
Pearl's Social & Billy Club
Dive Bar, Cocktail Bar
Average price: Moderate
District: Bushwick
Address: 40 Saint Nicholas Ave
Brooklyn, NY 11237
Phone: +1 (347) 627-9985

#385
Lunasa Bar & Restaurant
Pub, Irish
Average price: Moderate
District: East Village
Address: 126 1st Ave
New York, NY 10009
Phone: +1 (212) 228-8580

#386
Ten Degrees Bistro
Brasserie, Wine Bar,
Breakfast & Brunch
Average price: Moderate
District: East Villagea, Alphabet City
Address: 131 Ave A
New York, NY 10009
Phone: +1 (212) 358-9282

#387
Fat Buddha
Bar, Asian Fusion, Korean
Average price: Moderate
District: East Villagea, Alphabet City
Address: 212 Ave A
New York, NY 10009
Phone: +1 (212) 598-0500

#388
Mad Donkey Beer Bar & Grill
Dive Bar
Average price: Inexpensive
District: Astoria
Address: 3207 36th Ave
Astoria, NY 11106
Phone: +1 (718) 204-2070

#389
Heavy Woods
Bar, Cafe, Cajun/Creole
Average price: Moderate
District: Bushwick
Address: 50 Wyckoff Ave
New York, NY 11237
Phone: +1 (929) 234-3500

#390
Bearded Lady
Bar
Average price: Moderate
District: Prospect Heights
Address: 686A Washington Ave
Brooklyn, NY 11238
Phone: +1 (469) 232-7333

#391
Cuckoo's Nest
Irish, Pub
Average price: Moderate
District: Woodside
Address: 6104 Woodside Ave
Woodside, NY 11377
Phone: +1 (718) 426-5684

#392
The Slipper Room
Adult Entertainment
Average price: Inexpensive
District: Lower East Side
Address: 167 Orchard St
New York, NY 10002
Phone: +1 (212) 253-7246

#393
Wogies
Bar, American
Average price: Moderate
District: West Village
Address: 39 Greenwich Ave
New York, NY 10014
Phone: +1 (212) 229-2171

#394
BXL East
Belgian, Pub
Average price: Moderate
District: Midtown East
Address: 210 E 51st St
New York, NY 10022
Phone: +1 (212) 888-7782

#395
Piper's Kilt
Bar, Karaoke, Music Venue
Average price: Moderate
District: Inwood
Address: 4946 Broadway
New York, NY 10034
Phone: +1 (212) 569-7071

#396
Terroir Tribeca
Wine Bar, American
Average price: Moderate
District: TriBeCa
Address: 24 Harrison St
New York, NY 10013
Phone: +1 (212) 625-9463

#397
The Wren
Bar, Breakfast & Brunch
Average price: Moderate
District: East Village
Address: 344 Bowery
New York, NY 10012
Phone: +1 (212) 388-0148

#398
Crocodile Lounge
Lounge
Average price: Inexpensive
District: Gramercy, East Village
Address: 325 E 14th St
New York, NY 10003
Phone: +1 (212) 477-7747

#399
Piccolo Cafe
Coffee & Tea, Italian, Wine Bar
Average price: Moderate
District: Midtown West, Theater District
Address: 274 W 40th St
New York, NY 10018
Phone: +1 (212) 302-0143

#400
bOb Bar
Lounge, Dance Club
Average price: Moderate
District: Lower East Side
Address: 235 Eldridge St
New York, NY 10002
Phone: +1 (212) 529-1807

#401
New Leaf Restaurant & Bar
American, Bar
Average price: Expensive
District: Washington Heights
Address: 1 Margaret Corbin Dr
New York, NY 10040
Phone: +1 (212) 568-5323

#402
Rated P the Musical
Music Venue
Average price: Moderate
District: Hell's Kitchen, Midtown West
Address: 407 W 43rd St
New York, NY 10036
Phone: +1 (212) 315-2244

#403
Mary's Bar
Pub
Average price: Moderate
District: South Slope
Address: 708 5th Ave
Brooklyn, NY 11215
Phone: +1 (718) 499-2175

#404
Paddy Reilly's Music Bar
Pub, Music Venue
Average price: Inexpensive
District: Midtown East, Kips Bay
Address: 519 2nd Ave
New York, NY 10016
Phone: +1 (212) 686-1210

#405
The Atlantic ChipShop
British, Pub, Fish & Chips
Average price: Moderate
District: Brooklyn Heights
Address: 129 Atlantic Ave
Brooklyn, NY 11201
Phone: +1 (718) 855-7775

#406
The 55 Bar
Jazz & Blues
Average price: Inexpensive
District: West Village
Address: 55 Christopher St
New York, NY 10001
Phone: +1 (212) 929-9883

#407
Mercury Lounge
Dive Bar
Average price: Moderate
District: Lower East Side
Address: 217 East Houston St.
New York, NY 10002
Phone: +1 (212) 260-4700

#408
The Four-Faced Liar
Pub
Average price: Inexpensive
District: West Village
Address: 165 W 4th St
New York, NY 10014
Phone: +1 (212) 206-8959

#409
The Crown Inn
Bar
Average price: Moderate
District: Crown Heights
Address: 724 Franklin Ave
Brooklyn, NY 11238
Phone: +1 (347) 915-1131

#410
Terraza 7
Bar, Music Venue, Jazz & Blues
Average price: Moderate
District: Elmhurst
Address: 40-19 Gleane St
Elmhurst, NY 11373
Phone: +1 (718) 803-9602

#411
Nurse Bettie
Bar
Average price: Moderate
District: Lower East Side
Address: 106 Norfolk St
New York, NY 10002
Phone: +1 (917) 434-9072

#412
The Gutter
Bowling, Dive Bar
Average price: Moderate
District: Williamsburg - North Side
Address: 200 N 14th St
Brooklyn, NY 11222
Phone: +1 (718) 387-3585

#413
William Barnacle Tavern
Bar
Average price: Moderate
District: East Village
Address: 80 St Mark's Pl
New York, NY 10009
Phone: +1 (212) 388-0388

#414
Barcibo Enoteca
Wine Bar
Average price: Moderate
District: Upper West Side
Address: 2020 Broadway
New York, NY 10023
Phone: +1 (212) 595-2805

#415
B Cafe
Bar, Belgian
Average price: Moderate
District: Yorkville, Upper East Side
Address: 240 E 75th St
New York, NY 10021
Phone: +1 (212) 249-3300

#416
Lillie's Victorian Bar & Restaurant
Lounge, American
Average price: Moderate
District: Midtown West, Theater District
Address: 249 W 49th St
New York, NY 10019
Phone: +1 (212) 957-4530

#417
Break Bar & Billiards
Pool Hall, Sport Bar
Average price: Moderate
District: Astoria
Address: 32-04 Broadway
Astoria, NY 11106
Phone: +1 (718) 777-5400

#418
National Comedy Theatre
Performing Arts, Comedy Club
Average price: Inexpensive
District: Hell's Kitchen, Midtown West
Address: 347 W 36th St
New York, NY 10018
Phone: +1 (212) 629-5202

#419
Deacon Brodie's
Pub
Average price: Inexpensive
District: Hell's Kitchen,
Midtown West, Theater District
Address: 370 W 46th St
New York, NY 10036
Phone: +1 (212) 262-1452

#420
The Breslin Bar & Dining Room
Pub, Gastropub
Average price: Expensive
District: Midtown West, Flatiron
Address: 20 W 29th St
New York, NY 10001
Phone: +1 (212) 679-1939

#421
Tiny's & the Bar Upstairs
Bar, American
Average price: Expensive
District: TriBeCa
Address: 135 W Broadway
New York, NY 10013
Phone: +1 (212) 374-1135

#422
Sample
Bar
Average price: Moderate
District: Cobble Hill
Address: 152 Smith St
Brooklyn, NY 11201
Phone: +1 (718) 643-6622

#423
The NoMad Library
Gastropub, Lounge
Average price: Expensive
District: Flatiron
Address: 1170 Broadway & 28th St
New York, NY 10001
Phone: +1 (347) 472-5660

#424
Aria Wine Bar
Wine Bar, Tapas, Small Plates
Average price: Moderate
District: West Village
Address: 117 Perry St
New York, NY 10014
Phone: +1 (212) 242-4233

#425
Banter Irish Bar and Kitchen
Pub, Irish, Breakfast & Brunch
Average price: Moderate
District: Forest Hills
Address: 108-22 Queens Blvd
Forest Hills, NY 11375
Phone: +1 (718) 268-8436

#426
The Dead Poet
Bar
Average price: Moderate
District: Upper West Side
Address: 450 Amsterdam Ave
New York, NY 10024
Phone: +1 (212) 595-5670

#427
Ayza Wine & Chocolate Bar
Desserts, Wine Bar, Mediterranean
Average price: Moderate
District: West Village
Address: 1 7th Ave S
New York, NY 10014
Phone: +1 (212) 365-2992

#428
Double Down Saloon
Dive Bar
Average price: Inexpensive
District: East Villagea, Alphabet City
Address: 14 Ave A
New York, NY 10009
Phone: +1 (212) 982-0543

#429
Landmark Tavern
Pub, American
Average price: Moderate
District: Hell's Kitchen, Midtown West
Address: 626 11th Ave
New York, NY 10036
Phone: +1 (212) 247-2562

#430
Nino's 46
Italian, Wine Bar, Gluten-Free
Average price: Moderate
District: Midtown West
Address: 39 W 46th St
New York, NY 10036
Phone: +1 (212) 719-4015

#431
Tolani Eatery & Wine
Wine Bar, South African
Average price: Expensive
District: Upper West Side
Address: 410 Amsterdam Ave
New York, NY 10024
Phone: +1 (212) 873-6252

#432
Arlene's Grocery
Karaoke, Music Venue, Dive Bar
Average price: Moderate
District: Lower East Side
Address: 95 Stanton St
New York, NY 10002
Phone: +1 (212) 358-1633

#433
Tarallucci E Vino Cafe
Coffee & Tea, Sandwiches, Wine Bar
Average price: Moderate
District: East Village
Address: 163 1st Ave
New York, NY 10003
Phone: +1 (212) 388-1190

#434
St. Andrews
Pub, Seafood, Scottish
Average price: Moderate
District: Midtown West, Theater District
Address: 140 W 46th St
New York, NY 10036
Phone: +1 (212) 840-8413

#435
Tutu's
Pub, American, Breakfast & Brunch
Average price: Moderate
District: East Williamsburg, Bushwick
Address: 25 Bogart St
Brooklyn, NY 11206
Phone: +1 (718) 456-7898

#436
Wasabassco Burlesque
Performing Arts, Adult Entertainment
Average price: Moderate
District: 54 North 11th St,
Address: Brooklyn, NY 11249
Phone: +1 (646) 559-1671

#437
The Belfry
Bar
Average price: Moderate
District: East Village
Address: 222 E 14th St
New York, NY 10003
Phone: +1 (212) 473-6590

#438
Measure
Lounge, Jazz & Blues,
Tapas, Small Plates
Average price: Expensive
District: Midtown West
Address: 400 5th Ave
New York, NY 10018
Phone: +1 (212) 695-4005

#439
Booker and Dax
Lounge
Average price: Expensive
District: East Village
Address: 207 2nd Ave
New York, NY 10003
Phone: +1 (212) 254-3500

#440
The Three Monkeys
Bar, American, Gastropub
Average price: Moderate
District: Midtown West, Theater District
Address: 236 W 54th St
New York, NY 10019
Phone: +1 (212) 586-2080

#441
**Upright Citizens Brigade
Theatre East**
Comedy Club
Average price: Inexpensive
District: East Villagea, Alphabet City
Address: 153 E 3rd St
New York, NY 10009
Phone: +1 (212) 366-9231

#442
ReSette
Bar, American, Italian
Average price: Expensive
District: Midtown West
Address: 7 W 45th St
New York, NY 10036
Phone: +1 (212) 221-7530

#443
BXL Cafe
Pub, Belgian, Breakfast & Brunch
Average price: Moderate
District: Midtown West, Theater District
Address: 125 W 43rd St
New York, NY 10036
Phone: +1 (212) 768-0200

#444
Daddy-O
Bar
Average price: Moderate
District: West Village
Address: 44 Bedford St
New York, NY 10014
Phone: +1 (212) 414-8884

#445
Rose Bar
Lounge
Average price: Moderate
District: Gramercy, Flatiron
Address: 2 Lexington Ave
New York, NY 10010
Phone: +1 (212) 920-3300

#446
Billymark's West
Dive Bar
Average price: Exclusive
District: Chelsea, Midtown West
Address: 332 9th Ave
New York, NY 10001
Phone: +1 (212) 629-0118

#447
One Mile House
Bar, American
Average price: Inexpensive
District: Lower East Side
Address: 10 Delancey St
New York, NY 10012
Phone: +1 (646) 559-0702

#448
Juke Bar
Bar
Average price: Moderate
District: East Village
Address: 196 2nd Ave
New York, NY 10003
Phone: +1 (212) 228-7464

#449
Lucien
French, Wine Bar
Average price: Moderate
District: East Village
Address: 14 1st Ave
New York, NY 10009
Phone: +1 (212) 260-6481

#450
B Cafe West
Belgian, Bar
Average price: Expensive
District: Upper West Side
Address: 566 Amsterdam Ave
New York, NY 10024
Phone: +1 (212) 873-1800

#451
Kazuza
Hookah Bar, Middle Eastern
Average price: Moderate
District: East Villagea, Alphabet City
Address: 107 Ave A
New York, NY 10009
Phone: +1 (212) 505-9300

#452
The Sampler Bushwick
Bar
Average price: Moderate
District: Bushwick
Address: 234 Starr St
Brooklyn, NY 11237
Phone: +1 (718) 484-3560

#453
Osteria Cotta
Italian, Wine Bar
Average price: Moderate
District: Upper West Side
Address: 513 Columbus Ave
New York, NY 10024
Phone: +1 (212) 873-8500

#454
Miles
Wine Bar, American,
Cocktail Bar
Average price: Moderate
District: Bushwick
Address: 101 Wilson Ave
Brooklyn, NY 11237
Phone: +1 (718) 483-9172

#455
Franklin Park
Bar
Average price: Moderate
District: Crown Heights
Address: 618 St John's Pl
Brooklyn, NY 11238
Phone: +1 (718) 975-0196

#456
Gotham City Lounge
Dive Bar
Average price: Moderate
District: Bushwick
Address: 1293 Myrtle Ave
Brooklyn, NY 11221
Phone: +1 (718) 387-4182

#457
Duane Park
American, Jazz & Blues
Average price: Inexpensive
District: East Villagea, NoHo
Address: 308 Bowery
New York, NY 10012
Phone: +1 (212) 732-5555

#458
ViV
Thai, Bar
Average price: Exclusive
District: Hell's Kitchen,
Midtown West, Theater District
Address: 717 9th Ave
New York, NY 10019
Phone: +1 (212) 581-5999

#459
Montero's Bar & Grill
Dive Bar, American
Average price: Moderate
District: Brooklyn Heights, Cobble Hill
Address: 73 Atlantic Ave
Brooklyn, NY 11201
Phone: +1 (646) 729-4129

#460
Boulton & Watt
Bar, American, Gastropub
Average price: Inexpensive
District: Lower East Side, Alphabet City
Address: 5 Ave A
New York, NY 10009
Phone: +1 (646) 490-6004

#461
Sindicato De Cocineros
Mexican, Cocktail Bar
Average price: Moderate
District: Greenpoint
Address: 57 Nassau Ave
New York, NY 11222
Phone: +1 (347) 422-0727

#462
L.I.C. Bar
Bar, Music Venue
Average price: Moderate
District: Hunters Point, Long Island City
Address: 4558 Vernon Blvd
Long Island City, NY 11101
Phone: +1 (718) 786-5400

#463
Epistrophy
Wine Bar, Italian
Average price: Moderate
District: Nolita
Address: 200 Mott St
New York, NY 10012
Phone: +1 (212) 966-0904

#464
G.Lee's Smokin BBQ
Cocktail Bar, Barbeque
Average price: Moderate
District: Crown Heights
Address: 813 Nostrand Ave
Brooklyn, NY 11225
Phone: +1 (347) 413-8680

#465
Rue B
Bar, Jazz & Blues, Brasserie
Average price: Moderate
District: East Villagea, Alphabet City
Address: 188 Ave B
New York, NY 10009
Phone: +1 (212) 358-1700

#466
Littlefield
Performing Arts, Art Gallery, Bar
Average price: Moderate
District: Gowanus
Address: 622 Degraw St
Brooklyn, NY 11217
Phone: +1 (718) 855-3388

#467
Lips
American, Gay Bar, Performing Arts
Average price: Moderate
District: Midtown East
Address: 227 E 56th St
New York, NY 10022
Phone: +1 (212) 675-7710

#468
Pine Box Rock Shop
Bar, Vegan, Karaoke, Shopping
Average price: Moderate
District: East Williamsburg, Bushwick
Address: 12 Grattan St
Brooklyn, NY 11206
Phone: +1 (718) 366-6311

#469
the 'dam
American, Pub
Average price: Moderate
District: Manhattan Valley
Address: 998 Amsterdam Ave
New York, NY 10025
Phone: +1 (212) 257-4998

#470
Mandarin Oriental Lobby Lounge
American, Lounge
Average price: Moderate
District: Upper West Side
Address: 80 Columbus Cir at 60th St
New York, NY 10023
Phone: +1 (212) 805-8800

#471
Turks & Frogs
Wine Bar, Turkish
Average price: Expensive
District: West Village
Address: 323 W 11th St #2
New York, NY 10014
Phone: +1 (212) 691-8875

#472
Press Lounge
Lounge
Average price: Moderate
District: Hell's Kitchen, Midtown West
Address: 653 11th Ave
New York, NY 10036
Phone: +1 (212) 757-2224

#473
Legends Bar & Grill
Bar, Barbeque
Average price: Expensive
District: Jackson Heights
Address: 7104 35th Ave
Jackson Heights, NY 11372
Phone: +1 (718) 899-9553

#474
Sea Witch
Lounge, Gastropub
Average price: Moderate
District: South Slope
Address: 703 5th Ave
Brooklyn, NY 11215
Phone: +1 (347) 227-7166

#475
Oxcart Tavern
American, Pub, Gastropub
Average price: Inexpensive
District: Flatbush
Address: 1301 Newkirk Ave
Brooklyn, NY 11230
Phone: +1 (718) 284-0005

#476
Negril Village
Caribbean, Lounge
Average price: Moderate
District: Greenwich Village
Address: 70 W 3rd St
New York, NY 10012
Phone: +1 (212) 477-2804

#477
The Stone
Music Venue, Jazz & Blues
Average price: Expensive
District: East Villagea, Alphabet City
Address: E 2nd St & Ave C
New York, NY 10009
Phone: +1 (212) 473-0043

#478
Biddy's Pub
Pub
Average price: Inexpensive
District: Yorkville, Upper East Side
Address: 301 E 91st St
New York, NY 10128
Phone: +1 (212) 534-4785

#479
Swing 46
American, Jazz & Blues
Average price: Inexpensive
District: Hell's Kitchen,
Midtown West, Theater District
Address: 349 W 46th St
New York, NY 10036
Phone: +1 (212) 262-9554

#480
The Sunburnt Cow
Bar, Breakfast & Brunch, American
Average price: Expensive
District: East Villagea, Alphabet City
Address: 137 Ave C
New York, NY 10009
Phone: +1 (212) 529-0005

#481
The Stonewall Inn
Gay Bar, American
Average price: Moderate
District: West Village
Address: 53 Christopher St
New York, NY 10014
Phone: +1 (212) 488-2705

#482
Pencil Factory Bar
Bar
Average price: Moderate
District: Greenpoint
Address: 142 Franklin St
Brooklyn, NY 11222
Phone: +1 (718) 609-5858

#483
Alfie's
Bar
Average price: Moderate
District: Hell's Kitchen,
Midtown West, Theater District
Address: 800 9th Ave
New York, NY 10019
Phone: +1 (212) 757-2390

#484
Cake Shop
Coffee & Tea, Bar, Music Venue
Average price: Moderate
District: Lower East Side
Address: 152 Ludlow St
New York, NY 10002
Phone: +1 (212) 253-0036

#485
Rapture Lounge
Lounge, American
Average price: Inexpensive
District: Astoria
Address: 3427 28th Ave
Astoria, NY 11103
Phone: +1 (718) 626-8044

#486
Hollow Nickel
Pub
Average price: Moderate
District: Boerum Hill
Address: 494 Atlantic Ave
New York, NY 11217
Phone: +1 (347) 236-3417

#487
Bar Reis
Bar
Average price: Moderate
District: Park Slope
Address: 375 5th Ave
Brooklyn, NY 11215
Phone: +1 (718) 974-2412

#488
Anfora
Wine Bar, Tapas, Small Plates
Average price: Moderate
District: West Village
Address: 34 8th Ave
New York, NY 10014
Phone: +1 (212) 518-2722

#489
Turkey's Nest Tavern
Dive Bar
Average price: Moderate
District: Williamsburg - North Side
Address: 94 Bedford Ave
Brooklyn, NY 11211
Phone: +1 (718) 384-9774

#490
Lucey's Lounge
Lounge
Average price: Inexpensive
District: Gowanus
Address: 475 3rd Ave
Brooklyn, NY 11231
Phone: +1 (718) 877-1075

#491
V Bar
Wine Bar, Italian
Average price: Moderate
District: East Village
Address: 132 1st Ave
New York, NY 10009
Phone: +1 (212) 473-7200

#492
The Brooklyn Inn
Bar
Average price: Moderate
District: Boerum Hill
Address: 138 Bergen St
Brooklyn, NY 11217
Phone: +1 (718) 522-2525

#493
Therapy
Gay Bar
Average price: Inexpensive
District: Hell's Kitchen,
Midtown West, Theater District
Address: 348 W 52nd St
New York, NY 10019
Phone: +1 (212) 397-1700

#494
The Ding-Dong Lounge
Dive Bar
Average price: Moderate
District: Manhattan Valley
Address: 929 Columbus Ave
New York, NY 10025
Phone: +1 (212) 663-2600

#495
Croxley Ales
Sport Bar, Pub
Average price: Inexpensive
District: East Villagea, Alphabet City
Address: 28 Ave B
New York, NY 10009
Phone: +1 (212) 253-6140

#496
Bar Tano
Bar, Italian
Average price: Inexpensive
District: Gowanus
Address: 457 3rd Ave
Brooklyn, NY 11215
Phone: +1 (718) 499-3400

#497
Smith and Mills
Lounge, American
Average price: Moderate
District: TriBeCa
Address: 71 N Moore St
New York, NY 10013
Phone: +1 (212) 226-2515

#498
Space Billiard Café
Pool Hall, Bar
Average price: Moderate
District: Midtown West, Koreatown
Address: 34 W 32nd St
New York, NY 10001
Phone: +1 (212) 239-4166

#499
Local 138
Bar
Average price: Inexpensive
District: Lower East Side
Address: 138 Ludlow St
New York, NY 10002
Phone: +1 (212) 477-0280

#500
The Ten Bells
Wine Bar, Tapas Bar
Average price: Inexpensive
District: Lower East Side
Address: 247 Broome St
New York, NY 10002
Phone: +1 (212) 228-4450

Printed in Great Britain
by Amazon